Contents

Series editor's preface

Sources in History is a new series responding to the continued shift of emphasis in the teaching of history in schools and universities towards the use of primary sources and the testing of historical skills. By using documentary evidence, the series is intended to reflect the skills historians have to master when challenged by problems of evidence, interpretation and presentation.

A distinctive feature of *Sources in History* will be the manner in which the content, style and significance of documents is analysed. The commentary and the sources are not discrete, but rather merge to become part of a continuous and integrated narrative. After reading each volume a student should be well versed in the historiographical problems which sources present. In short, the series aims to provide texts which will allow students to achieve facility in 'thinking historically' and place them in a stronger position to test their historical skills. Wherever possible the intention has been to retain the integrity of a document and not simply to present a 'gobbet', which can be misleading. Documentary evidence thus forces the student to confront a series of questions with which professional historians also have to grapple. Such questions can be summarised as follows:

1. *What* type of source is the document?
- Is it a written source or an oral or visual source?
- What, in your estimation, is its importance?
- Did it, for example, have an effect on events or the decision-making process?
2. *Who* wrote the document?
- A person, a group, or a government?
- If it was a person, what was their position?
- What basic attitudes might have affected the nature of the information and language used?
3. *When* was the document written?
- The date, and even the time, might be significant.
- You may need to understand when the document was written in order to understand its context.
- Are there any special problems in understanding the document as contemporaries would have understood it?
4. *Why* was the document written?
- For what purpose(s) did the document come into existence, and for *whom* was it intended?

- Was the document 'author-initiated' or was it commissioned for somebody? If the document was ordered by someone, the author could possibly have 'tailored' his piece.
5 *What* was written?
- This is the obvious question, but never be afraid to state the obvious.
- Remember, it may prove more revealing to ask the question: what was *not* written?
- That is, read between the lines. In order to do this you will need to ask what other references (to persons, events, other documents, etc.) need to be explained before the document can be fully understood.

Sources in History is intended to reflect the individual voice of the volume author(s) with the aim of bringing the central themes of specific topics into sharper focus. Each volume will consist of an authoritative introduction to the topic and chapters will discuss the historical significance of the sources. Authors will also provide an annotated bibliography and suggestions for further reading. These books will become contributions to the historical debate in their own right.

Philip Boobbyer's *The Stalin Era* will prove to be an important addition to the literature on Stalin's Soviet Union. It is an ambitious book that embraces political, social, cultural and intellectual history. Dr Boobbyer has established an international reputation as a specialist in intellectual history, an area that is often overlooked in the voluminous literature on twentieth-century Russian history.

Boobbyer places Stalin's rule in the wider European perspective. He examines the extent of Stalin's power and his style of decision-making together with the changes that occurred in Stalinist ideology over time. The author contends that Stalinism was an attempt to challenge the dominant ideology of Western capitalism. Confronted with Russia's lack of economic progress, Stalin used the state to force its citizens and institutions to embrace 'progress' by means of a series of modernisation programmes. For Boobbyer, this 'revolution from above' was hampered by an impatience with historical processes that was also a feature of the Russian revolutionaries before 1917. The desperate need for Russia to modernise and the thinking of its revolutionary intelligentsia proved a volatile and explosive mixture. Everything had to be achieved in a hurry to short-circuit historical processes, with the result that while there were some economic successes, they were invariably counter-productive in the long term.

Moreover, Stalin did not possess the pragmatism or flexibility that Lenin occasionally revealed during his period in power. Boobbyer suggests that the essence of Stalinism can be found not only in Stalin's strategy of modernisation but also in his consolidation of power for its own sake. Again, while there were some 'successes' in a quantitative sense (clearly outlined by the author), Stalin created a monolithic political and economic system based on arbitrary personal despotism that was incapable of facilitating an efficient command economy or indeed of establishing a functioning civil society. For Boobbyer, Stalinism represents a classic case study in the complex juxtaposition of ends and means.

The Stalin Era provides a succinct and critical analysis of the intense historiographical debates surrounding different aspects of Stalinism. The author also includes new documentary material previously unavailable in English.

David Welch
Canterbury 2000

Preface

The revolution that Stalin launched at the end of the 1920s eventually transformed the Soviet Union into a superpower. Yet, as has often happened in Russian history, the population endured great hardship as the state expanded and grew powerful. How did this happen? What were the origins of Stalin's extraordinary personal dictatorship? How did the wider Soviet population come to participate in Stalin's terror? What was the fate of education, the family, religion and the arts in the Stalin era? How did the Stalin regime mobilise the Soviet population during the Second World War? This book is a resource for scholars and students who seek to answer such questions.

The chapters are structured around documents, some of which have only become available since the collapse of the Soviet Union, and a few of which are translated into English for the first time. Documents include speeches, party and government resolutions, NKVD reports, newspaper articles, academic works, letters, diaries, memoirs, novels and poetry. There are a significant number of visual sources, relating to the art and propaganda of the period. Sources are always placed in their historical context. Cross-references have been added to the text to suggest documents that can usefully be compared with one another, but readers are also advised to make good use of the index to locate comparative material. While each chapter is devoted to a particular topic, documents on themes like nationalism, propaganda and popular opinion run through the whole text. Reference is made throughout to secondary literature and relevant historiographical debates, and Chapter 1 contains a selection of extracts from important secondary sources. Students can use the book as a pointer to the most recent research in the field.

The book embraces political, social, cultural and intellectual history. Scholarship on the Stalin era, in concentrating on one or another of these aspects of Soviet history, sometimes lacks a broader perspective. This book attempts to offer a wider synthesis. There were, of course, limits to what could be included. Unfortunately, there was no room for a separate chapter on foreign policy, and the book does not do justice to the extraordinary ethnic diversity of the Soviet Union under Stalin. Nevertheless, the book remains broad in its scope and ambition. While it can be used simply for reference purposes, it can also be read in its entirety as an attempt to capture the 'total history' of the period. Scholars and students are thus encouraged to reflect on a wide range of subjects; in a world of increased specialisation, there is still room for the generalist.

Philip Boobbyer
Canterbury, April 2000

Glossary of Russian terms and abbreviations

ACP(b)	All-Union Communist Party (Bolsheviks), also VKP(b)
aktif/aktiv	party activists
ASSR	Autonomous Soviet Socialist Republic
batrak	rural labourer, landless peasant
bedniak/*pl* bedniaki or bednota	poor peasant(s)
Black Hundreds	extreme right-wing pre-revolutionary groups
brigade	work group in a kolkhoz or factory
cadres	key party members
CC	Central Committee (also TsK)
Cheka	Political Police during Civil War
CPSU(b)	Communist Party of the Soviet Union (Bolsheviks)
desiatina	measure of land
DC	district committee
Gosplan	State Planning Commission
GPU	State Political Directorate, formerly Cheka, later OGPU and NKVD
Gubernia	province
Gulag	main administration of labour camps
izba	peasant hut
kolkhoz	collective farm
Komsomol	Communist League of Youth
Komvuz	higher educational institution
krai	territory
kraikom	territorial party committee
kulak	rich peasant
LMG	League of the Militant Godless
MGB	Ministry of State Security
MGK	Moscow City Party Committee
MTS	Machine Tractor Station
MVD	Ministry of Internal Affairs
NEP	New Economic Policy
Nepman	A man made rich during NEP
NKGB	People's Commissariat of State Security
NKTP	People's Commissariat of Heavy Industry

NKVD	People's Commissariat of Internal Affairs
obkom	province party committee
oblast	province
OGPU (GPU)	Unified State Political Administration, Political Police
okrug	administrative unit, between region and district
Oprichnina	Ivan IV's (the Terrible) security police
Orgburo	organisational bureau of party's Central Committee
Party Conference	meeting of party delegates, constitutionally inferior to a congress
Party Congress	theoretically the party's sovereign body
People's Commissar	Minister of Soviet government, 1917–46
plenum	a full meeting of an organisation
Politburo	political bureau of party's Central Committee
politotdel	political department
Pravda	main party newspaper
raikom	district party committee
raion	district
RAPP	Russian Association of Proletarian Writers
RC/RK	regional committee
RCP	Russian Communist Party
RS	regional council/soviet
RSFSR	Russian Soviet Federative Socialist Republic
selsoviet	village soviet
skhod	gathering of the peasant commune
smychka	alliance
SNK	Sovnarkom
soviet	elected body with administrative functions
sovkhoz	state farm
Sovnarkom	Council of People's Commissars
Stakhanovite	peasant or worker recognised for achieving high production targets
TASS	Telegraph Agency of the Soviet Union
toilers	workers and peasants
troika	group of three persons
TsIK	Central Executive Committee of the Soviets of the USSR
TsK	Central Committee of the Communist Party
TsKK	Central Control Commission of the party
uezd	district
Vesenkha	Supreme Council of the National Economy
VKP(b)	All-Union Communist Party (Bolsheviks)
volost	small rural district
vozhd'	leader
Yezhovshchina	period when Yezhov headed NKVD

Acknowledgements

There are many people who have helped me with this book. Professors R.W. Davies and Arfon Rees made detailed comments on an early draft of the book, and pointed me in the direction of certain documents. I had many discussions with Professor Richard Sakwa, who also gave me access to his extensive personal library. Professor Richard Taylor gave advice on the material on film. Dr Mark Harrison, Dr Chris Ward and Alex and Joy Bache commented on particular extracts or chapters. Dr John Barber took time to discuss the project with me. Nikita Petrov was a very helpful source of information. For all this I am very grateful. I am thankful too to Gillian Oliver at Routledge for her work in dealing with permissions, and for the input of Susan Dunsmore as copy-editor. In addition, I wish to express my appreciation to Bill Jaeger for encouraging my interest in the Soviet Union over many years. Finally, I am grateful to Professor David Welch, the editor of the series, for encouraging me to write this book. I have enjoyed the project very much.

Philip Boobbyer

The author and publishers gratefully acknowledge permission from the following to reproduce from copyright material:

From *The Family in the USSR* edited by Rudolf Schlesinger, 1949, with kind permission of Routledge and Kegan Paul. From *Khrushchev Remembers* by Nikita Khrushchev, © 1970 by Little, Brown and Company (Inc.), by permission of Little, Brown and Company (Inc.). Reprinted with the permission of Scribner, a Division of Simon & Schuster from *Hope Against Hope* by Nadezhda Mandelstam, translated from the Russian by Max Hayward, © 1970 Atheneum Publishers, English translation © 1970 Atheneum Publishers and also with permission from HarperCollins Publishers Ltd. Nadezhda Mandelstam: extracts from *Hope Abandoned*, first published by Editions YMCA Press, Paris, 1972, first published in Great Britain in 1974 by Harvill, © Atheneum Publishers 1972, © English translation, Atheneum Publishers, New York and Harvill, 1973, 1974, reproduced by permission of The Harvill Press. Aleksandr Solzhenitsyn: lines from *The Gulag Archipelago: 1918-1956, III-IV*, © Aleksandr I Solzhenitsyn 1974 © in the English language translation Harper & Row, Publishers Inc. 1975, reproduced with the permission of The Harvill Press. From *A Documentary History of Communism* by Robert Daniels with kind permission of I.B. Tauris & Co. Ltd. From *Resolutions and Decisions of the Communist Party of the Soviet Union, Volume 3,*

The Stalin Years: 1929-1953 by Robert McNeal, with kind permission of Toronto University Press. From *Religion in the Soviet Union: An Archival Reader* by Felix Corley © 1996 with kind permission of Macmillan Press Ltd. From *The Rise and Fall of T.D. Lysenko* by Zhores Medvedev, 1969, with kind permission of Columbia University Press and the Copyright Clearance Center, Inc. For two photographs of Stalin at the Moscow-Volga Canal, with kind permission of RIA-Novosti. From *Stalin* by Dmitri Volkogonov with kind permission of Weidenfeld and Nicolson. From *To Build A Castle* by Vladimir Bukovsky with kind permission of Andre Deutsch Ltd. Extract from *The Revolution Betrayed* by Leon Trotsky, 1937, © 1937, 1972 by Pathfinder Press, reprinted with permission. From *Magnetic Mountain: Stalinism as a Civilization* by Stephen Kotkin, with permission from the Regents of the University of California and the University of California Press. From *Stalin's Letters to Molotov: 1925–1936* edited by Lars H. Lih, Oleg V. Khlevniuk and Oleg V. Naumov, *The Road to Terror* edited by J. Arch Getty and Oleg V. Naumov and *Stalinism as a Way of Life* edited by L. Siegelbaum and A.K. Sokolov, with kind permission from Yale University Press. From *Soviet Documents on Foreign Policy* edited by Jane Degras published by Oxford University Press for the Royal Institute of International Affairs, London, with permission of the Royal Institute of International Affairs. The photograph of Ernst Neizvestnyi's sculpture of Khrushchev at Khrushchev' s grave, with kind permission of Vagrius Publishers, Moscow. From the second edition of *Behind the Urals* by John Scott, with kind permission of Indiana University Press. Photo of Stalin as 'friend of the little children' and photo of the design for the palace of the Soviets from *The Commissar Vanishes* by David King, published in 1997 by Canongate Books, 14 High Street, Edinburgh. Stills from the feature films *October, The Circus, Lenin in 1918, The Tractor-Drivers, The Fall of Berlin* with kind permission of Mosfilm International Inc. The image of *Stalin: Leader, Teacher, Friend* with kind permission of The State Russian Museum, St. Petersburg. The image of *The Struggle for the Polytechnical School is the Struggle for the Five Year Plan*, 1931, with permission of The Merrill C. Berman Collection. Map adapted from one from *America in a Divided World, 1945–1972: a social and economic history of the USSR in World War II* by John Barber and Mark Harrison © Longman Group UK Limited 1991.

Every attempt has been made to obtain permission to reproduce copyright material. If any proper acknowledgement has not been made, we would invite copyright holders to inform us of the oversight.

Notes on the text

I have used the Library of Congress system of transliteration. However, the following changes have been made: at the ending of words, 'ii' in the LOC system becomes 'y', as in Trotsky rather than Trotskii; and at the beginning of surnames, 'E' and 'Ia' become 'Ye' and 'Ya': Yezhov rather than Ezhov; Yaroslavsky rather than Iaroslavsky.

In their use of italics the Documents reflect emphasis in the original.

Republics, major cities and other towns in the USSR, 1945

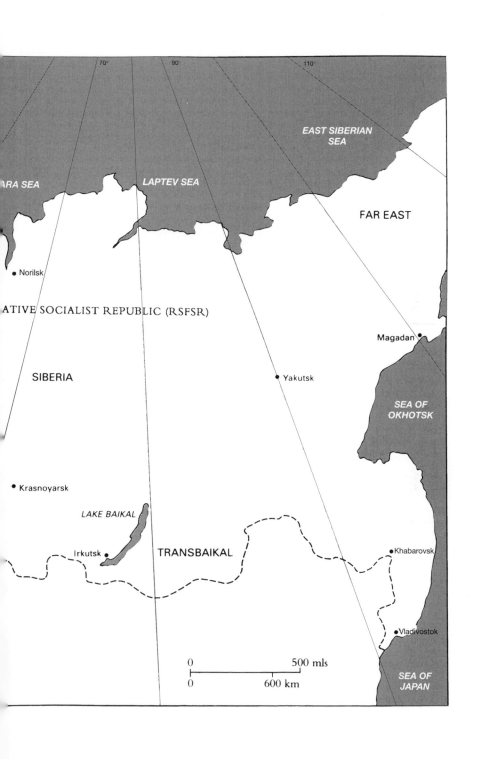

70°   90°   110°

EAST SIBERIAN
SEA

ARA SEA   LAPTEV SEA

FAR EAST

• Norilsk

ATIVE SOCIALIST REPUBLIC (RSFSR)

Magadan •

SIBERIA

• Yakutsk

SEA OF
OKHOTSK

• Krasnoyarsk

LAKE BAIKAL

Irkutsk •   TRANSBAIKAL

• Khabarovsk

• Vladivostok

0   500 mls

0   600 km

SEA OF
JAPAN

Interpreting the Stalin era | **1**

At Joseph Stalin's death in 1953, the Soviet Union was one of the two dominant world powers, and Soviet ideology continued to find adherents across the world. Stalin's political achievements, in spite of all the victims, seemed remarkable. Yet it is testimony to how historical judgments can owe their persuasiveness to political circumstances that almost half a century later Stalin's legacy looks very different. The Soviet empire has collapsed, and socialism as an ideology been in many ways discredited.

Certainly, for some critics, there seemed something to admire in Stalin's rule. After all, under Stalin the Soviet Union had developed a powerful industrial base, educated its people and defeated fascism in a terrible war. A backward society had been hauled into the modern age. In a biography that first appeared in 1949, the socialist historian Isaac Deutscher, although he believed that Stalin had betrayed many of the promises of the Bolshevik revolution, nevertheless credited him with building on positive strands in the Leninist tradition.

Document 1.1   Stalin in Comparative Perspective

Stalin cannot be classed with Hitler, among the tyrants whose record is one of absolute worthlessness and futility. Hitler was the leader of a sterile counter-revolution, while Stalin has been both the leader and the exploiter of a tragic, self-contradictory but creative revolution. Like Cromwell, Robespierre, and Napoleon, he started as the servant of an insurgent people and made himself its master. Like Cromwell he embodies the continuity of the revolution through all its phases and metamorphoses, although his role was less prominent in the first phase. Like Robespierre he has bled white his own party; and like Napoleon he has built his half-conservative and half-revolutionary empire and carried revolution beyond the frontiers of his country. The better part of Stalin's work is as certain to outlast Stalin himself as the better parts of the work of Cromwell and Napoleon have outlasted them. But in order to save it for the future and give to it its full value, history may yet have to cleanse and reshape Stalin's work as sternly as it once cleansed and reshaped the work of the English revolution after Cromwell and of the French after Napoleon.

Source: Isaac Deutscher, Stalin, *1967, pp. 569–70.*

Deutscher's comments illustrate the value of putting Stalin's rule into a wider European perspective; it is undoubtedly possible to find parallels between his dictatorship and the autocratic or ideological leadership of pre-twentieth-century revolutionary leaders. At the same time, in the decades after the Second World War, it was a more common opinion that the dictatorships of Stalin, Hitler and Mussolini were something unique. These new regimes were deemed to be qualitatively different from previous dictatorships in that they aspired after and were able to achieve, on the basis of new technologies and means of communication, levels of control previously unthinkable. In this context, political scientists and historians were attracted by the theory of 'totalitarianism', an interpretative model designed to highlight the key features of this kind of dictatorship. The American political scientists Carl Friedrich and Zbigniew Brzezinski, attempting to quantify the key features of 'totalitarianism', suggested six characteristics of totalitarian regimes: an ideology to which everyone is supposed to adhere; a mass, hierarchically organised party, led by one man, which is superior to or intertwined with the government apparatus; police control; monopoly of communication; monopoly of weaponry; a command economy (Friedrich and Brzezinski 1956: 21–2). The political philosopher, Hannah Arendt, writing in 1951 in *The Origins of Totalitarianism* (1979), suggested that totalitarian regimes aim to break down class loyalties and civil society in order to create lonely, atomised individuals with no private space of their own, who can thus be easily used to serve the state's interests.

Document 1.2   Totalitarianism

Totalitarian movements are mass organizations of atomized, isolated individuals. Compared with all other parties and movements, their most conspicuous external characteristic is their demand for total, unrestricted, unconditional, and unalterable loyalty of the individual member . . .

It is in the very nature of totalitarian regimes to demand unlimited power. Such power can only be secured if literally all men, without a single exception, are reliably dominated in every aspect of their life. In the realm of foreign affairs new neutral territories must constantly be subjugated, while at home ever-new human groups must be mastered in expanding concentration camps, or, when circumstances require, liquidated to make room for others. The question of opposition is unimportant both in foreign and domestic affairs. Any neutrality, indeed any spontaneously given friendship, is from the standpoint of totalitarian domination just as dangerous as open hostility, precisely because spontaneity as such, with its incalculability, is the greatest of all obstacles to total domination over man . . .

By pressing men against each other, total terror destroys the space between them . . .

Totalitarian government, like all tyrannies, certainly could not exist without destroying the public realm of life, that is, without destroying, by isolating men, their political capacities. But totalitarian domination as a form of government is new in that it is not content with this isolation and destroys private life as well. It bases itself on loneliness, on the experience of not belonging to the world at all, which is among the most radical and desperate experiences of man.

Loneliness, the common ground for terror, the essence of totalitarian government, and for ideology or logicality, the preparation of its executioners and victims, is closely connected with the uprootedness and superfluousness which have been the curse of modern masses since the beginning of the industrial revolution and have become acute with the rise of imperialism at the end of the last century and the breakdown of political institutions and social traditions in our own time.

Source: Hannah Arendt, The Origins of Totalitarianism, *1979, p. 323, 456, 466, 475.*

Hannah Arendt describes how individuals, cut off from their traditional social networks, can become slavishly subservient to the state. Literary works, such as Arthur Koestler's *Darkness at Noon* ([1940] 1985) and George Orwell's *Nineteen Eighty-Four* ([1949] 1984) have also attempted to describe the processes of psychological enslavement in modern dictatorships, and their power has been one of the reasons for the enduring attraction of totalitarian explanations. Robert Conquest's *The Great Terror* ([1968] 1992) was one of the more influential historical studies which reflected a totalitarian approach.

Another influential scholar who accepted the basic thrust of the totalitarian argument was Leonard Schapiro. He believed that the Stalin regime had its roots in the revolutionary violence and disregard of the law that were distinctive features of Lenin's regime; he suggested that totalitarian regimes are distinguished by their contempt for moral and legal norms.

Document: 1.3   The Lack of Moral and Legal Restraint

There are many examples in the history of the last fifty years alone to show that where a minority seeks to impose its will, in the profound conviction that it alone has possession of the truth, and the historic right to enforce it in defiance of all the legal and moral rights of those over whom it rules, the amount of violence which it employs will steadily and inexorably increase . . .

[T]he key to a society is its attitude to law . . . The whole point about a modern, totalitarian society is that it is not just a more elaborate kind of tyranny, with harsher laws, and more of them. It is, on the contrary, a system of arbitrary rule which has discovered a convenient formula in order to ensure that law and the judges can be utilized as instruments for that arbitrary rule; and can never act as a barrier against such rule . . . If once law . . . is turned into an instrument of arbitrary rule . . ., the position of the individual is beyond hope. In this respect . . ., there was no difference between Lenin and Stalin.

Source: Leonard Schapiro, The Origin of the Communist Autocracy, *1977, pp. xix–xxi.*

The 'totalitarian' school set the intellectual agenda for historians of the Stalin era, indeed, for Soviet studies as a whole, in the decades following the Second World War. Sophisticated advocates of the totalitarian school did not argue that the Stalinist polity perfectly fitted the model of a regime of total control. They saw it rather as a tendency than an established fact. Leonard Schapiro suggested that totalitarianism should not be taken as an immutable model of government, but more as an approximation (Schapiro 1972: 124). The American historian, Merle Fainsod, noted the existence of 'clique rivalries' amongst Stalinist elites, and observed that reality fell short of totalitarian aspiration (Fainsod 1963: 177). Although many historians are now sceptical of the value of the term, popular judgment still refers to the Stalin regime as 'totalitarian', and in post-Soviet Russia the term is widely accepted amongst scholars.

From the late 1950s onwards, many scholars reacted against the totalitarian school. Some claimed that it was a politicised term that had been designed to highlight differences between the Soviet Union and the West. Its relevance as a term would diminish as the Cold War came to an end (Spiro 1968: 108, 112). At an analytical level, it was seen to be a static model, which could not embrace the dynamic, changing nature of Soviet reality or differences between communist regimes (Curtis 1969: 105). Another criticism was that it was too general a term. American historian Robert Tucker argued that 'Stalinism' should be treated as a phenomenon in its own right and not just as a variant of totalitarianism (Tucker 1977: xiii). Tucker's own analysis of the Stalin regime led him to argue that the Stalin regime employed methods that were reminiscent of certain features of pre-revolutionary Russian political culture. Stalin, like Ivan the Terrible and Peter the Great before him, sought to create a powerful state to defeat his enemies and transform a backward society (see also Document 9.7).

Document 1.4   Stalinism as Revolution from Above

The basic underlying fact confronting us is that when the Russian revolutionary process resumed in the Stalinist stage, it had a different character from the revolutionary process of destruction of the old order and makeshift creation of the new that had marked the earlier, 1917–1921 stage; and this change of character is to be understood in terms of a reversion to a revolutionary process seen earlier in Russian history . . .

Stalinism as revolution from above was a state-building process, the construction of a powerful, highly centralized bureaucratic, military-industrial Soviet Russian state. Although it was proclaimed 'socialist' in the mid-1930's, it differed in various vital ways from what most socialist thinkers – Marx, Engels, and Lenin among them – had understood socialism to mean. Stalinist 'socialism' was a socialism of mass poverty rather than plenty; sharp social stratification rather than relative equality; of universal, constant fear rather than emancipation of personality; of national chauvinism rather than brotherhood of man; and of a monstrously hypertrophied state power rather than the decreasingly statified commune-state delineated by Marx in *The Civil War in France* and by Lenin in *The State and Revolution.*

It was not, however, by mere caprice or accident that this happened. Stalinist revolutionism from above had a prehistory in the political culture of Russian tsarism; it existed as a pattern in the Russian past and hence *could* be seen by a twentieth-century statesman as both a precedent and legitimation of a political course that would, in essentials, recapitulate the historical pattern . . .

Confronted in the aftermath of the two-century long Mongol domination with hostile and in some cases more advanced neighbor-states . . ., the princes – later tsars – of Muscovy undertook the building of a powerful 'military-national' state capable of gathering the Russian lands under its aegis. Given the primacy of the concern for external defence and expansion and the country's relative economic backwardness, the government proceeded by remodeling the social structure, at times by forcible means, in such a way that all classes of the population were bound in one or another form of compulsory service to the state . . .

[Under Peter I] the pattern of revolution from above emerged most distinctly, one of its most prominent aspects being an industrial revolution from above aimed at building a powerful Russian war-industrial base.

Source: Robert Tucker, 'Stalinism as Revolution from Above', in Stalinism, *1977, pp. 95–9*

The term 'Stalinism', embracing as it does the uniqueness of the Stalin regime, has become a more popular descriptive device than 'totalitarianism'. However, even that can pose problems. For Stalin was in power for long enough for his system to undergo considerable change. For example, the extent of Stalin's power and his style of decision-making changed throughout his rule. Furthermore, his ideology also changed. Many historians observe that in the 1930s there was a break with revolutionary approaches to education, the family and the arts (and in the 1940s to religion), and a turn to conservative policies; egalitarianism was set aside; Russian nationalism was embraced. Trotsky, using the language of the French Revolution, suggested that there was a 'Thermidorian reaction' against revolutionary principles (Trotsky 1972: 86–114). The Russian émigré historian, Nikolai Timasheff, in his *The Great Retreat* ([1946] 1972) argued that in the 1930s and 1940s in the USSR an amalgamation of pre-revolutionary Russian values with the communist system of beliefs occurred.

Document 1.5 'The Great Retreat'

The main pattern of the Great Retreat has been the amalgamation of traits of the historical and national culture of Russia with traits belonging to the Communist cycle of ideas and behavior patterns . . .

The pattern of amalgamation may be demonstrated in a large number of fields of sociocultural activity. The Russian Orthodox Church is once more a recognized, even partly privileged body; this is in accordance with historical tradition. But the State teaches antireligion in schools; this is in accordance with Communist principles. The *kolkhoz* is a Communist institution, but individual allotments and cattle-breeding revive parts of the old order. Painting repeats the style of the 'eighties' of the nineteenth century, but it is used to produce portraits of the heroes of our day. In literature, Alexis Tolstoy's masterpiece, *Peter the Great*, is written in the grand style of pre-Revolutionary days, but is conceived in such a way as to show that Stalin is a dignified successor of the greatest of Russian monarchs. . . .

The old school order, the old-fashioned type of family, the gamut of titles, ranks and orders of merit, even Church discipline all proved to be very helpful in consolidating the dictatorial system.

Source: Nikolai Timasheff, The Great Retreat, 1972, pp. 354, 355, 358.

The idea that a 'great retreat' had occurred has retained its popularity since Timasheff proposed it (see Fitzpatrick 1982: 147). However, the nature of this retreat or reaction has been disputed. American historian Martin Malia has argued that 'there never was a Soviet Thermidor', that Russian Jacobinism remained in control, and that nationalism was a misleading term to describe the ideology which took over in the mid-1930s (Malia 1994: 235). Another perspective is that this shift was not so much a retreat as a move away from the construction of socialism to its defence against external threats (Kotkin 1995: 357). Whichever approach one takes, it is difficult to maintain that Stalinist ideology was unchanging. It has been persuasively argued, for example, that Stalinism really encompasses four historical periods: the revolution from above of 1928–31; the great retreat and purges of the 1930s; the patriotic war; and the final post-war years (Reichman 1988: 74).

The argument that there was a continuity between Stalinism and the tsarist period has been popular with scholars (see Rees 1998b: 94). Another approach is to stress that 1917 involved a break in the organic development of Russian history and the beginning of a new ideological experiment (Heller and Nekrich 1986: 11; Malia 1994: 16). Such an approach does not deny the influence of longer-term factors, but stresses rather the crucial importance of the ideological dimension of Soviet rule. In this perspective, both Leninism and Stalinism grew out of Marxism and, beyond that, an Enlightenment worldview which saw human nature as essentially plastic and shaped by the economic and social environment. Soviet ideology grew out of a radical, utopian tradition which was highly optimistic about the potential of politics to change the world. The Polish philosopher Leszek Kolakowski was one of those who argued most forcefully that Stalinism could be best explained in terms of the ideological heritage of Marxism and Leninism (Kolakowski 1977: 283–98). Another Polish intellectual, Andrei Walicki, has recently reiterated this position.

Document 1.6   Marxism and Stalinism

It goes without saying that totalitarianism was not a necessary consequence of Marxism. It is the ABC of intellectual history that every ideology or trend of thought is subject to different interpretations and that the practical consequences of these interpretations depend on concrete historical circumstances. There is no such thing as one true Marxism; the search for a correct and binding account of Marx and Engels's legacy is an infantile disease afflicting true believers . . .

Nonetheless, it is a fact that Marxism proved to be very well suited to the legitimization of the most consistent and long-lived form of totalitarian regime known, that the crimes of this regime were meant to serve the cause of the Marxist utopia, and that almost all Marxists in the world supported this regime without questioning its ideological legitimacy. We can readily concede that it was not unavoidable but that it was not accidental. Leninism and Stalinism, both as theory and as practice, were not the products of an erroneous reading, much less a deliberate distortion, of Marxism; they were the dominant form of Marxist thought in the twentieth century . . .

We can go even further. Marxist totalitarianism was the *predictable* outcome of a Marxist-inspired revolutionary communist movement. It is quite obvious that Marxism as a theory of socioeconomic development contained many reasonable warnings against reckless revolutionism and utopianism; hence it could evolve (and did evolve in the West) in the direction of a democratic socialism that was increasingly compatible with bourgeois democracy and capitalist economy. However, . . . the inevitable price of such evolution was to abandon the essential elements of Marxist identity: its commitment to revolutionary radicalism and its communist ideals.

Source: Andrei Walicki, Marxism and the Leap to the Kingdom of Freedom, *1995, pp. 497–8.*

The relationship between Leninism and Stalinism has been one of the most contentious issues in Soviet studies. Was Stalinism a natural development from Leninism or a deviation? The controversies surrounding the relationship between Leninism and Stalinism have been particularly acute because the reputation of the revolution and thus of revolutionary socialism has been to some extent at stake. The totalitarian school was traditionally inclined to see the two periods as part of one continuum. 'Revisionist' historians, beginning in the 1960s, began to argue that Leninism, for all its violence, did not necessarily lead to Stalinism. There were other options. For example, Stephen Cohen in an acclaimed biography of Bukharin, suggested that the more moderate, 'Bukharinist' road to socialism had been a genuine option in the 1920s (Cohen 1973: 208).

Other work has suggested that even within the framework of the command-administrative system, Stalin's terroristic strategy was not the only option. Using the newly-opened Soviet archives, the young Russian historian, Oleg Khlevniuk, has suggested that a more moderate strategy of rapid industrialisation was represented in the Politburo of the 1930s by Commissar of Heavy Industry, G.K. Ordzhonikidze.

Document 1.7 Alternatives to Stalinism

Although Ordzhonikidze never spoke out against the purges as such and took a hand in organizing many acts of state terror, he considered some of the repressions excessive and actively tried to defend his friends and comrades. Overall, Ordzhonikidze's position can be called one of 'soft Stalinism', oriented toward the Stalinist general line, but rejecting extremes of terror, mainly in relation to 'his own people'. . . .

The so-called command-administrative economy clearly is not the same as Stalinism. Even in the 1930s, preconditions existed in society for the successful implementation of a more moderate, less arbitrary, and less terroristic command-administrative system . . .

At the same time it is unlikely that Ordzhonikidze was ready to get involved in a serious struggle with Stalin. He was too much a Stalinist and too dependent a political figure . . . It is not surprising, therefore, that the available facts suggest that Ordzhonikidze only tried to make Stalin change his mind, although he did so insistently, and, it can be said, fearlessly.

After his death, Stalin's comrades-in-arms, many of who, like Ordzhonikidze, were 'soft Stalinists', partly dismantled the system and rejected the extremes of state terrorism. They opted for a variant that germinated back in the 1930s and was in some measure connected with Ordzhonikidze.

Source: Oleg Khlevniuk, In Stalin's Shadow: the Career of 'Sergo' Ordzhonikidze, *1995b, pp. 175–8.*

Khlevniuk's argument points to Stalin's own personality as the crucial component in the formation of the Stalinist regime. It also suggests that that there were political differences in Stalin's Politburo, and this is a theme which has aroused considerable interest amongst Western historians. In addition to assessing the origins of Stalinism, some revisionists have argued that Stalin was not the all-powerful dictator that tradition has it. The American historian John Arch Getty went as far as to argue that factional struggles within the elite indicate that there was a 'lively politics' in the 1930s (Getty 1985: 199), although this has been widely disputed. To a large extent, the questions asked about Stalin are similar to those that have been asked about Hitler. The picture of a Hitler in total control of Nazi Germany was challenged in the 1960s by historians like Hans Mommsen and Martin Broszat, who suggested that Hitler usually delegated responsibility to others and that his decision-making was very haphazard (Mommsen 1966; Broszat 1969). Few have argued that Stalin was lazy and indolent like Hitler. Furthermore, the evidence suggests that Stalin achieved a greater everyday control of his system than did Hitler (Bialer 1980: 370). Nevertheless, it has been argued that there is little clear evidence that Stalin was a 'master planner'; sometimes, it seems, he reacted to events rather than planned them ahead of time (Getty 1985: 203; see also Thurston 1996: 17).

The most common critique of the traditional totalitarian interpretation has been that beneath the façade of total control, the Stalin administration was inefficient and chaotic, and hindered by bureaucratic struggles. Frequently, its policies had unintended consequences. Trotsky argued that the regime's democratic and revolutionary energy degenerated into 'bureaucratic centralism' (see Document 6.14). More recently, the historian Moshe Lewin has argued that Stalin was constrained by the very bureaucracy which he created.

Document 1.8   Bureaucracy and the Stalinist State

We see therefore a phenomenon with a Catch-22 quality to it: the growing Stalinist centralisation has as its counterpart, unavoidably, the growth (over-growth) of party and state *apparaty*, proverbially inefficient. But it also worked the other way round: the growth of large inefficient bureaucracies seems to call for . . . more centralisation . . .

As long as there was a Stalin at the top, he could use fear to force people to work – but not to work efficiently. His terror was arbitrary, not really a retribution for anything particular or predictable, and even the best performance was no shield against repressions.

The monopoly and supposed cohesion that the popular totalitarian model implied were, in many ways, a fiction in these conditions: the specialised functional administrations became a basis for the crystalisation of powerful departmental vested interests and the overall system turned out extremely refractory to effective coordination. The perennial bargaining and infighting actually blocked the system's capacity to act – despite the illusion that a strong top leadership in a dictatorship can always have things its way.

Source: Moshe Lewin, 'Bureaucracy and the Stalinist State', Stalinism and Nazism, 1997, pp. 69–70.

Much scholarship of the Stalin era has been labelled 'revisionist'. Yet 'revisionist' historians often differ widely amongst themselves. To distinguish them, it has been helpfully suggested that there have been two generations of revisionists: first-generation revisionists, like Stephen Cohen, Moshe Lewin and Robert Tucker declared that the 'totalitarian' model did not apply to the pre-Stalin regime; a second generation, often with a particular interest in social history, argued against totalitarian perspectives in general (Manning 1987: 409–10). Yet, the term 'revisionism' should be treated with some caution. Indeed, sometimes there is considerable common ground between totalitarian and revisionist interpretations, which can be obscured by an overuse of the terms (see also Getty and Manning 1993: 13).

The revisionist trend in studies of the Stalin period cannot be separated from the rise in Western scholarship of revisionist assessments of the events of 1917. Traditionally, liberal historians interpreted the February and October revolutions in terms of politics: a full understanding of the Bolshevik seizure of power could best be attained by looking at the weaknesses of the Provisional Government, the leadership of Lenin and the particular circumstances of the First World War. Revisionists, reacting against the perceived narrowness of this approach, attempted to introduce 'society' into the picture: politics could be understood as reflecting wider social processes; revolutionary upheaval occurred because of deep-seated divisions in Russian society (Acton 1990: 28–48.) The same difference of emphasis has also embraced the debate about the Stalin regime. Instead of analysing the state's impact on society during the Stalin era, social historians have focused on the reverse process, whereby policy was shaped by social forces. Writing in 1979, Sheila Fitzpatrick took the view that upwardly-mobile social groups, trained during the first Five Year Plan, had been the beneficiaries of Stalin's purges; Stalin's policies were in part the result of pressure from below (Fitzpatrick 1979b: 398). The revisionist argument has not been that politics were somehow irrelevant, but that it is impossible to understand Stalinist politics without seeing how policies were adapted or even reshaped by different social groups. Events can be seen from above and below (Manning 1987: 409).

A recent example of this social history is Sheila Fitzpatrick's *Stalin's Peasants* (1994). The book is an attempt to describe the often-hidden, mental universe of the Soviet peasant in the 1930s, and the different peasant strategies of resistance. Fitzpatrick uses the metaphor of 'negotiation' to describe the complex process of bargaining by which the state and the peasantry tried to impose their wills on one another.

Document 1.9   A Process of Negotiation

Much of what happened in the 1930s can be seen as a process of pushing and pulling as the various interested parties strove to define the kolkhoz to serve their purposes. In the first years, the great issue was the struggle over compulsory procurements levels that culminated disastrously for both sides in the 1932–1933 famine. Although quotas had to be lowered temporarily in response to the famine, the state did not abandon its determination to take a much larger share of the harvest than peasants would willingly have marketed . . .

On other issues there was more room for compromise and the kind of everyday negotiation that is part of most human transactions. On some questions, such as the size of the kolkhoz, the state modified its original preferences. On other questions, such as the obligatory collectivization of horses, the state held its ground despite persistent peasant pressure. Still other questions, such as the size of the private plot and the extent of the kolkhoznik's labor obligations, became subjects of endless contestation, with the boundaries of permissible practice shifting back and forth.

Source: Sheila Fitzpatrick, Stalin's Peasants, *1994, pp. 8–9.*

The nature of resistance strategies is also a central issue in Stephen Kotkin's recent, acclaimed study of Magnitogorsk in the 1930s, *Magnetic Mountain* (1995). Kotkin is interested in what French philosopher Michel Foucault called the problem of 'subjectivity': the processes by which individuals are made. Kotkin argues that the struggle between state and society in the 1930s resulted in a new Bolshevik culture; Stalinism is best understood as a system embracing new social and cultural patterns of behaviour. Although Kotkin argues that Stalinist ways of thinking and practices had much in common with other industrial countries (Kotkin 1995: 366), he also suggests that Stalinism had a cultural distinctiveness all of its own.

Document 1.10   Stalinism as a Way of Life

Stalinism was not just a political system, let alone the rule of an individual. It was a set of values, a social identity, a way of life . . .

Such activities [as the trade in forged or stolen documents], if they have been studied at all, have usually been attributed to the moral bankruptcy of individuals forced to live under an illegitimate regime. But far from showing depravity, the proliferation of illegalities may indicate, if not opposition to Bolshevik rule, creative resistance to a set of written and unwritten rules governing appropriate behavior . . .

The urban inhabitants knew how to make the best of their lot; they knew what should be avoided and which rules could be bent under what circumstances and which could not . . . The inhabitants of Magnitogorsk were experts in what they perceived to be the rules of the game. That these new rules of urban life were often unspoken did not mean they were less real . . .

Within the framework provided by the new rules of urban life, the inhabitants of Magnitogorsk were confronted and in turn confronted others with various attitudes, self-understandings and behavior. These constituted what has already been referred to as the little tactics of the habitat, through which life in Magnitogorsk was lived and made sense. Such petty maneuvers and modest stratagems hold an essential clue, for in them the basic outlines of the new socialist society made themselves manifest . . .

'[A]tomization,' if not as total as some commentators have claimed, was considerable. At the same time, however, the terms of the new social identity also forged the people into a larger political community.

Source: Stephen Kotkin, Magnetic Mountain: Stalinism as a Civilization, *1995, pp. 23, 154, 236.*

The study of the social history of the Stalin era has been a very influential tendency in the 1980s and 1990s. In addition to the above, such research has, for example, resulted in detailed studies of the Stalinist terror (Getty and Manning 1993), the popular culture of the war era (Stites 1995), the popular mood during the Leningrad seige (Lomagin 1995), peasant opposition movements of the early 1930s (Viola 1996), patterns of denunciation (Fitzpatrick 1996; Kozlov 1996), popular opinion of the 1930s (S. Davies 1997a), and urban, social and cultural history (Fitzpatrick 1999). Although the work of social historians has not reversed the traditional picture of a highly centralised and coercive state, it has led to a much more nuanced understanding of the relationship between state and society.

Some fascinating material has been released with the opening up of the Soviet archives (see R.W. Davies 1989a, 1997). Dmitri Volkogonov's biography of Stalin was one of the first books to give a taste of the range of materials which were available (Volkogonov 1991). Important collections of documents have appeared, covering Stalin's letters to Molotov (Lih et al. 1995); the Politburo in the 1930s (Khlevniuk et al. 1995); NKVD interrogations of writers (Shentalinsky 1995); wartime Moscow (Gorinov et al. 1995); censorship (Goriaeva 1997); social history (Sokolov 1998); the terror (Getty, Manning and Naumov 1999); as well as Soviet history in general (Koenker and Bachman 1997). So much information is being released that it is impossible for any one scholar to keep abreast of it. However, it is possible to say, in very general terms, that the new material has not led to a major theoretical reassessment of the Stalin regime. Much of what the totalitarian school originally stated about the extent of Stalin's power has been confirmed. His will and ambition remain crucial determinants of the system he created (Suny 1997: 48). At the same time, the complexity of the Stalin regime, which is not really conducive to 'models' of analysis, has also been brought out. Society as well as politics, has been given a voice. In many ways, it is clear that political and social history need not conflict; biographical and social approaches complement one another (Shearer 1996: 20).

From Lenin to Stalin $\Big|$ **2**

The relationship between Lenin and Stalin has always been a matter of controversy. Some historians have seen a continuous path from Lenin's regime to Stalin's dictatorship. From that point of view, Lenin's ideology and tactics were essentially dictatorial and provided the basis for Stalin's system of rule. Lenin was a ruthless, cynical and aggressive dictator who had nothing but scorn for humankind (see Pipes 1996: 10–13). Another perspective is that there was no such inevitable development. Although a dictatorship, Lenin's regime functioned very differently from Stalin's. Furthermore, Lenin's vision of a rational dictatorship with responsible leadership and efficient working institutions, was credible (Lewin 1975: 136).

Part of the dilemma is that Lenin introduced sharply contrasting policies at different times. During the Civil War, he advocated what later became known as War Communism. This involved the nationalisation of all industries, a state trade monopoly and the requisitioning of peasant produce. Peasant opposition was mercilessly crushed. At the same time, peasant unrest and the Kronstadt revolt forced Lenin into a radical change of course. At the 10th Party Congress in March 1921, against considerable opposition from within the party, Lenin brought in the New Economic Policy (NEP), which introduced a mixed economy. Instead of requisitioning grain from the peasants, the regime introduced a graduated, agricultural tax in kind (from 1923 in money only), which gave the peasant the chance to improve the productivity of his land and sell his produce for profit. War Communism and NEP represented two approaches to building a socialist society: the first involved a policy of state-led social engineering and modernisation; in the second, the state still played a central role, but the approach was more evolutionary. The fact that Lenin was associated with both these approaches was very convenient for later Soviet leaders, who could legitimise either their extreme or more moderate policies by claiming them to be truly Leninist.

In 1917, it appears that Stalin spent considerable time as Lenin's assistant (Radzinsky 1996: 107, 115), but he did not play an important role in the October revolution itself. After the Bolsheviks seized power, he was made Commissar of Nationalities. In March 1919, he was appointed to the newly-created Politburo and Orgburo. In April 1919, he was made head of the Workers' and Peasants' Inspectorate, a post he held until April 1922 when he was made General Secretary of the upgraded party Secretariat. This accumulation of offices was a remarkable achievement for a man who was little known in the wider party and certainly not in the country at large.

Lenin had a stroke in May 1922, and at that time his relationship with Stalin remained good. However, in subsequent months their relationship started to deteriorate. During the autumn of 1922, the two men had a dispute over how to organise the integration of non-Russian nationalities into the state structure. Stalin wanted to include the non-Russian nationalities as autonomous republics within a wider Russian state. Lenin, reacting against what he saw as Russian chauvinism, successfully argued for a federal structure, where the Russian republic was one amongst many.

Lenin was annoyed by an occasion in the autumn of 1922 when Ordzhonikidze, trying to impose his will on a Georgian communist called A. Kabakhidze, had beaten him up. Stalin and Dzerzhinsky took a relaxed attitude to the problem. Lenin saw in this the emergence of a crude and dictatorial method of working. It was in the context of such behaviour and the discussions of the nationality question in the autumn of 1922 that Lenin, on 24–25 December 1922, dictated his famous Testament, in which he criticised Stalin and the other Bolshevik leaders, and called for a collective party leadership. On 4 January 1923, he added a postscript to the Testament, in which he suggested that Stalin be removed from his post.

Document 2.1   Lenin's Testament

24 December 1922 . . . The prime factors in the question of stability are such members of the Central Committee as Stalin and Trotsky. I think the relationship between them constitutes the greater part of the danger of a schism, which could be avoided, and this purpose, in my opinion, would be served, among other things, by increasing the number of Central Committee members to 50 or 100.

Comrade Stalin, having become general secretary, has boundless power concentrated in his hands, and I am not sure whether he will always be capable of using that power with sufficient caution. Comrade Trotsky, on the other hand, . . . is distinguished not only by his outstanding ability. He is personally perhaps the most capable man in the present Central Committee, but he has displayed excessive self-assurance and shown excessive preoccupation with the purely administrative side of the work.

These two qualities of the two outstanding leaders of the present Central Committee can inadvertently lead to a schism, and if our party does not take steps to avert this, the schism may come unexpectedly.

I shall not give any further appraisals of the personal qualities of other members of the Central Committee; I shall just recall that the October episode with Zinoviev and Kamenev was, of course, no accident but neither can the blame for it be laid upon them, any more than unbolshevism can upon Trotsky . . .

Bukharin is not only the most valuable and important theorist of the party; he is also rightly considered the favorite of the whole Party, but his theoretical views can be classified as fully Marxist only with great reserve, for there is something scholastic about him (he has never made a study of dialectics, and, I think, never fully understood it).

25 December 1922. As for Piatakov, he is unquestionably a man of outstanding will and outstanding ability, but he shows too much zeal for administration and the administrative side of the work to be relied on in a serious political matter . . .

4 January 1923. Stalin is too crude, and this defect, although quite tolerable in our midst and in dealings with us Communists, becomes intolerable in a general secretary. That is why I suggest that the comrades think about a way of removing Stalin from that post and appointing another man in his stead who in all other respects differs from Comrade Stalin in having only one advantage, namely in being more tolerant, more loyal, more polite, and more considerate to the comrades, less capricious, etc. This circumstance may appear to be an insignificant trifle. But I think from the standpoint of safeguards against a split and from the point of view of what I wrote about the relationship between Stalin and Trotsky, it is not a trifle, or it is a trifle that can assume decisive significance.

Source: Lars H. Lih et al. (eds), Stalin's Letters to Molotov, *1995, pp. 241–2.*

There is evidence to suggest that Lenin had been preparing to attack Stalin publicly at the 12th Party Congress in April 1923. Fortunately for Stalin, Lenin had another stroke on 7 March, and was unable to pursue his concerns. After Lenin died, the Testament was brought to the attention of the 13th Party Congress in May 1924. However, it was not discussed by the Congress as a whole. A resolution was tabled in which Stalin was enjoined simply to take account of Lenin's criticisms, and after that the matter was dropped (Volkogonov 1991: 93–4). Stalin was helped by the fact that the other rivals for leadership did not emerge well from the document either. Furthermore, Zinoviev and Kamenev regarded Trotsky as the chief contender for leadership and Stalin was happy to operate in their shadow while he continued to build up his power base.

Although his relationship with Lenin had cooled in these years, Stalin also recognised the value of presenting himself as the guardian of Lenin's legacy. A cult of Lenin had begun to emerge during Lenin's lifetime (Tumarkin 1983: 64–111), and after his death Stalin encouraged its development. For example, on 26 January 1924, two days after Lenin's death and on the eve of his funeral, Stalin gave a speech at the Second All-Union Congress of Soviets in which he read out an oath of allegiance to Lenin. The style of the speech had a pseudo-religious quality to it; Lenin was becoming a new 'icon', in place of the symbols of traditional religion.

Document 2.2 Stalin's Oath to Lenin

Comrades, we Communists are people of a special cut. We have been cut out of peculiar stuff . . . There is no loftier title than that of a member of the party, of which Comrade Lenin has been founder and leader . . . It is not given to everyone to endure the hardships and storms that go with membership of such a party. Sons of the working class, sons of misery and struggle, sons of incredible privation and heroic endeavour, these, above all, ought to be the members of such a party . . .

In leaving us, Comrade Lenin ordained us to hold high and keep pure the great title of member of the party. We vow to thee, Comrade Lenin, that we shall honourably fulfil this thy commandment . . .

In leaving us, Comrade Lenin ordained us to guard the unity of our party like the apple of our eye. We vow to thee, Comrade Lenin, that without sparing our strength, we shall fulfil honourably this thy commandment, too . . .

In leaving us, Comrade Lenin ordained us to guard and strengthen the dictatorship of the proletariat. We vow to thee, Comrade Lenin, that without sparing our strength we shall honourably fulfil this thy commandment, too . . .

In leaving us, Comrade Lenin ordained us to strengthen with all our might the alliance of workers and peasants. We vow to thee, Comrade Lenin, that we shall fulfil honourably this thy commandment, too . . .

In leaving us, Comade Lenin ordained us to strengthen and broaden the Union of the Republics. We vow to thee, Comrade Lenin, that we shall honourably fulfil this thy commandment, too . . .

In leaving us, Comrade Lenin ordained us to keep faith with the principles of the Communist International. We vow to thee, Comrade Lenin, that we shall not spare our lives in the endeavour to strengthen and broaden the alliance of the workers of the whole world – the Communist International.

Source: Isaac Deutscher, Stalin, *1967, p. 270.*

Encouraged by Stalin, the cult of Lenin became very strong in the following years. Furthermore, a myth was created around the revolution itself. In his film, *October* (1927), Sergei Eisenstein presented the storming of the Winter Palace as a spontaneous explosion of popular anger by workers and soldiers, whereas the original event was low-key by comparison. Although the film emphasises the influence of 'the people', rather than the personalities of history, Lenin, speaking to the crowd following his arrival at the Finland Station in April 1917, was depicted in a memorably heroic pose (see also Document 12.7).

Document 2.3   Lenin at the Finland Station in Eisenstein's *October*

[See screen shot opposite]

Source: October, *1927.*

Stalin used Lenin to legitimise his position in his ideological battles with political opponents. At the end of 1924, Stalin introduced the idea of 'socialism in one country'. In theory, the revolution in Russia was to be accompanied by revolution

across Europe. When this did not happen, Stalin, quoting selectively from Lenin's writings, advocated 'socialism in one country': the idea that it was possible to build socialism in Russia before the international revolution took place. 'Socialism in one country' was designed to differ from Trotsky's theory of 'permanent revolution', and in attacking Trotsky's position, Stalin identified his own approach as the truly Leninist one. 'Socialism in one country' appealed to those who wanted the country to settle down after the troubles of the previous decade. It also appealed to latent feelings of Russian nationalism. In 1920, a collection of essays had appeared in the Russian emigration entitled *Change of Landmarks*, which suggested that the Bolshevik ideology was acquiring nationalistic characteristics. It had found a number of adherents amongst the Soviet intelligentsia. Stalin discreetly touched a similar chord when, in his 'Foundations of Leninism' (1924), he attacked the 'permanentists' for failing to appreciate the strength of the Russian peasantry and proletariat.

Document 2.4   Stalin's Critique of 'Permanent Revolution'

Why did Lenin combat the idea of 'permanent (uninterrupted) revolution'?

Because Lenin proposed that the revolutionary capacities of the peasantry be utilized 'to the utmost' and that the fullest use be made of their revolutionary energy for the complete liquidation of tsarism and for the transition to the proletarian revolution, whereas the adherents of 'permanent revolution' did not understand the important role of the peasantry in the Russian revolution, underestimated the strength of the revolutionary energy of the peasantry, underestimated the strength and ability of the Russian proletariat to lead the peasantry, and thereby hampered the work of emancipating the peasantry from the influence of the bourgeoisie, the work of rallying the peasantry around the proletariat.

Because Lenin proposed that the revolution *be crowned* with the transfer of power to the proletariat, whereas the adherents of 'permanent' revolution wanted to *begin* at once with the establishment of the power of the proletariat, failing to realise that in so doing they were closing their eyes to such a 'minor detail' as the survivals of serfdom and were leaving out of account so important a force as the Russian peasantry, failing to understand that such a policy could only retard the winning of the peasantry to the side of the proletariat . . .

The idea of 'permanent' revolution is not a new idea. It was first advanced by Marx at the end of the forties in his well-known *Address to the Communist League* (1850). It was from this document that our 'permanentists' took the idea of uninterrupted revolution. It should be noted, however, that in taking it from Marx our 'permanentists' altered it somewhat, and in altering it spoilt it and made it unfit for practical use. The experienced hand of Lenin was needed to rectify this mistake, to take Marx's idea of uninterrupted revolution in its pure form and make it a cornerstone of his theory of revolution . . .

That is why Lenin regarded this theory as a semi-Menshevik theory and said that it 'borrows from the Bolsheviks their call for a decisive revolutionary struggle and the conquest of political power by the proletariat, and from the Mensheviks the "repudiation" of the role of the peasantry'.

Source: J. Stalin, 'The Foundations of Leninism', Leninism, 1940, pp. 24–6.

Trotsky was forced to resign as Minister of War in January 1925, and the theory of 'socialism in one country' was accepted as official party policy at the 14th Party

Conference in April 1925. However, by then, Stalin was encountering opposition from another quarter. During the years 1923–25, the USSR was led by a 'triumvirate' consisting of Zinoviev, Kamenev and Stalin. Outwardly, Zinoviev was the most powerful of the three, but in practice it was increasingly Stalin who held the levers of power. The 'triumvirate' were united by their hostility to Trotsky, but with Trotsky's power fading, their differences soon came into the open. The unity of the triumvirate was always shaky. As early as July 1923, Zinoviev was expressing concern about Stalin's rising power (R.W. Davies 1997: 141). At the 14th Party Congress in December 1925, Kamenev attacked the dominance of Stalin in the leadership. However, he had difficulty making himself heard. Stalin's control of the party machine meant that it was very hard to express a dissonant word publicly.

Document 2.5   Kamenev Attacks Stalin

We are against creating the theory of the 'leader', we are against making a 'leader'. We are against the Secretariat, which in practice unites policy and organisation, standing above political organs. We believe that our leadership should be organised so that the Politburo is truly all powerful, bringing together all the policies of our party, and that together with that the Secretariat is subject to it and technically carrying out its commands. (Noise.) We cannot consider it normal and think that it is harmful for the party if the position continues whereby the Secretariat unites the policy and organisation and in practice decides policy beforehand . . . I have come to the conclusion that Comrade Stalin cannot carry our the task of uniting the Bolshevik staff. (Voices from seats: 'That is not true', 'Rubbish', 'That is what it is about', 'They have shown their hand!' Noise. Applause from the Leningrad delegation. Cries: 'We won't surrender the command posts to you.' 'Stalin!', 'Stalin!' The delegates rise and salute Comrade Stalin. Stormy applause. Cries: 'Here's where the party's united. The Bolshevik general staff must be united.') . . .

'Long live Comrade Stalin.' (Prolonged stormy applause, cries 'Hurrah!' Noise.)

Source: M. Glavatsky et al. (eds), Khrestomatia po istorii Rossii, 1917–1940, *1995, pp. 223–4.*

At the 10th Party Congress in 1921, Lenin had pushed through a ban on factions in the party. While an issue was being discussed, it was possible to suggest diverse points of view. However, when the party had come to a particular conclusion, it was essential to accept it. Failure to do so was factionalism and merited severe punishment. The strengthening of central control over the party was a response to two opposition groups: the Democratic Centralists, who wanted a return to genuine elections and debate within the party; and the Workers' Opposition, which sought to combat a perceived rift between the party and the working class. It was also an attempt by the leadership to preserve its political control while the market was introduced. It has been argued that the ban on factions paved the way for Stalin to gain control of the party

(Schapiro 1977: xvii, 314–42). Certainly, Stalin made full use of the ban on factions. Writing in *The Foundations of Leninism*, he placed great emphasis on party unity.

Document 2.6   Stalin on Party Unity

The achievement and maintenance of the dictatorship of the proletariat are impossible without a party which is strong by reason of its solidarity and iron discipline. But iron discipline in the Party is inconceivable without unity of will, without complete and absolute unity of action on the part of all members of the Party. This does not mean, of course, that the possibility of conflicts within the Party is thereby precluded. On the contrary, iron discipline does not preclude but presupposes criticism and contest of opinion within the Party. Least of all does it mean that discipline must be 'blind'. On the contrary, iron discipline does not preclude but presupposes conscious and voluntary submission, for only conscious discipline can be truly iron discipline. But after a contest of opinion has been closed, after criticism has been exhausted and a decision has been arrived at, unity of will and unity of action of all Party members are the necessary conditions without which neither Party unity nor iron discipline in the Party is conceivable.

Source: J. Stalin, 'The Foundations of Leninism', Leninism, 1940, p. 80–1.

In his battles with his rivals in the Politburo, Stalin would often avoid substantive issues and instead accuse his opponents of factionalism. For example, moving against Zinoviev in 1926, Stalin noted Zinoviev's association with M.M. Lashevich, an old Bolshevik who was first deputy of the USSR Revolutionary Military Council. Stalin decided to use the fact that Lashevich had spoken at a meeting of oppositionists outside Moscow as an excuse to strike against Zinoviev himself. Stalin planned the attack on Zinoviev very carefully, accusing him primarily of factionalism (see R.W. Davies 1997: 147).

Document 2.7   Stalin on Zinoviev

Sochi, [25 June 1926]

To Molotov, Rykov, Bukharin, and other friends,
    I have long pondered the matter of the Lashevich affair, going back and forth, linking it with the question of the opposition groups in general; several times I came to various opinions and have finally settled on the following:
1. Before the appearance of the Zinoviev group, those with oppositional tendencies (Trotsky, the workers' opposition, and others) behaved more or less loyally and were more or less tolerable;
2. With the appearance of the Zinoviev group, those with the oppositional tendencies began to grow arrogant and break the bounds of loyalty;

3. The Zinoviev group became the mentor of everyone in the opposition who was for splitting the party; in effect it has become the leader of the splitting tendencies in the party; . . .

10. Previously I had thought that a *broad* resolution on unity was needed *at the plenum*. Now I think that it would be better to leave a resolution for the [XV] *Conference* ([where we could provide] a theoretical foundation and so on) or the *Congress*. At the plenum, we can and should limit ourselves to a *brief* resolution on unity in the narrow sense of the word *in connection with the Lashevich affair*, citing Lenin's resolution on unity at the Tenth Congress. This resolution should say that Zinoviev is being removed from the Politburo not because of differences of opinion with the Central Committee – there are no less profound disagreements with Trotsky, after all, although the issue of removing Trotsky from the Politburo is not on the agenda – but because of his [Zinoviev's] policy of *schism*. I think this will be better: the workers will understand it, since they value party unity, and this will be a serious warning for the other opposition groups. Dzerzhinsky can be brought into the Politburo to replace Zinoviev. The party will take this well. Or the number of Politburo members can be raised to ten by bringing in both Dzerzhinsky and Rudzutak. Obviously with a *broad* plenum resolution (the previous plan), we would be forced to *unite* Zinoviev and Trotsky *officially* in one camp, which is perhaps premature and strategically irrational now. Better to break them individually. Let Trotsky and Piatakov defend Zinoviev, and we will listen. At any rate that will be better at this stage. Then we'll see.

Source: Lars H. Lih et al. (eds), Stalin's Letters to Molotov, *1995, pp. 115–16.*

At a joint plenum of the Central Committee and the Central Control Commission in July 1926, Stalin magnified the issue to suggest that Zinoviev's activity was part of a wider conspiracy against the party, and factionalism was condemned (see Gregor 1974: 286–8).

At the same plenum in July 1926, the forces of the left, including Trotsky, Zinoviev, Kamenev came together to form a United Opposition. Their 'declaration of the thirteen' advocated greater party democracy and criticised the moderate economic policy of the time, which was based around the idea of an alliance (*smychka*) between the proletariat and peasantry.

Document 2.8   Declaration of the Thirteen

Lenin always took into account the danger that the concentration of administrative power in the hands of the party would lead to bureaucratic pressure on the Party. Precisely from this arose Vladimir Ilich's idea about organizing the Control Commission, which, while it had no administrative power in its hands, would have all the power essential for the struggle with bureaucratism, for the defense of the right of a party member to express his convictions freely and to vote according to his conscience without fearing any punitive consequences . . .

Meanwhile . . . the Central Control Commission itself has become a purely administrative organ, which assists the repression conducted by other bureaucratic organs, executing for them the punitive part of the work, prosecuting any independent thought in the party . . .

All this is gravely reflected in the internal life of the party organization. Members of the party are afraid openly to express aloud their most cherished thoughts, wishes, demands. This is what constitutes the cause of the 'affair' of Comrade Lashevich et al.

The present year again reveals with all clarity that state industry is lagging behind the development of the economy as a whole. The new harvest again catches us without supplies of goods. But movement towards socialism is assured only when the tempo of development of industry does not lag behind the general development of the economy . . .

The question of the *smychka* is under present conditions above all a question of industrialization . . .

The fact is that under the guise of a union of the poor peasantry with the middle peasant, we observe steadily and regularly the political subordination of the poor peasantry to the middle peasants, and through them to the *kulaks*.

Source: Robert Daniels, A Documentary History of Communism, *vol. 1, 1985, pp. 187–8.*

At the 15th Party Conference in October 1926, when Trotsky was expelled from the Politburo, the opposition tried to present their arguments but were denied the right to speak. During subsequent weeks, they attempted to mount demonstrations in order to appeal to a wider audience, but their meetings were broken up.

In 1927, Stalin's disputes with the United Opposition involved differences over foreign affairs. In April 1927, the Soviet strategy of encouraging the Chinese Communist Party to join the Chinese nationalist Kuomintang, began to go disastrously wrong. The Kuomintang leader, Chiang Kai-Shek, after capturing Shanghai with communist support, then proceeded to instigate a massacre of local communists. Stalin then switched Soviet support to a rival left Kuomintang organisation, based in Wuhan. However, by the end of July 1927, that had begun to disintegrate. An attempted communist uprising was suppressed in the middle of 1928. The United Opposition had bitterly criticised this support of the left Kuomintang, declaring that the Chinese proletariat and poor peasants had an inherent strength of their own. However, members of the United Opposition were forbidden to publish their views (Ulam 1974a: 178–9).

Trotsky and Zinoviev had also been very critical of the policy of support for moderate, reformist trade unions in Britain, and in particular the Anglo-Soviet Committee which acted as a link between Soviet trade unions and the General Council of the British Trades Union Congress. After the involvement of British trade union leaders in the ending of the British General Strike in 1926, the United

Opposition demanded that Soviet members should quit the Committee. In May 1927, the British government ordered a raid on the Soviet Embassy and then severed diplomatic relations. A 'war scare' ensued, which Stalin exploited to appeal for greater party unity.

Stalin's policies, both in regard to China and Britain, had not proved a success, and in a speech of August 1927 to a joint meeting of the Central Committee and the Central Control Commission, he was forced to defend his strategy. He suggested that his opponents were adventurists, who did not appreciate the need for the sort of tactical flexibility which Lenin had emphasised in his pamphlet, *'Left Wing' Communism, an Infantile Disorder* (1920) (see Lenin 1947 vol. 2: 571–644).

Document 2.9   Stalin Defends Soviet Foreign Policy, 1927

[Our policy] was to turn the Wuhan Kuomintang into a centre of struggle against the counter-revolution, into the kernel of the future revolutionary-democratic dictatorship of the proletariat and the peasantry.

Was this policy right?

The facts have shown that it was the only correct policy capable of training the broad masses of the workers and peasants in the spirit of the further development of the revolution.

The opposition at the time demanded the immediate formation of Soviets of workers' and peasants' deputies. But that would have been adventurism, an adventurist leap ahead, for the immediate formation of Soviets would have meant jumping the left-Kuomintang phase of development. Why? Because the Kuomintang in Wuhan, having supported alliance with the communists, had not yet been discredited and exposed in the eyes of the broad masses of the workers and peasants, had not yet exhausted itself as a bourgeois-revolutionary organization . . .

What is the Anglo-Soviet Committee? It represents one of the means by which our trade unions are connected with the English unions, with reformist unions, with reactionary unions . . .

In proceeding to the formation of the Anglo-Soviet Committee, we managed to establish open contact with the trade union organizations of the working masses of England. What for? Firstly, to facilitate the creation of a united front of the workers against capital, or, at least, to make more difficult the struggle of the reactionary leaders of the unions against the formation of such a united front . . .

Are communists in general permitted to work in reactionary trade unions? This is not only permitted, but is sometimes obligatory, for in the reactionary unions there are millions of workers, and communists have no right to refrain from entering these unions, finding the way to the masses, and winning them for communism.

Look at Lenin's little book on *'Left Wing' Communism, an Infantile*

Disorder, and you will see that the Leninist tactic obliges communists not to refuse to work in reactionary trade unions . . .

Why do certain imperialist circles regard the USSR with hostility, organizing a united front against it? Because the USSR is a rich market for goods and for the export of capital . . .

There is the basis and origin of the inevitability of a new war, whether it is between separate imperialist coalitions, or against the USSR.

Source: Jane Degras (ed.), Soviet Documents on Foreign Policy, *vol. 2, 1925–1932, 1952, pp. 239–44.*

At the 15th Party Congress in December 1927, Trotsky, Zinoviev and Kamenev were accused of refusing to accept party discipline and were expelled from the party altogether. Charges of factionalism against the opposition were always likely to resonate with party members. Bolshevik ideology assumed that a scientific knowledge of history was possible. Lenin's particular contribution to Marxist thought had been to present the party, interpreted as the vanguard of the proletariat, as the primary interpreter of the historical process. This made it very difficult to criticise the party, for to disagree with the party line meant to stand outside of history. Even Trotsky, who so frequently disagreed with Stalin, was compelled to protest his loyalty in such terms at the 13th Party Congress in 1924 (see also Document 13.12).

Document 2.10   Trotsky on the Party

The party in the last analysis is always right, because the party is the single historic instrument given to the proletariat for the solution of its fundamental problems . . . I know that one must not be right *against* the party. One can be right only with the party, and through the party, for history has created no other road for the realization of what is right. The English have a saying: 'Right or wrong – my country.' With far greater historic justification we may say: right or wrong, on separate particular issues, it is my party.

Source: Isaac Deutscher, Stalin, *1967, p. 278.*

It would be wrong to assume that all party members were wholly subservient in the 1920s, or indeed later. Stalin did not have everything his own way, and it was not until late 1929 that he had a Politburo that he could really rely on. After the defeat of the Left and United Oppositions, Stalin took on the Right Opposition and its main representatives, Bukharin, Rykov and Tomsky. The following letter to Stalin from Rykov, the Prime Minister, in which Rykov comments on Stalin's pamphlet of January 1926, *On the Problems of Leninism*, suggests a man who was willing to speak to Stalin on equal terms, and with a more moderate frame of mind. Rykov accepts the assumption that all methods are valid for the sake of the revolution, but he also indicates an openness to a freer and less coercive political system.

Document 2.11   Rykov on Dictatorship

6 February 1926

Com[rade] Stalin.

I have read your brochure. I read it between receptions, telephone calls, signing papers etc. So I could have missed a lot. It seems to me that the most crucial chapter is the one on dictatorship. Dictatorship is interpreted as violence and that, of course, is in all respects correct. But in the brochure there are no adequately clear precise formulations on the fact that the forms of dictatorship and the forms of violence change according to the circumstances, that dictatorship does not exclude, for example, 'revolutionary legality', and even a certain expansion of suffrage. In conditions of civil peace, of course, a dictatorship runs differently than in conditions of civil war. The extra-judicial use of violence becomes less frequent and will diminish where there is a weakening of hostile forces. This relates, for example, to the use of the highest form of punishment. The growing vibrancy of the soviets and the increase in rights of volost and uezd soviets, with the influx into them of wide circles of the non-party peasantry – in no way contradicts the dictatorship of the proletariat and can be realized in life only in certain conditions (the unification of all working and exploited people around the working class and the communist party). There should be something on this theme, it seems to me, so that the reader would find in the brochure an answer to certain topical questions of contemporary reality.

The brochure, it seems to me, is correct. Grisha [Zinoviev] will answer it and I fear that we will have to conduct a new literary battle, although it won't be possible to avoid that in any case.

A.I. Rykov

Source: 'Znaio, Chto Vy ne Nuzhdaetsia v Pokhvaklakh', Istochnik, no. 6, 1994, pp. 85–6.

Bukharin had been on the left of the party during the early Civil War years, but during NEP his outlook had become more moderate. He was prepared to countenance a mixed economy, and argued that a rich peasantry would provide a good base for the industrialisation of the country. He argued that a large income for agriculture would lead to increased revenue for state industry. In January 1929, on the fifth anniversary of Lenin's death, he wrote an essay, 'The Political Testament of Lenin'. Referring to Lenin's article of March 1923, 'Better Fewer, but Better', which was a defence of NEP as a strategy for industrialisation, Bukharin reiterated his own his vision of an alliance between the proletariat and peasantry, and called for a focus on quality and productivity. It was a very different strategy from the one that Stalin was by then pursuing.

Document 2.12 Bukharin Defends the *Smychka*

In his well-known essay 'Better Fewer, but Better', Lenin develops his plan in two directions, which relate to the directives on the union of workers and peasants, and the economy. This is the plan of *industrialisation* and the plan of *the cooperation* of the population. Having stated that we must preserve the trust of the peasants . . ., reduce the state apparatus to a minimum, accumulate gradually, com. Lenin then asks: 'Won't this mean the region of peasant narrowmindedness?'

In answer to this Vladimir Ilich says:

'No. If we preserve for the working class leadership over the peasantry, we shall be able, by exercising the greatest possible economy in the economic life of the state, to use everything we save to develop our large-scale machine industry, . . . electrification, the hydraulic extraction of peat . . .'

What here distinguishes the Leninist approach from any other? Firstly, at the basis of the whole plan lies a union of workers and peasants and the 'greatest carefulness' about this matter, a carefulness which sharply distinguishes the Leninist 'earth' from the Trotskyite 'heavens'; secondly, there is here a clearly defined answer as to . . . the *sources of additional sums* which we must increasingly spend on the industrialisation of the country . . . These sources come from first of all a maximum reduction in all unproductive expenses, which are truly huge, and a raising of qualitative indices, in the first place a raising of the productivity of people's work. No issues [of money], no eating through our stocks (gold, goods or currency), no overtaxation of the peasantry, but a *qualitative improvement in the productivity of public work and a decisive struggle against unproductive expenditure – these are the main sources of accumulation.*

Source: Nikolai Bukharin, 'Politicheskoe zaveshchanie Lenina', Kommunist, 1988, no. 2, p. 97.

The importance of Bukharin is that for some historians he represents the human face of Soviet socialism, and his ideology the road not taken by the Bolsheviks but which perhaps could have one day converged with the Western European social democratic tradition. Stalin was associated with this kind of approach in the mid-1920s, but with the defeat of the Left and United Oppositions, he moved sharply away from such moderation. Indeed, it was ironic that Stalin now appeared to draw instead from the economic thinking of the left. E.A. Preobrazhensky was one of the foremost advocates of the left's approach. In his *The New Economics* (1926), he argued for a process of 'primitive socialist accumulation', where instead of a partnership between town and countryside, the peasantry would be taxed unequally in order to build up savings for investment. The following document is taken from an essay which Preobrazhensky published in 1927, in which he predicted that there would be growing class differentiation in the countryside, and suggested that a war between the party and the rich peasantry was inevitable. A class analysis was central to the Bolshevik perception of the world, and this kind of thinking played a major role in the decision to collectivise agriculture in the autumn of 1929.

Document 2.13   Preobrazhensky on NEP

Although during the period of primitive socialist accumulation we *hold to* nonequivalent exchange (*obmen*), using it for the reconstruction of our technological base, that does not mean that we will *hold out* for very long in such an extreme position if we do not overtake capitalism but continue to lag behind it or, while moving forward, nevertheless maintain the same relative distance from it in technology and in the development of our productive forces . . .

The kulak tries to offset the nonequivalence of exchange with the town, hoping that by not selling in months when the poor and middle peasant strata are marketing grain at the prices fixed by the state, he can thereby drive up grain prices in the spring. He experiments with replacing certain crops with other, more profitable ones. He tries to avoid the market and accumulate in kind by raising more livestock and poultry from his own production, by constructing new farm buildings, and so on. But the possibilities for such economic manoeuvers are not very great, and in the end the kulak is forced into a confrontation with the entire Soviet system. And the longer it takes for this confrontation, the more the kulak will be inclined to seek a solution to the problem not by economic means within the Soviet system, not in a partial adjustment of the equilibrium in his favor, but by attempting to force his way through to the world market by counterrevolutionary means. Here the problem of economic equilibrium rests squarely on the problem of social equilibrium, that is, the relation of class forces for and against the Soviet system. Two systems of equilibrium are struggling for supremacy: on the one hand, equilibrium on a capitalist basis – which means participation in the world economy regulated by the law of value – by abolishing the Soviet system and suppressing the proletariat, and on the other hand, equilibrium on the basis of a temporarily nonequivalent exchange serving as the source of socialist reconstruction and *inevitably signifying the suppression of capitalist tendencies of development, particularly in agriculture.*

Source: E.A. Preobrazhensky, 'Economic Equilibrium in the System of the USSR', The Crisis of Soviet Industrialisation, 1979, pp. 176–7, 179.

To what extent did Stalin always intend to launch the so-called 'Stalin revolution' at the end of the 1920s? Some, following 'circumstantial' explanations, argue that the new policy was a response to crisis. They argue that the war scare of 1927 created considerable tension (Reiman 1987: 12–13), that an apparent shortfall in grain supplies in 1928 suggested a serious social crisis was emerging (Deutscher 1967: 313), and that the collectivisation policies were not premeditated, but a response to the serious economic situation (Carr and Davies 1969: 269). Another argument is that Stalin had long-standing ideological inclinations, pushing him in the direction of terror, statism and anti-peasantism (Service 1998: 23). It has been suggested that the importance of the war scare and the grain crisis was exaggerated in order to justify the shift to a more extreme policy (Tucker 1977: 88).

A related question is how viable was the policy of NEP, irrespective of whether the Bolsheviks could have found it ideologically acceptable? One view is that NEP was unlikely to provide the conditions for rapid economic development, because peasant demand would not have provided a sufficient internal market for rapid industrial expansion (Gerschenkron 1962: 144). Another perspective that there was a contradiction in NEP between the principles of the free market and the idea of state planning (Carr 1978: 278). More positively, however, it has been argued that the Right Opposition's plan for an alliance between the city and the countryside offered a coherent long-term programme, which would have achieved many of the objectives of the first Five Year Plan without the suffering entailed (Cohen 1973: Chapter 9; Millar 1976). Much has been written on this question; an answer to it largely depends on an assessment of the importance of quickly establishing a heavy industrial base (R.W. Davies 1998: 37).

Collectivisation | 3

Although the Bolsheviks claimed that the peasants were their allies, in practice they always suspected that they were in some way hostage to them: peasant interests stood in the way of their advance to a proletarian state. The Russian peasantry was fiercely independent, and had its own values and traditions. Rural life was based on a pre-capitalist economy, in which the family was the basic unit of production. Work was regulated not by the clock, but by the needs of the seasons. Holidays coincided with Orthodox festivals. The village, the *mir*, was a 'world in itself' (Altrichter 1991: 192).

During the crisis of NEP, Stalin decided that this kind of traditional peasant society stood in the way of progress; either it would have to be destroyed or it would destroy the revolution itself. The harvests of 1927 and 1928 were both poor. The low level of state grain procurement in the autumn of 1927 led Stalin to suggest that the peasants were deliberately hoarding grain. In a telegram sent to all party organisations on 6 January 1928, Stalin warned party leaders that they would lose their jobs if they did not achieve grain procurement targets swiftly (see Hughes 1996: 250), and he himself visited Siberia to encourage the forcible procurement of grain. Anyone who resisted was to be branded a kulak and arrested under Article 107 of the criminal code. In July 1928, although apparently still open to the possibilities offered by small-scale agriculture, Stalin gave a speech in which he suggested that the peasantry should pay a 'tribute' or surtax, to finance industrialisation (Carr and Davies 1969: 78).

In the autumn of 1928, a new method of grain collection began to be introduced, which had clear parallels with the policy of War Communism. Stalin called it the 'Ural-Siberian method' because it had been piloted by certain districts in Siberia. The method, sometimes called 'self-taxation', involved the use of 'social pressure' against kulaks (Hughes 1996: 73–91). Bolshevik analysis, assuming growing class division in the countryside, divided the peasantry into rich peasants (kulaks), middle peasants (seredniaks), poor peasants (bedniaks) and agricultural wage labourers or landless peasants (batraks). In spite of attempts to define these groups precisely, the divisions were in practice very arbitrary (Lewin 1985: 121–41). In the Ural-Siberian method, local village gatherings, *skhody*, made up of middle, poor and landless peasants, were encouraged to call for grain to be procured from kulaks, or for the confiscation of kulak property. This gave the coercive extraction of grain the appearance of being a voluntary measure.

By early 1929 the Ural-Siberian method was being applied in many parts of the country. It was formally sanctioned for use in Kazakhstan, the Urals and Siberia by the

Politburo on 21 March 1929, and was given legal status on 28 June 1929. The Right Opposition expressed deep misgivings about it; for example, Bukharin warned at the April plenum of the Central Committee that it meant the end of NEP (Taniuchi 1981: 521).

Document 3.1   The 'Ural-Siberian Method'

PROTOCOL 69 OF POLITBURO SESSION, 21 MARCH 1929

Attended: Voroshilov, Kalinin, Kuibyshev, Molotov, Rykov, Tomsky, Stalin. Cand[idate member]s: Mikoyan; plus 29 others.

Decided: To approve decision of Politburo of 20 March on grain procurement and apply this method in Kazakhstan, Urals, Siberia.

Decision of Politburo, 20 March 1929

To adopt the suggestion of comrade Kaganovich on measures for improving grain procurement.

a) The decision to use compulsory quotas to fulfil the grain plan in villages should be an open initiative not of grain procurement representatives or organs of power but of social organizations (bednota groups and actifs) and then promulgated by the general meeting of citizens.
b) In fulfilling the grain plan adopted by the general meeting it is necessary to separate out the kulak *verkhushka* [upper echelon] in the village from the mass of the peasants in order to apply against them the fixed compulsory duties to sell grain to the state from their surpluses, either through the general meeting or by special commissions acting on its decisions.
c) The remainder of the grain plan, after kulaks have fulfilled their duties, is to be divided up among the peasantry according to self-taxation rates. The whole process should be conducted with active agitational work and the mobilization of proletarian social influence on the peasant masses.

Signed: Stalin

Source: James Hughes, Stalinism in a Russian Province, 1996, pp. 251–2.

This move towards a coercive solution to the peasant problem was very much Stalin's own policy. Although the left of the party had advocated greater investment in industry, financed by taxing the peasantry, it had never contemplated the kind of drastic approach Stalin now put forward. Certainly, it was in Stalin's character to use aggressive, administrative methods to achieve his ends. His recently published letters to Molotov bear out this side of his character. They reveal a man obsessed with checking up on whether officials had carried out orders, and keen on punitive measures against apparently hostile behaviour (see Lih 1995: 14). For example, in reference to a draft of a Central Committee decree on grain procurements, Stalin wrote the following letter to Molotov on 10 August 1929. All his suggestions were incorporated into a decree on grain procurements, issued on 15 August 1929 (see Lih *et al.* 1995: 14, 166–7).

Document 3.2 Stalin to Molotov on Grain Procurements

Hello, Com. Molotov,

I read the Central Committee's decree on grain procurements. Despite all its merits, I think it is *completely inadequate*. The main problem with grain procurements at present is 1) the presence of a large number of *urban speculators* at or near the grain market who take the peasants' grain away from the government and – the main thing – create a wait-and-see attitude among the grain holders; 2) *competition between procurement organizations*, which creates the opportunity for grain-holders to be obstinate and not give up the grain (while waiting for higher prices), to hide the grain, to take their time turning over the grain; 3) *the desire of a whole number of collective farms* to hide grain surpluses and sell grain on the side . . .

My advice:

1) give a directive *immediately* to the [local] GPUs to *immediately* start punitive measures regarding urban (and urban-related) speculators in grain products (that is, arrest them and deport them from grain regions) in order to make the grain-holders feel *right now* (at the beginning of the grain procurement campaign) that little can be gained from speculation, that the grain can be given without trouble (and without loss) only to state and cooperative organizations;

2) give a directive *immediately* to the directors of the *cooperatives, Soiuzkhleb* [state grain purchasing agency], *OGPU*, and the *judicial agencies* to expose and *immediately* hand over to the courts (with *immediate* dismissal from their posts) all those procurement officials caught [trying to obtain grain by competing with other state agencies], as indisputably alien and Nepman elements (I don't exclude 'Communists') who have burrowed into our organizations like thieves and maliciously helped to wreck the cause of the workers' state;

3) establish surveillance of collective farms (through the Collective Farm Center, the party organizations, the OGPU), so that those *directors* of collective farms caught holding back grain surpluses or selling them on the side will be *immediately* dismissed from their posts and *tried* for defrauding the state and for wrecking . . .

Regards,
J. Stalin

I agree wholly.

Voroshilov

Source: Lars H. Lih et al. (eds), Stalin's Letters to Molotov, *1995, pp. 165–6.*

The Right Opposition were, of course, extremely unhappy with these developments. However, although their gradualist strategy was admired in some circles, they lacked the skills of political infighting of the Stalin faction. They lost their hold on the Moscow Party organisation in the autumn of 1928 and Tomsky lost his post as leader of the trades unions in early 1929. Bukharin was removed from the Politburo in November 1929.

A campaign to collectivise the mass of the peasantry was launched in the autumn of 1929. Middle and poor peasants were forced to enter collective farms, *kolkhozy*, white kulaks had their wealth confiscated and were usually deported or sent to labour camps. In a speech of 27 December 1929 at a conference of Marxist agronomists, Stalin called for the 'elimination of the kulaks as a class'.

Document 3.3 The Offensive Against the Kulaks

We have passed from the policy of *restricting* the exploiting tendencies of the kulaks to the policy of *eliminating* the kulaks as a class . . .

Until recently the Party adhered to the policy of *restricting* the exploiting tendencies of the kulaks . . .

Was this policy correct? Yes, it was absolutely correct at the time. Could we have undertaken such an offensive against the kulaks some five years or three years ago? Could we then have counted on success in such an offensive? No, we could not. That would have been the most dangerous adventurism. It would have been a very dangerous playing at an offensive. For we should certainly have failed, and our failure would have strengthened the position of the kulaks. Why? Because we did not yet have in the countryside strong points in the form of a wide network of state farms and collective farms which could be the basis for a determined offensive against the kulaks. Because at that time we were not yet able to *replace* the capitalist production of the kulaks by the socialist production of the collective farms and state farms.

In 1926–1927, the Zinoviev-Trotsky opposition did its utmost to impose on the Party the policy of an immediate offensive against the kulaks. The Party did not embark on that dangerous adventure, for it knew that serious people cannot afford to play at an offensive. An offensive against the kulaks is a serious matter. It should not be confused with declamations against the kulaks. Nor should it be confused with pin-pricks against the kulaks, which the Zinoviev-Trotsky opposition did its utmost to impose upon the Party. To launch an offensive against the kulaks means that we must smash the kulaks, eliminate them as a class. Unless we set ourselves these aims, an offensive would be mere declamation, pin-pricks, phrasemongering, anything but a real Bolshevik offensive. To launch an offensive against the kulaks means that we must prepare for it and then strike at the kulaks, strike so hard as to prevent them from rising to their feet again.

Today, we have an adequate material base for us to strike at the kulaks, to break their resistance, to eliminate them as a class, and to *replace* their output with the output of the collective farms and state farms.

Source: J. Stalin, Works, vol. 12, 1955, pp. 173–5.

The number of people involved in collectivisation and dekulakisation was enormous. About 2 million households had already been collectivised by October 1929. By March 1930 that had risen to 15 million. At that point, faced with widespread social unrest, Stalin wrote an article in *Pravda* (2 March) in which he stated that some overzealous officials had got carried away – were 'dizzy with success' – and noted that the process was supposed to be voluntary. The speech is a good illustration of the way Stalin would dissociate himself and the top leadership from controversial policies, when it was expedient.

Document 3.4 'Dizzy with Success'

Successes have their seamy side, especially when they are attained with comparative 'ease' – 'unexpectedly', so to speak. Such successes sometimes induce a spirit of vanity and conceit: 'We can achieve anything!', 'There's nothing we can't do!' People not infrequently become intoxicated by such successes; they become dizzy with success, lose all sense of proportion and the capacity to understand realities: they show a tendency to overrate their own strength and underrate the strength of the enemy; adventurist attempts are made to solve all questions of socialist construction 'in a trice' . . .

The successes of our collective-farm policy are due, among other things, to the fact that it rests on the *voluntary character* of the collective-farm movement and on *taking into account the diversity of conditions* in the various regions of the U.S.S.R. Collective farms must not be established by force. That would be foolish and reactionary.

Source: J. Stalin, Works, *vol. 12, 1955, pp. 198–9.*

Following the article, many peasants left the collective farms and by August the numbers fell back to around 6 million. However, in the autumn of 1930 the process was resumed and by 1936 some 90 per cent of all peasant households had been collectivised.

Approximately 5–6 million peasants, over 1 million out of a total of 25 million peasant households were direct victims of dekulakisation between 1930–33. Of these, an estimated 2.1 million were sent into exile, usually to remote parts of the country; 2–2.5 million were resettled on the edge of their villages or in their district or region; and approximately 1–1.25 million 'dekulakised themselves', fleeing to the towns or other regions (R.W. Davies *et al.* 1994: 68).

The application of 'social pressure' against kulaks became an important part of the process of collectivisation. Kulaks would appear before tribunals to explain failures to supply sufficient grain, and they frequently had to answer charges before village gatherings. The following document, from the protocols of a village meeting in Siberia, offers an insight into how an individual family might be expelled from a village. The head of a family from the Siberian village of Mochishe is found guilty of hiring batraks, owning considerable property, renting out a house, and paying a considerable amount of tax. The fact that the government mobilised social support for its policies by encouraging such class antagonism has been used to suggest that the Stalin revolution in the countryside was as much a 'revolution from below' as it was a 'revolution from above' (Hughes 1996: 3).

Document 3.5   Expulsion of Sizov Family from Moshiche Village, Siberia

Extract

From the protocol of the general meeting of members of the agricultural artel 'OGPU', Mochishe rural soviet, Novosibirsk raion, together with the *bednota* [poor peasant] group and the bedniak-seredniak actif on 10 May 1931.

Participated: 77 kolkhozniks and 25 individual peasants
Chairman: Bochkarev
Secretary: Myrenov

Agenda: On the kulak Sizov, Yacov Nikolaevich

Discussion

Shchanova, A: Sizov employed a batrak woman, Glukova, in 1926.

Aganov: comrade [unreadable] confirms this and adds that he hired another batrak in 1927, Laptev. In 1928 Solov'ev and Kharlamov lived there, Kharlamova from 1927.

Decided: the household of Sizov, Yacov Nikolaevich is a clear kulak, having hired batraks: from 1926 to 1927, Glukova. In 1928 Solov'ev, Kharlamov and Kharlamova, and Laptev right up to 1931. In 1928 he owned – 3 horses, 5 cows, 10.05 hectares of sown area. He was taxed 107 roubles 87 kopecks. He owned a repair shop. He rented out a house.

In 1929 he owned 3 horses, 3 cows, a sown area of 7.54 hectares: his tax was 488–70. In 1930 he owned 2 horses, 2 cows, 5 calves, a sown area of 3.76 hectares, and was taxed 17r–93k.

For this reason the household Sizov, Yacov Nikolaevich is expropriated and sent off into exile to uninhabited areas beyond the borders of the West Siberian Krai.

Approved: Chairman Bochkarev, Secretary Myrenov

Source: James Hughes, Stalinism in a Russian Province, *1996, pp. 256–7.*

For many, it was very hard to comprehend what had happened. In the following letter to state President, Mikhail Kalinin, a deported kulak, Petr German, originally from the Bobruisk region of Belorussia, complains that he had been unjustly required to pay the individual tax, a special tax on kulaks which had been introduced in 1929. He argues that his years of working to buy off his father's land made him a wage labourer (batrak). The letter, which is written with a clear lack of literary sophistication, conveys the man's despair very eloquently; it also illustrates a faith in Soviet officialdom, which suggests that the higher leadership were not always blamed for the excesses of collectivisation. There are diverse ways in which letters to the authorities in Russian and Soviet history can be interpreted: some letters reflect a traditional paternalistic relationship between ruler and subject; others can best be seen in terms of the letter-writer as a citizen (see Fitzpatrick 1997: 4–7). This letter is expressive of a traditional paternalism, reflective of pre-revolutionary attitudes. Indeed, it is not possible to understand peasant society generally during collectivisation without taking traditional rural political culture into account (see also Viola 1993: 97–8).

Document 3.6 Letter to President Kalinin

To the All-Union Head (*Staroste*)
Mikhail Ivanovich Kalinin
From Petr Leonidovich German, Babich-Liadia farmstead, Bobruisk okrug and raion, Borovitsky village soviet

Application

4 April 1930

I genuinely appeal to you for pardon (*pomilovanii*).

I was sent from my native land with my ill wife Anna 40 years old, my children Maria 8 years, Petr 6 years, Pavl 3 years, Elena 2 years to the Siberian taiga to the certain death of me and my family because this year I paid an individual tax, which had been wrongly imposed upon me.

I had 2 horses, 2 cows, 5 sheep. Surely Soviet power cannot treat so inhumanely those who have not deserved it.

I and my wife are hired labourers (*batraki*), because we worked all the time to pay off the land bought by my father. I had worked off the redemption payments for the fifteen desiatinas of land. I was a shepherd for four years. Surely I am not guilty for the fact that my father bought the land, but was it necessary for this reason to send me to certain death with my family? Surely I am not guilty, that in our village soviet 50% of people have been deported purely because of slander.

We were driven into exile in the Tabarinsky raion, the Irkutsk okrug in Petrovsky settlement. We are perishing here from hunger, the children will die, there is no bread and food. I cannot work at timber cutting, I have cancer of the stomach, for this reason I must perish with my family.

An individual tax of 185 rubles was imposed on me. I paid this sum, all my property and goods were taken away, if that could have been the end of it, but why deport me, what kind of criminal am I. Let soviet power immediately take from me the children, they are swelling up with hunger, I and my wife will perish simply because we were building soviet power. . . .

Send rather help or give some work, so that the children do not peg out, give some land so that I can work on it, or let us settle somewhere in a colony.

I ask you, Com. Kalinin, to pay attention to the fact that of 1500 families, which were sent from Bobruisk, 50% are suffering innocently. Let the kulaks suffer, who exploited our labour, but I have nothing, I go in sandals.

Petitioner – German

Source: L. Larina (ed.), Istoriia otechestva v dokumentakh 1917–1993, vol. 2, 1921–1939, *1994, pp. 108–9.*

This kind of despair led frequently to serious unrest. It should not be forgotten that such was the opposition to collectivisation that the regime itself was threatened and Stalin's own leadership was put into question. Peasant opposition to the process of dekulakisation took various forms. One common reaction was the slaughtering of animals; better to kill and eat the farm animals, thought the peasant, than let the state gets its hands on them. It was reported, for example, that between March 1929 and March 1930, the number of cattle declined by one-fifth, sheep by one-third and pigs by two-fifths. The state called this *razbazirovanie*, literally 'squandering'. There were riots, ritualised diplays of rage and clandestine meetings (Viola 1996: 69–70, 153–54). Frequently, it was women who took the lead in opposing the collectivisation process or in protecting village churches from closure and pillage (see Document 11.9).

The slaughter and consumption of livestock were memorably described by the Soviet writer Mikhail Sholokhov in his novel *Virgin Soil Upturned*, a sanitised view of collectivisation which began to appear in 1932. Sholokhov, a loyal servant of the Soviet state, won the Nobel Prize for literature in 1965 for his *The Quiet Don*, an account of cossack life during the revolution which first started to appear in 1928. In *Virgin Soil Upturned*, Sholokhov describes the slaughter of livestock as a deliberate attempt to sabotage Bolshevik policy. One of the principal characters in the novel, Yakov Lukich Ostrovnov, is a wealthy cossack who has become the manager of a kolkhoz in order to destroy it from within. In the following extract, he teams up with Alexander Polovtsiev, a former captain in the Imperial Army and now the organiser of an anti-Soviet conspiratorial organisation, to organise the slaughter of cattle. Reference is also made to Shchukar, an old man and member of the kolkhoz.

Document 3.7 The Slaughter of Livestock

Yakov Lukich had a good eye to business. He did not want the meat from his sheep to feed Red Army soldiers, or workers in some factory dining-room. They were Soviet, and for the past ten years, the Soviet government had burdened him with taxes and exactions, and had not allowed him to develop his farming on a large scale, to grow rich and fatter than the fat. The Soviet government and Yakov Lukich were mutual enemies, at daggers drawn . . . In his thoughts, Yakov Lukich used to picture himself attired not in the cossack trousers of cheap leather, but in a pair made of silk, with a gold chain across his belly . . . His son would become a colonel and wed an educated young lady . . . He must either take sides with Polovtsiev, in order to bring back the life which formerly had glittered and crackled like a hundred-rouble note, or he must throw up his present life!

And that was why Yakov Lukich, a member of the management committee of the Gremyachy Collective farm 'Stalin', was slaughtering fourteen of his sheep. 'Better to throw the carcasses to that black hound which is greedily licking the steaming sheep's blood at Polovtsiev's feet, than allow a single sheep to pass into the collective farm pen, for it to grow fat and multiply to feed the enemy government,' thought Lukich . . .

Through the influence of Yakov Lukich livestock began to be slaughtered every night in Gremyachy. Hardly had darkness fallen when the brief and stifled bleating of a sheep, the mortal scream of a pig or the bellowing of a calf would be heard piercing the silence . . .

Old Shchukar was one of the first to slaughter a calf born the previous summer. With his wife's help he tried to hang the carcass from a crossbeam in order to flay it the more easily . . . [O]ld Shchukar himself did the cooking the next day, and . . . he ate so much of the stewed beast that for some days he did not go farther than the yard, did not fasten up his sack-cloth trousers, and suffered for twenty-four hours on end in the terrible cold among the sunflower stalks behind the shed.

Source: Mikhail Sholokhov, Virgin Soil Upturned, *1977, pp. 120–2, 127–8.*

The peasantry never accepted the idea of public ownership of land, and the Soviet government was forced to admit this by granting peasants the right to have their own private plots. At the Second Congress of Outstanding Kolkhozniks (Collective Farm Workers) in February 1935, there was much debate about how large a private plot should be. After the Congress, an editorial commission of 170 persons, including Stalin and Chernov, the then Commissar of Agriculture, worked on a Kolkhoz Charter. A Leningrad delegate on the editorial commission published the following account of its discussions, in which Stalin appears in a very benevolent light, in *The Peasant Newspaper*, 27 February 1935.

Document 3.8 Discussion of the Private Plot

There was a particularly large amount of discussion on the second section of the Charter – the part on land . . . Comrade Chernov [in the chair] asked: 'Who wants to speak?' So many hands went up that they didn't know who to let speak first . . . The big argument was over the size of the private plot. Some people suggested allocating 0.12 hectares for the private plot, others suggested 0.25 hectares. I personally suggested 0.45 hectares. A few said that the [size of] private plots ought to be determined by the number of people in the household . . .

After he had listened to everyone else, comrade Stalin then expressed his own opinion. 'You are all progressive people that are gathered here,' he said, 'and it's very good that you think more of working on the kolkhoz land than on your own plots. But you must not forget that the majority of kolkhozniks want to plant an orchard, cultivate a vegetable garden, or keep bees. The kolkhozniks want to live a decent life, and for that this 0.12 hectares is not enough. We need to allocate a quarter to half a hectare, and even as much as one hectare in some districts.'

Source: Sheila Fitzpatrick, Stalin's Peasants, *1994, p. 122.*

Stalin's proposal was accepted. The Kolkhoz Charter of 1935 stipulated that plots should be between 0.25 and 0.5 hectares, and it was left to local authorities to stipulate the amount. In practice the system caused the government some headaches. In certain cases, plots were located not just around peasants' houses, but also in the kolkhoz area itself, and they easily became the major preoccupation of the peasant household. Furthermore, peasants were sometimes entitled to additional 'add-ons' to their plots. In reaction to these developments, the government in 1939 tried to restrict the size of plots. Plots expanded again during the more liberal war period, after which there were similar attempts to curtail their activity.

Ownership of the private plot gave peasants a way to play the system to their advantage. For example, of those collective farm workers who left for the city in the early 1930s, some illegally profited from leasing out their private plots. Other subtle forms of resistance were typical of the post-collectivisation countryside. Sometimes, it seems, peasants could take real revenge on party officials. It has been suggested, for example, that peasants took advantage of the regional show trials of 1937, to express their genuine grievances against state officials (Fitzpatrick 1994: 134–5, 166, 286–312).

In some places, opposition to collectivisation acquired an overtly political nature. Not surprisingly, in non-Russian areas of the USSR, the mood of opposition to the regime could easily acquire a nationalist element. For example, the following proclamation from Krutianskii raion village of Strimbakh in Ukraine was discovered in July 1930. It indicates that opposition to Soviet rural policies was strongly tied to Ukrainian nationalism. Other similar proclamations contained strongly anti-semitic sentiments, attacking, for example, the 'Communist *zhidy*' (a pejorative term for Jews). The exact origins of such proclamations are uncertain. However, they indicate a general consciousness that collectivisation was a war on the peasantry (Viola 1996: 121).

Document 3.9   Ukrainian National Consciousness

Citizens, down with the bandit gangs, down with the villainous communars. Long live free Ukraine.

The destruction of communism is the responsibility of each [person]. Dear citizens address yourselves to the request to distribute these proclamations in the village. Villagers, be prepared for the struggle with bolshevism. The Ukraine is defecting from Russia. The time is come and we from the underground will go out and show ourselves in the villages in order to smash the enemy with you.

The destruction of communism is the responsibility of each [person]. The Bolsheviks know that the Ukrainian people do not like the government and fear that Ukrainians are not connected to the Ukrainian democratic parties.

Source: Lynne Viola, Peasant Rebels under Stalin, *1996, p. 121.*

The impact of collectivisation in Ukraine was particularly bad. In 1932–33, there was widespread famine and up to 5 million people starved to death (the figures are still disputed). There are some horrific eye-witness accounts of what happened (see Kravchenko 1947: 91). In the 1920s, the Soviet government had fostered the policy of 'nativisation': the development of the cultures and languages of the non-Russian peoples of the USSR. By the end of the 1920s, the growing use of the Ukrainian language in Ukrainian public life signalled a dramatic rise in Ukrainian national consciousness, and this was a cause for concern for Stalin. It has been argued by some historians that the Stalinist leadership knew of the famine and used it to destroy Ukrainian nationalism (Conquest 1986: 322–30). Others have argued that Stalin's responsibility for the famine may have been exaggerated (Tauger 1991: 70–89). Certainly, the Soviet leadership can be accused of criminal negligence in this matter, although the question of motivation has not yet been proven (Marples 1992: 23).

The British journalist, Malcolm Muggeridge, who was able to travel to the North Caucasus and Ukraine in 1933, reported the following in the *Fortnightly Review*.

Document 3.10   Famine

On a recent visit to the North Caucasus and the Ukraine, I saw something of the battle that is going on between the government and the peasants. The battlefield is as desolate as in any war and stretches wider; stretches over a large part of Russia. On the one side, millions of starving peasants, their bodies often swollen from lack of food; on the other, soldier members of the GPU carrying out the instructions of the dictatorship of the proletariat. They had gone over the country like a swarm of locusts and taken away everything edible; they had shot or exiled thousands of peasants, sometimes whole villages; they had reduced some of the most fertile land in the world to a melancholy desert.

Source: Robert Conquest, Harvest of Sorrow, *1986, p. 260.*

Party activists involved in these campaigns were encouraged to see the process of collectivisation as a kind of heroic struggle against dark forces. Implementation of the campaign fell in part to a group of urban party activists called the 'twenty-five-thousanders'. Their achievements acquired legendary status in Soviet mythology, achieving 'official historical infallibility' (Viola 1987: 4). The journalist Lev Kopelev was a young 'twenty-five-thousander' in Ukraine. Years later he recalled the way in which he came to justify what he was doing on ideological grounds.

Document 3.11   How the Activists Justified the Policy

I was convinced that we were warriors on an invisible front, fighting against kulak sabotage for the grain which was needed by the country, by the five-year plan. Above all, for the grain, but also for the souls of these peasants who were mired in unconscientiousness, who succumbed to enemy agitation, who did not understand the great truth of communism . . .

A team consisting of several young kokhozniks and members of the village soviet . . . would search the hut, barn, yard, and take away all the stores of seed, lead away the cow, the horse, the pigs.

In some cases they would be merciful and leave some potatoes, peas, corn for feeding the family. But the stricter ones would make a clean sweep. They would take not only the food and livestock, but also 'all valuables and surpluses of clothing', including icons in their frames, samovars, painted carpets and even metal kitchen utensils which might be silver . . .

Several times Volodya and I were present at such plundering raids. We even took part: we were entrusted to draw up inventories of confiscated goods . . .

The women howled hysterically, clinging to the bags . . .

I heard the children echoing them with screams . . . And I saw the looks of the men: frightened, pleading, hateful, dully impassive, extinguished with despair or flaring up with half-mad, daring ferocity . . .

And I persuaded myself, explained to myself. I mustn't give in to debilitating pity. We were realizing historical necessity. We were performing our revolutionary duty. We were obtaining grain for the socialist fatherland. For the five-year plan . . .

Some sort of rationalistic fanaticism overcame my doubts, my pangs of conscience and simple feelings of sympathy, pity and shame, but this fanaticism was nourished not only by speculative newspaper and literary sources. More convincing than these were people who in my eyes embodied, personified our truth and our justice, people who confirmed with their lives that it was necessary to clench your teeth; clench your heart and carry out everything the party and the Soviet power ordered.

Source: Lev Kopelev, The Education of a True Believer, *1981, pp. 226, 234–5.*

It was intended that collectivisation would lead to the modernisation of a backward rural economy. The peasantry were still using practices which were outdated. Certainly, this was how it was seen to many at the time. Maurice Hindus, an American journalist with socialist sympathies who was born in Russia, returned to his native village in 1930, and reported on what he saw. Although he noted with sympathy the great hardships faced by the peasants, he concluded that the collectivisation policy contained some healthy features.

Document 3.12   Modernisation of the Russian Village

Indeed, if peaceable methods alone had been pursued and the principle of voluntary choice faithfully observed, a decade or more might have been required to bring the *kolkhoz* to its present stage of development, and time was precious. The city was threatened with famine. A crisis might have been averted by acceptance of the policy of the right opposition which counselled compromise with private enterprise. But since this policy was thrust aside, immediate and drastic action was imperative. In Revolution, as in war, it is the objective that counts, and not the price, whether in gold or blood . . .

The disappearance of individual ownership of land, the coming of large-scale industrialized farming, the collapse of the village, the rise of rural townships, the growing sophistication of the peasant women and its effect on the nation's birth rate, the collapse of religion and the transformation of the individualistic family – these are the unmistakeable guideposts of the approaching civilization in the Russian village. They are rooted in the very principle of the *kolkhoz*, and as the *kolkhoz* strengthens, they will strengthen.

Source: Maurice Hindus, Red Bread, *1988, pp. 357, 369.*

The regime used all resources at its disposal to convince the public of the rightness of its policy in the countryside. The following poster by Vera Korableva was widely disseminated. It was first issued in 1930, then reissued in 1931 and reproduced in many different national languages. The circulation of the 1931 Russian language edition was 40,000 copies alone. It is notable that the young woman in the poster is in the foreground and in an active pose, for it was a feature of the poster art of this time that woman were consistently portrayed in a positive light (Bonnell 1997: 101–2). The tractor's presence in the poster highlights the regime's consistent stress on the advantages of mechanisation.

Document 3.13 'Come, Comrade, Join Us on the Collective Farm'

[See page 42]

Source: Russian State Library Collection.

Painters were also engaged in the propaganda campaign. For example, Arkady Plastov's painting, 'A Collective Farm Festival' (1937), offers a vision of a happy and abundant Soviet countryside. In artistic terms, there was a rich variety of colour in the painting which reflected the increased use of bright colour and sunshine in the art of the late 1930s; and the vigorous, even vulgar quality of the picture could be considered a class gesture against 'bourgeois' values, offering a link with folk-art and the home-made icon (Bown 1998: 182).

Document 3.14 'A Collective Farm Festival'

[See page 43]

Source: Mathew Bown, Socialist Realist Painting, *1998, p. 158.*

Film was another important medium in communicating these messages. The emphasis on experimentalism of the 1920s was replaced in the 1930s with a very different

[Document 3.13]

genre. The Soviet film-maker of the 1930s was expected to entertain mass audiences, present Soviet life in an idealised light, and communicate the qualities of happiness and joy (Taylor 1996: 602; 1999: 145). A famous example was Ivan Pyriev's musical comedy *The Tractor-Drivers* (1939). The film tells the story of a demobbed Soviet soldier, returning from the conflict with Japan in Manchuria. He goes to Ukraine, where he helps with the mechanisation of a collective farm. He also falls in love with a beautiful and politically aware young woman. The screen shot above is of a tractor-driver singing the 'tractor-driver's march'. The cited verse and chorus of the song remind the viewer of the possibility of war. The reference to 'flashing steel' is an implicit reference to Stalin, the 'man of steel'.

[Document 3.14]

Document 3.15   Screen Shot from *The Tractor-Drivers*

Source: The Tractor-Drivers, *1939.*

Document 3.16   Extracts from The 'Tractor-Driver's March'

Let the enemy remember as he lies in wait
That we are on our guard, on the lookout for him.
We don't want an inch of foreign soil,
But we won't give up an inch of ours!

> Thundering fire and flashing steel,
> The violent stream of our weaponry will advance
> When we are sent to war by Comrade Stalin
> Our First Marshal will lead us into the fight.

Source: Richard Taylor, 'Singing on the Steppes for Stalin: Ivan Pyr'ev and the Kolkhoz Musical in Soviet Cinema', Slavic Review, *vol. 58, no. 1, 1999, p. 152; and also* The Tractor-Drivers, *1939.*

The countryside, of course, was far from idyllic, and the difficulties continued after the war. Recovery was slow after 1945, and a severe drought in the summer of 1946 contributed to a very poor harvest. An estimated 1 million people died in the subsequent famine that hit the Central Black-Earth oblasts, Ukraine and Moldavia in 1946–47. The following document is a resolution of the Council of Ministers of the USSR, 'On Economies in Distribution of Bread', to reduce grain rations to rural areas and to dependants in the cities. Out of 27.5 million rural inhabitants entitled to rations, only 4 million remained in October 1946. It has been suggested that these reductions were forced on the government, but it also has been argued that there was actually sufficient grain to feed the population adequately, but that instead the government chose to sharply export grain in 1947 (Popov 1992: 39–40; Channon 1998: 203–4).

Document 3.17 Grain Crisis of 1946

27 September 1946

Moscow, Kremlin

Secret

To add to the strong drought, which this summer has hit a significant proportion of the oblasts in the country, there have in the last two weeks been some new undesirable occurrences. The grain harvest in the most productive regions, Siberia, Kazakhstan, the central and nothern oblasts, has been taking place in unpleasant climatic conditions, in constant rain. For this reason there has been a further reduction in state grain resources . . .

[T]he Council of Ministers of the USSR and the TsK of the VKP(b) have deemed it necessary now to reduce somewhat the distribution of state grain resources . . .

The Council of Ministers of the USSR and the Central Committee of the VKP(b) . . . RESOLVES . . .

1 . . . :

a) to reduce from 1 October by 70% the stocks of grain allotted for supply to the population living in rural areas, which gives a saving of 121,200 tons of grain per month . . .;

b) to remove from those receiving a ration supply of grain in cities and worker settlements non-working adult dependants (except students and those responsible for young children) by a total of 3.5 million people . . .;

c) to terminate the distribution of bread and cereals of the best quality by ration cards . . . to all categories of the population, which will give a saving of grain of 48,900 tons per month;

d) to reduce from 1 October the norm of bread given to all dependants by between 300 and 250 grams per day for a person, but for children from 400 to 300 grams, which gives a saving of grain of 47,300 tons per month;

e) to reduce the distribution of cereals in rations and replace them with potatoes, which will give a saving of grain of 20,000 tons per month . . .

2. to require Minister of Trade of the USSR c. Liubimov:

a) to strictly limit the contingent of the population, supplied with rationed bread in October [this year] in towns and villages to no more than 60 million people, instead of the current 87 million . . .

President of the Council of Ministers of the USSR	J. Stalin
Secretary of the TsK VKP(b)	A. Zhdanov

Source: V.P. Popov, 'Golod i gosudarstvennaia politika', Otechestvennye arkhivy, *1992, no. 6, pp. 45–6.*

Just as the peasants learned to play the system to their own advantage, so too did rural party officials. Since the party was not accountable to any other institutions, its regional bosses had a free hand to do what they liked. 'Blat' was the name given to the system of influence and favours which became a central feature of the way the Soviet system worked. In the following letter of November 1948 to Collective Farm Secretary A.A. Andreev, three collective farm workers, invalids of the war, complain of the corrupt practices which had become endemic in the collective farms of their region. The Russian historian, Vladimir Kozlov has suggested that denunciations were sometimes a means through which the Soviet regime kept control over local authorities. Furthermore, he describes Soviet letters of denunciation as 'disinterested' and 'interested', the former being sincere and reflecting a traditional respect for authority, the latter motivated by a desire to protect the interests of the writer and carefully codified in the appropriate ideological terms (Kozlov 1996: 891, 872–82; see also Fitzpatrick 1996). The naïveté of expression of this letter (which is also rather disjointed) clearly puts it in the first of these two categories.

Document 3.18 'Blat is Greater than the People's Commissariat'

We beg your direct intervention in the following matter. Specifically . . ., in the 'Road to Victory' kolkhoz of the Ivanovsky village soviet in the Pokrovsky raion of Vladimirsky oblast, [in] November 1947, the squandering of kolkhoz resources was discovered – both of money and products, the embezzlement of the kolkhoz hay by the very chair[woman] of the kolkhoz and the sale of the kolkhoz forest. The money gained was made over to herself, by the chair-[woman] of the collective farm, Koriagina . . . Koriagina, bypassing the decisions of the leadership, on her own initiative at extraordinarily low prices sold vegetables to the officials of the organisations of the Pokrovsky raion. At the same time when all these acts were discussed . . . at the general meeting of the kolkhoz, the collective farmer workers did not agree to write into the budget of the kolkhoz the illegally spent resources.

The next day the chair[woman] of the kolkhoz brought in the leader of the raion agricultural department, com. Korchin . . . [He] said to the meeting that if your chair[woman] had not sold vegetables to our officials at low prices

. . . , then they would not have measured the soil, and the vet would not have stitched the bull-calf.

'Blat,' says com. Korchin, 'is greater here than the People's Commissariat and you will not do anything without it, and the actions of your chair[woman] Koriagina do not represent anything important, and it is necessary to write the squandered sums into the kolkhoz budget, and those collective farm workers who object to writing the spent sums into the kolkhoz budget, are alien elements. And I will write their names on a piece of paper and settle accounts with them later.' Here all the collective farm workers became afraid in case com. Korchin put their names on the paper and out of fear began to gradually go home.

Chair[woman] Koriagina, accountant Deliagin, chairman of the village soviet Kliukvin and com. Korchin made the most of this . . . , [they] wrote a protocol and everything was in order. Subsequently, the local authorities with the support of raion organisations began to persecute and take revenge on those who here tried to uncover the illegal actions and abuses, but . . . Kliukvin was her lover (. . . Koriagina's), stayed over with her etc.

Source: V. P.Popov, Rossiiskaia derevnia posle voiny (Iiun' 1945–Mart 1953), *1993, p. 34–5.*

The collective farm system never flourished. The Soviet government thought that it had conquered the countryside. In a way that only became clear after Stalin's death, it also became hostage to it. The inefficiencies of the collective farm would haunt the Soviet leadership in subsequent decades, and would never be resolved.

4 | Industrialisation

Vesenkha, the Supreme Council of National Economy, was founded in December 1917. Gosplan, the State Planning Commission, was set up in 1921 to set production targets and national economic plans. In the last years of NEP, planning strategy became a crucial issue, and divisions appeared within the planning agencies. A debate took place between the so-called 'geneticists' and 'teleologists'. Geneticists considered that it was important to prioritise industrial expansion, but they also argued that growth should proceed in an organic and gradualist fashion. Teleologists were less cautious. They believed that higher targets were achievable, and that a massive transformation in the economy was possible in a short space of time. This debate to some extent reflected traditional divisions between Mensheviks and Bolsheviks about strategies for building socialism; indeed, one of the chief proponents of the geneticist school in Gosplan, V.G. Groman, was a former Menshevik. A chief advocate of the teleological model in Gosplan and Vesenkha was S.G. Strumilin. The following document, an extract from an article he wrote for the journal *Planned Economy* in 1927 in which he attacked the 'geneticist' N.D. Kondratiev, reflects the emphasis which he and other Soviet central planners placed on the power of the will to transform reality.

Document 4.1 The Purpose of Central Planning

If our future national economy were to be 100% determined by circumstances, which were not dependent on our will, then it would be pointless to construct any plans for the economy. And a capitalist system, subject in its development to the spontaneous laws of the market, does not have them. But we to a large degree have freed ourselves from the *complete* domination of this blind spontaneity. The October revolution has already partly opened for us the door from the kingdom of necessity to the kingdom of freedom. And now we are more than ever right to follow Marx in setting ourselves a new task: up till this point we have simply studied the world, but the task is to change it.

For this reason, in distinction from prof. Kondratiev, we do not consider elements of scientific foresight sprinkled into a plan to be the characteristic feature of any economic plan, but rather the complete establishment of a plan as a *system of economic tasks and predictions*. This does not free us of course from a real assessment of our objective possibilities in the construction of such a system of tasks . . . To concentrate and mobilise the collective will of producers for one or another economic task – that is what we see as the basic task of the plan. And this goes far beyond the bounds of the purely analytical purposes of armchair science . . .

We will never draw back from targets simply because their realisation is not a 100% certainty, since it is *the will of the proletariat and our plans*, concentrating that will on the struggle to achieve the task at hand, that themselves can and must be the *decisive* factor needed for their successful fulfilment.

Source: S.G. Strumilin, 'Industrializatsiia SSSR i epigony narodnichestva', Izbrannye proizvedeniia (2): na planovom fronte, *1963, pp. 218–20.*

This strong belief in the power of the will was shared by figures on the Trotskyite left of the party, such as the prominent Bolshevik leader G.L. Piatakov. Indeed, the Trotskyite wing of the party had traditionally advocated an industrial dictatorship to bring about the economic transformation of the country (Deutscher 1959: 413–14; Shearer 1996: 82–4). It was ironic that Stalin, once he had defeated the left, quickly moved to embrace many of their policies.

At the 15th Party Congress in December 1927, the party voted to introduce a Five Year Plan. The first Five Year Plan ran from October 1928 to December 1932. The first version of the plan was subsequently revised upwards on two occasions, as planners came under political pressure to set higher and higher targets. With the Right Opposition out of the way, Stalin had a free hand to embrace or encourage the most extreme visions of transformation. Resolutions were made to fulfil five-year production targets in four or even three years. Stalin was always attracted to the idea that, with sufficient will-power, everything could be different. In a well-known speech to leading business executives on 4 February 1931, Stalin called on managers to promise to fulfil the Five Year Plan in three years. He seems to have believed that to make a promise is the same thing as to carry it out. The speech also reveals a certain kind of chauvinistic Russian nationalism. Even before 1917, Stalin had a tendency to associate Bolshevism and Russian interests (Tucker 1974: 140, 247). In referring here to the way Russia had suffered in the past at the hand of foreign powers, Stalin appealed to national as well as socialist instincts and suggested that the USSR was the inheritor of Russia's imperial legacy.

Document 4.2 Stalin's Speech at the First All-Union Conference of Leading Personnel of Socialist Industry

[W]hat does the pledge to fulfil the control figures for 1931 mean? . . . Such a pledge means that you not only pledge yourselves to fulfil our five-year plan in four years . . . , *it means that you promise to fulfil it in three years in all the basic, decisive branches of industry* . . .

To slacken the tempo would mean falling behind. And those who fall behind get beaten. But we do not want to be beaten. No, we refuse to be beaten! One feature of the history of old Russia was the continual beatings she suffered because of her backwardness. She was beaten by the Mongol khans. She was beaten by the Turkish beys. She was beaten by the Swedish feudal lords. She was beaten by the Polish and Lithuanian gentry. She was beaten by the British and French capitalists. She was beaten by the Japanese barons. All beat her – because of her backwardness, because of her military backwardness, cultural backwardness, political backwardness, industrial backwardness, agricultural backwardness. They beat her because to do so was profitable and could be done with impunity. You remember the words of the pre-revolutionary poet: 'You are poor and abundant, mighty and impotent, Mother Russia.' Those gentlemen were quite familiar with the verses of the old poet. They beat her, saying: 'You are abundant', so one can enrich oneself at your expense. They beat her, saying: 'You are poor and impotent', so you can be beaten and plundered with impunity. Such is the law of the exploiters – to beat the backward and the weak. It is the jungle law of capitalism. You are backward, you are weak – therefore you are wrong; hence you can be beaten and enslaved. You are mighty – therefore you are right; hence we must be wary of you . . .

Do you want our socialist fatherland to be beaten and to lose its independence? If you do not want this, you must put an end to its backwardness in the shortest possible time and develop a genuine Bolshevik tempo in building up its socialist economy. There is no other way. That is why Lenin said on the eve of the October Revolution: 'Either perish, or overtake and outstrip the advanced capitalist countries.'

We are fifty or a hundred years behind the advanced countries. We must make good this distance in ten years. Either we do it, or we shall go under. That is what our obligations to the workers and peasants of the U.S.S.R. dictate to us.

Source: J. Stalin, Works, vol. 13, 1955, pp. 31, 40–1.

The rhetoric was magnificent. The reality was very different. The industrialisation drive was a chaotic process, which was characterised by much waste and inefficiency. A culture was created where to avoid high output targets, factory managers would frequently belittle their output potential (Dyker 1985: 23). Managers had to improvise as best they could to cope with orders coming from the centre, and had to compete with one another for scarce resources. Labour was at times plentiful, but at other times scarce (Rassweiler 1983: 245). The command system was plagued with perpetual imbalances (Lewin 1993: 272–84). Such problems were the inevitable result of the regime's attempt to achieve rapid results in every area of the economy at the same time (Schultz 1990: 212). This was a point made in the following criticisms of the first Five Year Plan in the summer of 1930 by a prominent member of the Trotskyite opposition, Christian Rakovsky (see also Document 12.1).

Document 4.3   The Problem with Increasing the Tempos

Today they increase the programme for coal and iron to make it possible to fulfil the programme for machine-building; tomorrow it will be necessary to expand the programme for machine-building to make it possible to fulfil the enlarged programme for coal and iron; later they will again find it necessary to increase the programme for coal and iron in order to guarantee the new programme for machine-building. In the midst of this spiral it suddenly turns out that it is posing tasks for transport that transport will not be able to cope with unless the latter receives an appropriate supply of iron and steel – and so the programme for coal and iron is boosted again and the circle begins anew.

Hence the exaggerated tempos, the exaggerated figures, the exaggerated plans which collapse as soon as they come into touch with reality. At this point appear comrades who . . ., talk about the 'rearmament' of the opposition, about the fact, (or so they claim) that the opposition, after having stood for high tempos in the past, now, when Stalin has finally gone after these tempos, comes out against them simply to be able to remain in opposition. With these comrades one has to drag them by the nose into the real world and show them that these high tempos exist only on paper, in books, in articles, and in plans, that any advance in one area comes at the expense of violating all proportions, of creating colossal disruptions in other areas, of creating huge new disproportions. To these comrades one has to explain that our weapon is never rigid formulae, but the marxist method, which allows us to work out the formulae most useful at any given stage along the way.

Source: Christian Rakovsky, 'The Five-Year Plan in Crisis', Critique, 1981, no. 13, pp. 48–9.

The problems created in the Soviet command economy were systemic. A centrally-planned economy lacks the accountability that the market can provide. The system of fixed prices, which came in with central planning, meant that the state lacked the mechanism of communication with the consumer offered by a market. G.F. Grinko, from October 1930 head of the People's Commissariat of Finance, suggested to a meeting of party activists in Nizhny Novgorod in April 1931 that coercion might provide the solution to the problem of managerial complacency; cost accounting (*khozraschet*) would be rigorously enforced. Grinko's speech illustrates the way in which the structure of the Soviet command economy led inexorably to the use of coercive methods.

Document 4.4   Enforcing Party Directives

It is necessary to thrash the psychology that unfortunately is widespread among our managers. This psychology could be characterized thus: 'We are state enterprises; we cannot be sold by auction, why [do we have to] worry?' Of course, the Sormovo Factory and the [Nizhny Novgorod] Automobile Plant won't be sold by auction. But the party and the government have many other, no less effective methods of teaching the leaders both of factories such as Sormovo and of construction [projects] such as the Automobile Plant to implement *khozraschet* unflinchingly. There will be show trials and much more that will force them to get cracking and carry out the directives of the party.

Source: Hiroaki Kuromiya, Stalin's Industrial Revolution, 1988, p. 271.

Although the Stalin regime put an end to a free price system, it did not abandon the market altogether. Indeed, in what appeared to be a rejection of the radical egalitarianism of the Marxist tradition, Stalin announced in June 1931, at a conference of business executives, that the government would now permit the introduction of wage differentials (see Document 9.8).

Show trials were an important element of the Stalinist model of industrialisation. For example, from 1928–31, there were a series of trials of specialists. In May 1928 at the 'Shakhty' trial in the Donbass, fifty-three engineers were accused of wrecking equipment, causing accidents and maintaining links with foreign owners. There is no evidence that any of the charges were true; rather, it appears that the cases were trumped up by Stalin to heighten tension. Speaking to a group of Moscow Communists about the Shakhty trial in April 1928, Stalin suggested that foreign powers were attempting to interfere with Soviet policy.

Document 4.5   Stalin on the Shakhty Trial

What is the class background of the Shakhty affair, where are its roots, and on what class basis could this economic counter-revolution arise?

There are comrades who think the Shakhty affair accidental. They usually say: we are really caught napping this time; we didn't have our eyes open, but if we had not been yawning we would not have had any Shakhty affair. That there was carelessness, and a good deal of it, there can be no doubt. But to explain everything by that is to miss the main point.

What do the facts, the material about the Shakhty affair, tell us?

They tell us that the Shakhty affair is economic counter-revolution plotted by some bourgeois specialists, who formerly controlled the mines . . .

[W]e are dealing here with economic intervention by west European anti-Soviet capitalist organizations in the affairs of our industry.

Source: Jane Degras (ed.), Soviet Documents on Foreign Policy, vol. II, 1925–1932, *1952, pp. 300–1.*

There were further trials. In 1930, some members of a so-called 'Industrial Party' were tried for sabotage and treason. In March 1931 former Menshevik and SR members of Gosplan were convicted of proposing criminally low production targets.

As well as seeking to rein in potential enemies amongst the so-called 'specialists', the regime sought also to control those likely to be more ideologically sympathetic – for example, the trade unions. This is illustrated by the following resolution taken at the 16th Party Congress in June–July 1930, in which 'trade unionistic' tendencies were fiercely condemned.

Document 4.6   On Opportunism in the Trade Union Movement

The present phase of socialist construction raises the problem of the complete reorganization of the activities of the proletarian mass organizations, and among others the trade unions. It is necessary to concentrate on production. The opportunistic ruling group of the old executive of the All-Russian Trade Union Central Committee not only showed itself unable to understand the problems of the proletarian dictatorship but opposed the party's reorganization of the work of the trade unions. Displaying 'trade unionistic' tendencies, this opportunistic leadership actually carried on a campaign to weaken the party's supervision over the trade union movement. Under the leadership of the party, the trade unions have now removed their bankrupt leaders and have begun a determined fight against the elements of 'trade unionism' and opportunism in the trade union movement. Today the basic factor in energizing and improving the entire work of the trade unions must be socialist competition and its offspring, the shock brigades. Socialist competition and the shock brigades must become the primary concern of all the constructive activities of the unions . . .

Source: Manya Gordon, Workers Before and After Lenin, *1941, quoted in Robert Daniels (ed.)*, The Stalin Revolution, *1972, pp. 70–1.*

In April 1929, measures were taken to set up a system of labour camps which would play a part in the economic life of the country. The possibility of using prison labour to increase timber exports had been raised in 1928 by People's Commissar of Justice, N.M. Yanson. The idea of using labour camps to support the national economy was again raised in the spring of 1929, when the Politburo sanctioned the creation of a system of labour camps under the control of the OGPU. The following document is a proposal from the Commissariats of Justice and Internal Affairs and the OGPU for the use of prison labour in the national economy. The first camp of the new type was to be set up in the Ukhta region on the model of the camp on the Solovetsky islands in the White Sea. The Politburo, after setting up a commission to investigate, confirmed the essential principles of the proposal in a resolution of 23 May 1929.

Document 4.7   The Economic Role of the Camps

13 April 1929

We put to [Sovnarkom] the following proposals:
1. To use all those condemned to three or more years for the colonisation of our northern regions and the cultivation of their natural resources.
2. For this purpose to charge the OGPU with the organisation of a concentration camp on the Solovetsky model in the Olonets region of Ukhta.
3. The capacity of camps is to be 30,000.

The carrying out of these suggestions . . . will lead to the abolition of all prisons with the exception of places of isolation for those under investigation or in transit, with a significant reduction in the expense of maintaining inmates from 250 roubles per year to 100 roubles . . .

1,200,000 roubles will be needed before the end of this financial year.

Source: S.A. Krasil'nikov (ed.), 'Rozhdenie GULAGA: Diskussii v verkhnikh eshelonakh vlasti', Istoricheskii arkhiv, *1997, no. 4, p. 144.*

The camp in the Ukhta region began to be constructed in the second half of 1929. By the summer of 1930, there were already six camp complexes in regions from Karelia to the Far East, containing almost 200,000 people (Krasil'nikov 1997: 142–3). There has been much debate about the size of the labour camp population under Stalin. Recent research suggests that about 3.3 million people were under the control of the Gulag (literally Chief Administration of Camps) on the eve of the Second World War, and that the numbers reached just under 5.5 million in 1953. These figures include those sent to work in colonies and special settlements. The Soviet regime used forced labour to tackle ambitious projects like the construction of the White Sea Canal in 1931–33 or the mining of the Kolyma gold fields. But it is doubtful whether the economic benefits outweighed the extreme inefficiency of the system (see R.W. Davies 1998: 48–51; for discussion about the numbers of those in camps, see Wheatcroft 1996, 1999; Getty and Naumov 1999: 587–94; Keep 1999).

The second Five Year Plan (1933–37) was more moderate than the first. Its original targets, which were introduced at the 17th Party Congress, were in fact subsequently reduced, and there has been considerable debate amongst Western historians as to whether there was a significant division over this in the Politburo between Molotov, who wanted the higher targets, and the more moderate Ordzhonikidze and Kuibyshev (see R.W. Davies and Khlevniuk 1997: 51).

The achievements of the Five Year Plans in the 1930s were remarkable: the Donbass coal industry and the Baku and Grozny oil fields were expanded; huge metallurgical factories were built in Western Siberia and the Urals, including at Magnitogorsk; a giant hydroelectrical scheme was created on the lower Dnieper; and there were tractor factories built in Stalingrad, Cheliabinsk and Kharkov. Much of this was established from scratch. Consumer goods fared less well.

The Soviet regime made extensive use of propaganda to persuade the population of the rightness of its policies. Posters of the time emphasised the dynamic nature of Soviet reality, and the possibility of building a better future. The 1930 poster, 'For the Five Year Plan in Four Years', by Yuri Pimenov, is an excellent example. Above the train is a slogan which says 'For the industrial finance plan'; beneath it, another slogan declares 'For the five year plan in four years'; to the right of the train, there is a phrase 'against religion'; and across the tracks, a number of hostile figures are trying to stop the train with ropes entitled 'religious prejudices', 'sabotage', 'religion', 'self-seeking', 'drunkenness', 'absenteeism', and 'marriage'.

Document 4.8 'For the Five Year Plan in Four Years'

Source: Russian State Library Collection.

The campaign to fulfil and over-fulfil production targets was given further momentum in the mid-1930s by the Stakhanovite movement. Alexei Stakhanov was a coalminer who in 1935 cut 102 tonnes of coal in a single session, instead of the 7 tonnes prescribed. This was achieved by halting other work in his section of the mine and allocating a special gang to do the auxiliary work he would normally have done. This kind of endeavour was attempted in other branches of industry and on the collective farms, and successful workers were rewarded with pay rises and good apartments. The Stakhanovite worker was to be an example of the 'new Soviet man': the kind of hero who would master the forces of nature and lead society into socialism. Pilots and arctic explorers also received attention in the 1930s for their supposedly Promethean feats (see Bergman 1998: 135–42).

A good example of Stakhanovite propaganda is Andrei Deineka's painting of 1937, 'The Stakhanovites'. Deineka, one of the most influential Soviet artists of the 1920s, was the prime link between the poster art of the revolution and socialist realist painting (Bown 1998: 93). In this piece, the workers are no longer rough types with their hands dirty. Dressed in white, they represent a new type of human being. The characters in front are doubtless Russians, but they are leading a multi-ethnic population.

Document 4.9   'The Stakhanovites'

Source: Irina Antonova and Iorn Merkert, Moskva-Berlin/Berlin-Moscau, 1900–1950, *1996, p. 402.*

The Stakhanovite movement undoubtedly generated some genuine enthusiasm, and it offered people opportunities for social advancement. Much of the cultural mythology of the 1930s revolved around it (Siegelbaum 1988: 210–46). However, the fact that others had to change their work patterns for Stakhanovite norms to be reached meant that the economic benefits of the whole process were doubtful. The reality was that while the state set the political agenda, managers and workers often colluded to disobey laws and plans (Filtzer 1998: 175). Furthermore, the regime's efforts to create a new social elite in the workplace created resentment among workers who were not part of that elite. The following document is an extract from the memoirs of Viktor Kravchenko, an engineer and party member who was assigned to work at a metallurgical plant in Nikopol in Ukraine, and who later defected to the West. In the extract, Kravchenko recalls the fraudulent nature of the 'speed-up' process and the discontent it created among many workers.

Document 4.10   The Stakhanovite Movement and Social Division

In the end, in my own sub-plant, I was obliged to resort to artificial speed-up which, in my heart, I considered a crime against the machines and the workers alike . . .

At eleven o'clock one evening, with reporters and photographers present, the 'Stakhanovite' shift got under way. As expected, it 'overfulfilled' the normal quota by 8 per cent . . . Congratulations arrived from officials in the capitals . . .

But this 'victory' on the industrial front merely left me heartsick. It was, at bottom, fraudulent and must boomerang. The other two shifts, deprived of their best personnel and their best tools, lost more than the favoured group had won. By contrast, they seemed ineffective if not actually 'lazy'. They naturally resented being made the scapegoats. They cursed the lucky ones and the officials . . .

And thus the Kremlin drove a wedge also between various categories of workers . . .

In my plant, of fifteen hundred men, perhaps two hundred qualified as Stakhanovites or speedkings. For the others the revision of norm meant simply a serious cut in earning power. The general resentment was silent, sullen, unmistakable.

To add insult to injury, the new norms had to be presented and accepted by the workers 'themselves', not only 'voluntarily' but enthusiastically. The farce was played out in a series of meetings.

Source: Viktor Kravchenko, I Chose Freedom, *1947, pp. 188–9.*

One of the distinctive features of the first Five Year Plan was extreme social mobility. From 1928–32, the combination of new employment opportunities in the towns and collectivisation led to an exodus of roughly 12 million peasants from the villages to the towns (Fitzpatrick 1994: 80). The social transformation which this engendered resulted in what one historian called a 'quicksand society' and the 'ruralization of the cities' (Lewin 1985: 220–3). Migration to the towns opened up social opportunities for people which would previously have been unthinkable. In 1933, the young American socialist John Scott went to work on the construction of Magnitogorsk and later wrote a description of his life there. He married a Russian girl Masha, who after finishing school in the small town of Udomlya, moved to Moscow for further studies, and then got a job teaching adults in a party higher education college (Komvuz) in Magnitogorsk (see also Document 9.9).

Document 4.11   Villagers Move to the Towns

The family lived in the Tverskaya Gubernia, roughly half way between Moscow and Leningrad, a part of Russia where poor soils and long winters have always kept agricultural production low and the population correspondingly poor.

Masha's mother and father were both descended from serfs, and were both illiterate. They were determined, however, that their children should go to school, and so, barefoot and ragged, Masha and her brothers and sisters started to study in the local village school . . .

Shortly a 'secondary' school was organized in Udomlya, and Masha enrolled. It was five miles each way every day, and when she was fourteen Masha got her first pair of shoes . . .

From the incredible poverty and suffering of the civil-war period, the Russian people were working their way up to a higher standard. All Masha's family were enthusiastic. Several of the children joined the Komsomol, and after years of argument, the mother succumbed to the pressures of her children and took down the icons from the walls of the hut. Then she too decided to study. Masha's mother learned to read and write at the age of fifty-five. She was taught by her youngest daughter.

On finishing the eight years of her secondary school in Udomlya, Masha decided to go to Moscow to continue her studies. One brother and one sister were there already, and had secured a room in a cellar. One by one during fifteen years the younger brothers and sisters came to Moscow, and lived in that little room while they went through one of Moscow's higher educational institutions. Masha went to the capital in 1929. At that time the industrialization of the country was just beginning. Russia's rapidly expanding economy was crying for every kind of professional skill, for engineers, chemists, teachers, economists, and doctors. The higher schools paid stipends to their students, and aided them in every way to get through their courses and out to factory and laboratory. Masha finished up her preparatory work, and then entered the Mendelyeyev Institute, where she worked part time as laboratory assistant to make a few roubles for bread.

In 1932, Masha's second oldest sister graduated from the Moscow University, married, and went off to Magnitogorsk. The following year, for personal reasons, Masha followed her. She went into the junior year of the Magnitogorsk Teachers' College, majoring in mathematics and physics. She lived with her sister, and got a job in the local Komvuz, where she spent four hours a day, most of it engaged in preparing her lessons for her next day's classes.

Masha was very happy in Magnitogorsk. She felt that the world was at her feet. She slept on the divan of her sister and brother-in-law's tiny hotel room, she had two or three dresses, two pairs of shoes and one coat. In two more years, she would graduate from the teachers' college. Then she would teach, or perhaps take graduate work. Not only this, she was living in a town which had grown up from nothing just as she herself had. Living conditions were improving as the pig-iron production of the mill increased. She felt herself a part of a going concern. Hence her spontaneous pity for me, whom she first saw as a cast-off from a bankrupt and degenerating society.

Source: John Scott, Behind the Urals, *1989, pp. 120–3.*

Such was the extent of social mobility during the first Five Year Plan, that in December 1932, the government moved to restrict access to the cities, introducing a passport system requiring citizens to remain in their designated regions without special permission.

Document 4.12   Passport System

27 December 1932

The Central Executive Committee and the Council of People's Commissars . . . RESOLVES:

1. To set up in the USSR a unitary passport system on the basis of a statute of passports.
2. To introduce a unitary passport system with mandatory registration throughout the USSR in 1933, embracing in the first place the populations of Moscow, Leningrad, Kharkov, Kiev, Odessa, Rostov-on-Don, Vladivostok . . .
4. To require the governments of union republics to introduce their own legislation to correspond with the current resolution and statute of passports.

Source: M.Glavatsky et al. (eds), Khrestomatiia po istorii Rossii, 1917–1940, 1995, p. 350.

Migration to the towns led to the construction of new social identities. People learned how to present themselves in the right ideological terms: to 'speak Bolshevik'. For example, a worker's record contained information about his or her working past; a person's labour history was recorded in terms of attendance at conferences and courses, or achieving norms. Workers thus had to present themselves using these new frames of reference. The following letter offers an example of this. It was written by Anna Kovaleva, the wife of the best locomotive driver in internal factory transport in Magnitogorsk to the wife of the worst driver, Marfa Gudzia, and it illustrates the 'politically correct' language of the time. It was not essential that Anna Kovaleva actually believed what she was saying, nor that she had actually written the letter herself (although she may have); the important thing is that she could play by the 'rules of the game' (Kotkin 1995: 216–20).

Document 4.13   Letter of Wife of Locomotive Driver

Dear Marfa!

We are both wives of locomotive drivers of the rail transport of Magnitka. You probably know that the rail transport workers of the MMK [Magnitogorsk Metallurgical Complex] are not fulfilling the plan, that they are disrupting the supply of the blast furnaces, open hearths, and rolling shops . . . All the workers of Magnitka accuse our husbands, saying that the rail workers hinder the fulfillment of the [overall] industrial plan. It is offensive, painful, and annoying to hear this. And moreover, it is doubly painful, because all of it is the plain truth. Every day there were stoppages and breakdowns in rail transport. Yet our internal factory transport has everything it needs in order to fulfill the plan. For that, it is necessary to work like the best workers of our country work. Among such shock workers is my husband, Aleksandr Panteleevich Kovalev. He always works like a shock worker, exceeding his norms, while economizing on fuel and lubricating oil. His engine is on profit and loss accounting . . . My husband trains locomotive drivers' helpers out of unskilled laborers. He takes other locomotive drivers under his wing . . . My husband receives prizes virtually every month . . . And I too have won awards.

My husband's locomotive is always clean and well taken care of. You, Marfa, are always complaining that it is difficult for your family to live. And why is that so? Because your husband, Iakov Stepanovich, does not fulfill the plan. He had frequent breakdowns on his locomotive, his locomotive is dirty, and he always overconsumes fuel. Indeed, all the locomotive drivers laugh at him. All the rail workers of Magnitka know him – for the wrong reasons, as the worst driver. By contrast, my husband is known as a shock worker. He is written up and praised in the newspapers . . . He and I are honored everywhere as shock workers. We will get an apartment with rugs, a gramophone, a radio, and other comforts. Now we are being assigned to a new store for shock workers and will receive double rations . . . Soon the Seventeenth Party Congress of our Bolshevik Party will take place. All rail workers are obliged to work so that Magnitka greets the Congress of Victors at full production capacity.

Therefore, I ask you, Marfa, to talk to your husband heart to heart, read him my letter. You, Marfa, explain to Iakov Stepanovich that he just can't go on working the way he has. Persuade him that he must work honorably, conscientiously, like a shock worker. Teach him to understand the words of comrade Stalin, that work is a matter of honor, glory, valor, and heroism.

You tell him that if he does not correct himself and continues to work poorly, he will be fired and lose his supplies. I will ask my Aleksandr Panteleevich to take your husband in tow, help him improve himself and become a shock worker, earn more. I want you, Marfa, and Iakov Stepanovich to be honored and respected, so that you live as well as we do.

I know that many women, yourself included, will say: 'What business is it of a wife to interfere in her husband's work? You live well, so hold your tongue.' But it is not like that . . . We all must help our husbands to fight for the uninterrupted work of transport in the winter. Ok, enough. You catch my drift. This letter is already long. In conclusion, I'd like to say one thing. It's pretty good to be the wife of a shock worker. It's within our power. Let's get down to the task, amicably. I await your answer.

Anna Kovaleva

Source: Stephen Kotkin, Magnetic Mountain, *1995, pp. 218–19.*

Soviet industrialisation has been so closely identified with Stalin that it is difficult to imagine a non-terroristic version of it. However, some historians do not feel that the Stalinist model of industrialisation was the only one available. For example, it has been argued that industrialisation need not have been accompanied by the appearance of a massive centralised bureaucratic apparatus (Shearer 1996: 12). A less terroristic command-administrative system was an option (Khlevniuk 1995b: 176).

One Politburo member who seems to have discretely questioned aspects of the terror was 'Sergo' Ordzhonikidze. Recent research notes the way in which Ordzhonikidze, as head of the People's Commissariat of Heavy Industry (NKTP), tried to protect some of his staff during the purges of 1936–37, and even tried to change Stalin's mind regarding the clampdown (Khlevniuk 1995b: 158, 175). On 5 February 1937, just before the opening of the February–March Party plenum which led to a further escalation of the terror, Ordzhonikidze made a speech at a conference of the heads of the NKTP Central Directorate, in which he accepted that his deputy Piatakov had been a spy and saboteur. However, he went on to defend factory directors against unfair accusations:

Document 4.14   Ordzhonikidze Defends Factory Directors

There are directors at several factories today who, in connection with the trial of the scoundrels, feel that they themselves are under attack as if they are criminals, and everyone must answer for Piatakov and the others. Nothing of the sort. They must be told directly that they're not criminals, they're our cadres. We caught the criminals, shot them, and we'll catch future criminals and shoot all the scum we find. We're not talking about them, but about the enormous mass of cadres, fine ones trained by us . . .

When you go to the directors and help them, they'll respect you more and take you more seriously. But if you only curse them, nothing will come of this. They're left to their own devices. They're put on the spot and harrassed by the party organization because of the trial. It's necessary to approach them, to talk with the workers, to talk with the directors, and to help and encourage them.

Source: Oleg Khlevniuk, In Stalin's Shadow: The Career of 'Sergo' Ordzhonikidze, *1995b, p. 130.*

Ordzhonikidze was evidently concerned that directors and workers were being needlessly persecuted. Unfortunately, a few days later on 18 February, he was found dead in his apartment. It appears to have been suicide, although there is some evidence, if ultimately inconclusive, that he was murdered at Stalin's orders. The party plenum of February–March 1937 subsequently singled out the commissariats of heavy industry and transport for their lack of ideological vigilance.

The attack on the NKTP suggests that there was an economic dimension to the terror. Key areas of the Soviet economy were having problems in the first half of 1936, and this likely contributed to the expansion of terror (Manning 1993b: 116–41). Industrial bosses were one group which particularly suffered in the repression; it has been noted, for example, that 60 per cent of senior officials in the NKTP disappeared from the telephone directories between 1937 and 1939 (Fitzpatrick 1993: 255).

One of the arguments for rapid industrialisation had been the threat of war. It is an indication of the priority of the arms industry that whereas it accounted for just 2.6 per cent of total industrial production in 1930, it had increased to 22 per cent by 1940. By 1932 armament production was greater than agricultural machinery, tractor and automobile industries combined, and accounted for over 11 per cent of total machine-building and metal-working production. In 1941, the arms industry absorbed up to 73 per cent of all investment in the machine-building and metal-working sub-sectors (R.W. Davies *et al.* 1994: 144–5).

The tractor factories at Stalingrad, Cheliabinsk and Kharkov had been designed to allow for a swift conversion to tank production. The following document relates to production of the famous T-34 tank. Soviet engineers initially imitated Western tank designs. However, they soon developed their own models; in particular, their own T-34 and KV heavy tanks were outstanding and proved more than a match for the Germans during the war. The T-34 had thick plated armour, heavy firepower and superb mobility. The following resolution of 5 June 1940 indicates that the Stalingrad factory started producing T-34s in the autumn of 1940. At that time, the Kharkov Locomotive Factory (No. 183 – Comintern) was the central location for the production of T-34s. However, prior to the German capture of Kharkov on 24 October 1941, it was evacuated to Nizhny Tagil in the Urals, where it was merged with parts of tank factory No.174 from Leningrad and the Ural Locomotive Factory to become the new Stalin Ural Tank Works (No.183) (Zaloga and Grandsen 1984: 127). Factory No. 75, which produced tank engines and was also in Kharkov, was evacuated to Cheliabinsk in 1941 (Cooper *et al.* 1999: 5, 9).

Document 4.15   The Production of the T-34

Ascribing particular significance to equipping the Red Army with T-34 tanks, the Council of People's Commissars of the USSR and the TsK of the VKP(b) resolves:

1. To require People's Commissar of Middle Machine-Construction com. I.A.Likhachev:

   a) to manufacture in 1940 600 T-34 tanks:

   500 of them at factory No. 183 (called The Comintern) and

   100 at the Stalingrad tractor factory [STF],

according to the following monthly figures:

	June	July	August	September	October	November	December
Factory 183	10	20	30	80	115	120	125
STF					20	30	50

   b) in order to supply diesel engines to fully meet the T-34 output target in 1940, factory No. 75 shall increase its output of B-2 motors, ensuring the output of 2000 engines by the end of 1940 . . .

Source: Izvestiia TsK KPSS, *1990, no. 2, p. 181.*

The initial batch of T-34s had technical difficulties. The above resolution was followed on 5 May 1941 by a similar decree calling for the production of a further 2,800 T-34s and technical improvements.

The Cheliabinsk tractor factory also switched to tank production, and was already producing the KV heavy tank by the middle of 1941. The growing use of Stalingrad and Cheliabinsk for tank production reflected a desire to locate armament production in the East, far from a possible front. By June 1941, almost 20 per cent of tank production was located in the East, and this made it possible for the Soviet Union, even in 1941, to outdo Germany in tank production (Bonwetsch 1997: 186). The fact that the tank industry was well prepared for a possible outbreak of war was not replicated in all other sectors. Although the tank-building and other armaments industries were well prepared for a possible war, there is some doubt as to whether there was a long-term plan for the conversion of the economy to a wartime footing.

Political factors often interfered with strategic thinking. For example, in 1937, military contingency plans for a German invasion had been denounced as defeatist (Harrison 1985: 58–60).

After 1945, Soviet politicians suggested that the Soviet victory demonstrated the superior qualities of the Soviet system. In the economic sphere, it is certainly true that the Soviet economy showed great resilience in the face of colossal pressure. In war, the economies of other newly-industrialising countries, such as Russia, Austria-Hungary and even Germany in the First World War, and of Japan and Italy in the Second World War had collapsed. At the same time, the human costs were considerable: while nearly three-fifths of the national product was devoted to the war effort, there was a lack of money for subsistence and for replacing lost resources (Harrison 1996: 170–1). In this sphere, the government inherited certain problems from the 1930s. Collectivisation and lack of investment in railroads meant that it was hard to supply unoccupied areas. In any case, the state often lacked the resources to supply. People were very much thrown back on their own resources; 'people were fed not because of the system but in spite of it' (Moskoff 1990: 238).

In 1947, State Planning Chief Nikolai Voznesensky, who had been responsible for the wartime economy, argued in his book *The Economy of the USSR in World War II* that a centrally-planned economy was ideally suited for such a colossal operation.

Document 4.16   Reasons for Success of the War Economy

The war economy of the USSR was based on the predominance of socialist ownership of the means of production. The concentration of the basic means of production in the hands of the state assured a rapid conversion of the USSR to a wartime footing. The predominance of private ownership of the means of production in pre-revolutionary Russia, a low level of development of productive powers, and the dependence on foreign capital created unsurpassable difficulties for Russia in the waging of the war of 1914–1917.

The socialist revolution had destroyed the dependence of our country on foreign capital and had radically altered the class composition of the population of the USSR. While in pre-revolutionary Russia in 1913 urban and rural workers and employees constituted less than 17 percent of the whole population, in the USSR in 1939 they comprised 48 percent, i.e. almost half of the whole population. As is known, there was no *kolkhoz* peasantry and there were no cooperatives of handicraftsmen and artisans in Russia prior to the socialist revolution of 1917, while in the USSR in 1939 they comprised 46 percent . . .

The wartime conversion of the economy of the USSR was carried out under the direction of the organizer of our great victories, the Great Stalin, in the course of the second half of 1941 and the first half of 1942. The nucleus of economic and political personnel, created and trained by the party of Lenin-Stalin during the period of peacetime construction, assured the wartime conversion of the economy without which our victory would have been impossible. The people of the Soviet Union who had given their heroic labor to the Soviet Army, had organizers and leaders that were devoted to their people and to their party until the end.

Source: Robert Daniels, A Documentary History of Communism, *vol. 1, 1985, pp. 285–6.*

In the decades after the war, the Soviet Union consolidated its global power and gained 'superpower' status. It was a remarkable achievement for a state which had been relatively backward at the end of the 1920s. Yet heavy industry grew much more rapidly after 1945 than light industry (Dunmore 1980: 117–19). Indeed, the Soviet economy, structurally well equipped to fight a war, was never suited to answering the needs of a consumer society. Adapting to a more complex society was the greatest challenge faced by the Soviet economy after 1953.

Terror | 5

Although the Great Terror is normally associated with the late 1930s, terror in various guises was a central feature of Stalinist rule from 1928 to 1953. Although it went in phases, and hit different institutions and groups at different times, the use of coercive means to implement policy and get rid of opponents was always central to Stalinist politics. That does not mean that the whole population was in a state of fear throughout Stalin's rule, or indeed that Stalin had no popular support. It is simply difficult to divorce the Stalin years from violence and terror.

On 1 December 1934, the Stalin regime introduced a law which gave the government legal sanction to eliminate its enemies at will. This occurred a few hours after the assassination of Sergei Kirov, head of the Leningrad Party. In January 1934, at the 17th Party Congress, there had been talk of replacing Stalin as General Secretary of the Party with Kirov, who was seen to be more moderate. This fact, together with a lot of circumstantial evidence, has meant that Stalin has been traditionally blamed for the murder, and Khrushchev concluded as much when he appointed an investigation into the whole affair in 1956. However, the question of Stalin's responsibility for the murder has never been satisfactorily resolved (see Getty and Naumov 1999: 140–7). Whether or not Stalin authorised the murder, he certainly made full use of it. The new law was to provide the legislative basis for the terror of subsequent years.

Document 5.1 Legislative Basis for Terror

The Central Executive Committee of the USSR resolves: to introduce the following changes to the current codes of criminal procedure of the union republics relating to the investigation and examination of matters concerning terrorist organisations and terrorist acts against the workers of the Soviet state:

1. An investigation of these matters must be completed in no more than ten days.
2. Those accused should be presented with charges twenty-four hours before the case comes to trial.
3. Matters should be heard without the participation of defence or prosecution.
4. Appeals, as also petitions for pardon, are not permitted.

5. A sentence for the most severe form of punishment should be carried out immediately on the issuing of the sentence.

President of the Central Executive
Committee of the USSR
M. Kalinin

Secretary of the Central Executive
Committee of the USSR
A. Yenukidze

Source: M. Glavatsky et al. (eds), Khrestomatiia po istorii Rossii 1917–1940, *1995, p. 358.*

A distinctive feature of the terror after Kirov's death was that it embraced the Communist Party itself. Zinoviev and Kamenev were arrested under suspicion of being involved in the murder; in Leningrad, Zinoviev's former power base, there were mass arrests and deportations. The assault on Zinoviev and Kamenev culminated in August 1936, when the two of them featured in the first major show trial, and were convicted of being members of a 'Trotskyite-Zinovievite Centre' which had conspired to assassinate Stalin and other Soviet leaders. Alongside these events, in 1935, an attempt to reorganise the party resulted in a verification of party documents, which involved an essentially administrative purge of unreliable party members (Getty 1985: 58–91).

On 25 September 1936 Stalin, while on vacation on the Black Sea, sent a telegram to Moscow demanding the replacement of G.G. Yagoda, NKVD chief, with N.I. Yezhov, then head of the Party Control Commission. It is likely that in the following document the reference to the OGPU 'lagging four years behind' refers to the existence of a united opposition bloc in 1932 headed by Trotsky and I.N.Smirov (Getty 1993: 60).

Document 5.2   Telegram on the Appointment of Yezhov

We regard it as absolutely necessary and urgent that Comrade Yezhov be appointed People's Commissar for Internal Affairs. Yagoda has shown himself to be utterly incapable of unmasking the Trotskyite-Zinovievite bloc. The OGPU is lagging four years behind on this matter. This has been noticed by all party workers and most representatives of the NKVD.

Source: Dmitri Volkogonov, Stalin, *1991, p. 270.*

Yezhov quickly purged the senior officers of the NKVD and replaced them with his own men. Methods of interrogation immediately became more aggressive. In these years, hundreds of thousands were subjected to torture, and then shot or sent to labour camps. On 10 January 1939, the Central Committee released a statement indicating that from 1937, torture had been a legal instrument of investigation. The following document, from the post-war era, illustrates the kinds of methods that were used to extract information. It is taken from a secret memorandum of 17 July 1947 from V.S. Abakumov, head of the MGB (Ministry of State Security, a successor to the NKVD) to Stalin.

Document 5.3   Interrogation Techniques

1 . . .

During the arrest of an important state criminal, when it is necessary to conceal his arrest from his near ones or impossible at the same time to arrest his accomplices, in order not to frighten them or give them the possibility of slipping out of responsibility, or of destroying primary evidence, – there takes place a secret arrest on the street or in some other specially conceived circumstances . . .

4 . . .

When the arrested person does not provide frank statements and avoids direct and truthful answers to the questions put, the investigator, in order to put pressure on the arrested person, makes use of compromising data which the MGB has at its disposal, which the latter is concealing.

Sometimes, in order to outwit the arrested person and give him the impression that the agencies of the MGB know everything about him, the investigator draws the arrested person's attention to particular intimate details from his personal life, vices which he conceals from his associates and others . . .

7. In relation to arrested persons who stubbornly oppose the demands of the investigator, and conduct themselves in a provocative manner, and seek in all ways to drag out the investigation or to deflect it from the right path, a strict regime under guard is to be strictly introduced.

This includes the following measures:

a) transfer to a prison with a more strict regime, where hours of sleep are restricted and the maintenance of the arrested person in regard to food and other domestic needs is worsened;

b) solitary confinement;

c) forbidding walks, food parcels and the right to read books;

d) placing in a punishment cell for a period up to 20 days.

Source: 'Dobit'sia Polnogo Razoblacheniia', Istochnik, *1994, 6, pp. 112–14; also R.W. Davies,* Soviet History in the Yeltsin Era, *1997, p. 176.*

According to Yezhov's deputy, M.P. Frinovsky, who was himself later shot, he also ensured that those in charge of interrogation themselves had some sins in their past which meant that they could be manipulated and kept in line (Starkov 1993: 33).

The second major show trial, involving the famous journalist Karl Radek and Piatakov amongst others, took place in January 1937, and following the party plenum of February–March 1937, the USSR was plunged into a frenzy of arrests and executions.

In her memoirs of this period, Evgenia Ginzburg, a loyal party member living in Kazan, describes the hysterical atmosphere which pervaded certain party circles in 1937. Public confessions of guilt became essential signals of political vigilance. Ginzburg herself was arrested for an association with a historian, Professor Elvov, who was accused of errors in his treatment of the theory of permanent revolution in a chapter he had written on the revolution of 1905. She also relates an episode when Emilian Yaroslavsky, founder of the League of the Militant Godless, argues that the question of motive is irrelevant to the issue of guilt. Through such dialectical arguments, the party could argue that, since it was at the vanguard of the 'objective' historical process, anyone was guilty if he or she stood in its way.

Document 5.4 'The Torrent of Confessions'

Great concert and leisure halls were turned into public confessionals. Although absolution was not easy to come by – expressions of contrition were more often than not rejected as 'inadequate' – the torrent of confessions grew from day to day. Every meeting had its chosen theme. People did penance for mis-understanding the theory of permanent revolution and abstaining from voting on the opposition programme of 1923; for failing to purge themselves of great-power chauvinism; for underrating the importance of the Second Five-year Plan; for remaining friends with sinners or liking Meyerhold's theatre . . . Beating their breasts, the 'guilty' would lament that they had 'shown political short-sightedness' and 'lack of vigilance', 'compromised with dubious elements', 'added grist' to this or that mill, and were full of the 'rot of liberalism' . . .

I left again for Moscow that very evening and saw Yaroslavsky, who accused me of 'not denouncing' Elvov's erroneous article – he had *himself* included the article in the four-volume *History of the All-Union Communist Party*, of which he was the editor. It was enough to make one's head spin . . .

My reason told me that there was absolutely nothing they could arrest me for. I realised, of course, that there was something wildly exaggerated and unreal about the monstrous accusations against enemies of the people, pub-lished in the newspapers. Still, I thought to myself, there must be something in it, some crumb of truth – they must at least have voted the wrong way on some occasion or other . . .

I would never have thought that Yaroslavsky, who was known as the 'conscience of the party' could have woven such a web of lying and syllogisms. It was he who first explained to me the theory which became popular in 1937, that 'when you get down to it, there is no difference between "subjective" and "objective".' Whether you had committed a crime or inadvertently 'added grist' to somebody's mill, you were equally guilty – even if you had not the slightest idea of what was going on. The chain of 'logical' reasoning in my case was as follows: 'Elvov's article contained theoretical errors – whether he intended them or not is beside the point. You who worked with him and knew he had written the article, failed to denounce him. This is collusion with the enemy.'

Source, Evgenia Ginzburg, Into the Whirlwind, *1967, pp. 17, 30–2.*

In March 1938, Bukharin, Rykov and Yagoda were the most prominent of the defendants at the third and final of the major show trials. Bukharin had been under threat since the first show trial, when he was implicated in the evidence gathered. While in prison, Bukharin wrote to Stalin frequently. On 10 December 1937, he wrote the following letter, revealing why he had decided to admit to the charges which had been put against him. It supports the idea that for many senior communists, it was too much to renounce their belief in the party, even if they had to admit to crimes that they had not committed (see also Conquest 1992: 117). The idea that senior communists falsely confessed to crimes for the sake of the party was one of the central themes of Arthur Koestler's novel *Darkness at Noon* (see Document 13.4).

Document 5.5 Bukharin's Letter to Stalin

I cannot leave this life without writing to you these last lines because I am in the grip of torments which you should know about.

1) Standing on the edge of a precipice, from which there is no return, I tell you on my word of honor, as I await my death, that I am innocent of those crimes which I admitted to at the investigation . . .

3) I had no 'way out' other than that of confirming the accusations and testimonies of others and of elaborating on them. Otherwise, it would have turned out that I had not 'disarmed'.

4) . . . I have formed, more or less, the following conception of what is going on in our country:

There is something *great and bold about the political idea* of a general purge. It is a) connected with the prewar situation and b) connected with the transition to democracy. This purge encompasses 1) the guilty; 2) persons under suspicion; and 3) persons potentially under suspicion. This business could not have been managed without me. Some are neutralized one way, others in another way, and a third group in yet another way. What serves as a guarantee for all this is the fact that people inescapably talk about each other and in doing so arouse an *everlasting* distrust in each other. (I'm judging from my own experience. How I raged against Radek, who had smeared me, and then I followed in his wake . . .) In this way the leadership is bringing about a *full guarantee* for itself . . .

I know all too well that *great* plans, *great* ideas, and *great* interests take precedence over everything, and I know that it would be petty for me to place the question of my own person *on a par* with the *universal-historical* tasks, resting, first and foremost, on your shoulders . . .

I believe that I am suffering retribution for those years when I really waged a campaign. And if you really want to know, more than anything else I am oppressed by one fact, which you have perhaps forgotten: Once, most likely during the summer of 1928, I was at your place, and you said to me: 'Do you know why I consider you my friend? After all, you are not capable of intrigues, are you?' And I said: 'No, I am not.' At that time, I was hanging around with Kamenev . . . Believe it or not, but it is *this* fact that stands out in my mind as original sin does for a Jew . . . For *this*, forgive me, Koba. I weep as I write . . . I ask you for forgiveness, though I have already been punished to such an extent that everything has grown dim around me, and darkness has descended upon me . . .

Oh, Lord, if only there were some device which would have made it possible for you to see my soul flayed and ripped open. If only you could see how I am attached to you, body and soul . . . Well, so much for 'psychology' – forgive me. No angel will appear now to snatch Abraham's sword from his hand. My final destiny shall be fulfilled.

Source: J. Arch Getty and Oleg V. Naumov (eds), The Road to Terror, *1999, pp. 556–9.*

The conversations which took place between Bukharin and the chief prosecutor Vyshinsky, during the trial of March 1938, have aroused much interest. Bukharin pleaded guilty to the charges in very general terms, but implied that in regard to specific accusations he was innocent. Some have suggested that this was a way of indicating the falsity of the whole proceedings, and that Bukharin was implicitly trying to condemn Stalin (Tucker 1972: 83). Others suggest that Bukharin had really capitulated to the regime, or that he was very naïve about what was going on (Medvedev 1989: 367; Radzinsky 1996: 363). It also has been suggested that Bukharin felt it necessary to confess to these crimes in order to save the life of his young wife, Anna Larina, and their son.

Document 5.6   Extracts from the Trial of Bukharin

BUKHARIN: . . . I plead guilty to being one of the outstanding leaders of this bloc of 'Rights and Trotskyites'. Consequently, I plead guilty to what directly follows from this, the sum total of crimes committed by this counter-revolutionary organization, irrespective of whether or not I knew of, whether or not I took a direct part, in any particular act. Because I am responsible as one of the leaders and not as a cog of this counter-revolutionary organization . . .

I shall now speak of myself, of the reasons for my repentance. Of course, it must be admitted that incriminating evidence plays a very important part. For three months I refused to say anything. Then I began to testify. Why? Because while in prison I made a reevaluation of my entire past. For when you ask yourself: 'If you must die, what are you dying for?' an absolutely black vacuity suddenly arises before you with startling vividness. There was nothing to die for, if one wanted to die unrepented. And, on the contrary, everything positive that glistens in the Soviet Union acquires new dimensions in a man's mind. This in the end disarmed me completely and led me to bend my knees before the Party and the country. And when you ask yourself: 'Very well, suppose you do not die; suppose by some miracle you remain alive, again what for? Isolated from everybody, an enemy of the people, in an inhuman position, completely isolated from everything that constitutes the essence of life . . .' And at once the same reply arises. And at such moments, Citizens Judges, everything personal, all the personal incrustation, all the rancour, pride, and a number of other things, fall away, disappear . . .

I am explaining how I came to realize the necessity of capitulating to the investigating authorities.

Source: Report of Court Proceedings in the Case of the Anti-Soviet 'Bloc of Rights and Trotskyites', *1938, pp. 370, 697, 777–8.*

From the trial of August 1936 to the summer of 1937, the terror mainly affected party members. However, from late June 1937 onwards, it escalated to embrace the population as a whole. The following document is of an NKVD operational order 'Concerning the operation of repressing former kulaks, criminals, and other anti-Soviet elements'. It was drawn up by Frinovsky, who was to take charge of the operation, and sent to the Politburo for its approval on 30 July. It was based on information supplied by the localities. Exact numbers to be arrested were provided, illustrating the way in which NKVD officials were required to fulfil quotas. Three-man courts, troikas, were set up around the country to resolve the guilt of those arrested. From late August to early December, following requests from local leaders for increased quotas, the Politburo sanctioned an increase of 22,500 in the first category, and 16,800 in the second category (Khlevniuk 1995a: 161–3).

Document 5.7   Operational Order No. OO447

30 July 1937

. . .

1. All kulaks, criminals, and other anti-Soviet elements subject to punitive measures are broken down into two categories:

a) To the first category belong all the most active of the above-mentioned elements. They are subject to immediate arrest and, after consideration of their cases by the troikas, to be shot.

b) To the second category belong all the remaining less active but nonetheless hostile elements. They are subject to arrest and to confinement in concentration camps for a term ranging from 8 to 10 years, while the most vicious and socially dangerous among them are subject to confinement for similar terms in prisons as determined by the troikas.

2. In accordance with the registration data presented by the people's commissars of the republic NKVD and by the heads of territorial and regional

boards of the NKVD, the following number of persons subject to punitive measures is hereby established:

	First Category	Second Category	Total
Azerbaijan SSR	1,500	3,750	5,250
Armenian SSR	500	1,000	1,500
Belorussian SSR	2,000	10,000	12,000
Georgian SSR	2,000	3,000	5,000
Kirghiz SSR	250	500	750
Tadzhik SSR	500	1,300	1,800
Turkmen SSR	500	1,500	2,000
Uzbek SSR	750	4,000	4,750
Bashkir ASSR	500	1,500	2,000
Buryat Mongolian ASSR	350	1,500	1,850
Dagestan ASSR	500	2,500	3,000
Karelian ASSR	300	700	1,000
Karbadino-Balkar ASSR	300	700	1,000
Crimean ASSR	300	1,200	1,500
Komi ASSR	100	300	400
Kalmyk ASSR	100	300	400
Mari ASSR	300	1,500	1,800
Mordvinian ASSR	300	1,500	1,800
German-Polvozhia ASSR	200	700	900
Northern Ossetian ASSR	200	500	700
Tatar ASSR	500	1,500	2,000
Udmurt ASSR	200	500	700
Chechen-Ingush ASSR	500	1,500	2,000
Chuvash ASSR	300	1,500	1,800
Azov-Black Sea territory	5,000	8,000	13,000
Far Eastern territory	2,000	4,000	6,000
Western Siberian territory	5,000	12,000	17,000
Krasnoyarsk territory	750	2,500	3,250
Ordzhonikidze territory	1,000	4,000	5,000
Eastern Siberian territory	1,000	4,000	5,000
Voronezh region	1,000	3,500	4,500
Gorky region	1,000	3,500	4,500
Western region	1,000	5,000	6,000
Ivanovo region	750	2,000	2,750
Kalinin region	1,000	3,000	4,000
Kursk region	1,000	3,000	4,000
Kuibyshev region	1,000	4,000	5,000
Kirov region	500	1,500	2,000
Leningrad region	4,000	10,000	14,000
Moscow region	5,000	30,000	35,000

Omsk region	1,000	2,500	3,500
Orenburg region	1,500	3,000	4,500
Saratov region	1,000	2,000	3,000
Stalingrad region	1,000	3,000	4,000
Sverdlovsk region	4,000	6,000	10,000
Northern region	750	2,000	2,750
Cheliabinsk region	1,500	4,500	6,000
Yaroslavl region	750	1,250	2,000

. . .

[N. YEZHOV]
Certified: M. Frinovsky

Source: J. Arch Getty and Oleg V. Naumov (eds), The Road to Terror, *1999, pp. 475–8.*

The party was devastated by the purges. Of the 139 members of the party Central Committee elected at the 17th Party Congress in 1934, 110 were arrested before the 18th Congress in March 1939. Certain regions were hit especially badly. Of the 86 members of the Ukrainian party Central Committee at the beginning of 1937, only 3 remained at the end of 1938. More widely, official figures suggest that 680,000 people were executed for political reasons in 1937–38, although the true figure may be some hundreds of thousands higher. It has been recently estimated that, excluding famine victims, the Stalinist regime was responsible for a total of about 1 million purposive killings, and through criminal neglect for the premature death of some 2 million more victims in camps, exile, prisons and POW camps for the Germans (Wheatcroft 1996: 1331–2). Previously, much higher estimates were offered, and there is still much controversy over the numbers.

The terror became less intense in the latter part of 1938, and Yezhov himself became a convenient scapegoat for the excesses of the purges. He was replaced in December 1938 by the Georgian Lavrenty Beria and shot in 1940. Like many of those demoted from power, Yezhov's place in history was also affected. Stalin evidently did not like having to recall the existence of those whom he had dispensed with. Photographs were often retouched to ensure the removal of repressed people. Even in their homes, it happened that people would cut out the heads of their own repressed relatives from pictures in their photo albums (see King 1997: 7). The following photograph portrays Voroshilov, Molotov, Stalin and Yezhov against the background of the Moscow–Volga canal; following his demise, Yezhov was removed from the photograph.

Document 5.8   Yezhov is Removed from History

[See page 74]

Source: Dmitri Volkogonov, Stalin, *1991, between pages 290 and 291.*

[Document 5.8]

Stalin was aware of the need to mobilise support for his policies, or at least present the country as behind them. In the summer of 1937, a closed trial took place of some of the top military leaders, including the Soviet Union's main military strategist, Marshal Tukhachevsky, and the Army Commanders I. Yakir and I. Uborevich. All were found guilty of plotting against the Soviet Union and were shot, and this set the scene for a massive purge of the army elite in subsequent months. At the end of the trial, Stalin sent a telegram to party committees instructing them to organise popular demonstrations against the accused.

Document 5.9   The Mobilisation of Support for Condemnation of Tukhachevsky

(In cipher)

National CCs, kraikoms and obkoms
   In connection with the current trial of the spies and wreckers Tukhachevsky, Yakir, Uborevich and others the CC suggests that you organise meetings of workers, and where possible peasants, and also meetings of red army units and put forward resolutions on the necessity of using the most extreme measures of repression. The trial must be finished tonight. An announcement about the sentence will be published tomorrow, that is the twelfth of July.
11. VI. 37. 16 h. 50 m.   Secretary of the CC Stalin

Source: L. Larina (ed.), Istoriia otechestva v dokumentakh 1917–1993 vol. 2 1921–1939, *1994, p. 154.*

In his memoirs, Molotov argues that the attack on the military elite, and particularly Tukhachevsky and Yakir, was necessary not because they were spies, but because they were a potential 'fifth column' which might have challenged Stalin during the war. In general, he argues that, in spite of mistakes, the terror was necessary.

Document 5.10   Molotov Justifies the Terror

Let us assume [Stalin] made mistakes. But name someone who made fewer mistakes. Of all the people involved in historic events, who held the most correct position? Given all the shortcomings of the leadership of that time, [Stalin] alone coped with the tasks then confronting the country . . .
   Stalin was, of course, distinguished by his rudeness. He was a very blunt person. But if not for his harshness I don't know how much good would have been accomplished. I think harshness was necessary otherwise there would have been even greater vacillation and irresolution . . .
   1937 was necessary. Bear in mind that after the Revolution we slashed right and left; we scored victories but tattered enemies of various stripes survived, and as we were faced by the growing danger of fascist aggression, they might have united. Thanks to 1937 there was no fifth column in our country during

the war . . . It's unlikely those people were spies, but they were definitely linked with foreign intelligence services. The main thing, however, is that at the decisive moment they could not be depended on . . .

Stalin, in my opinion, pursued a correct line: let innocent heads roll, but there will be no wavering during and after the war. Yes, mistakes were made. But look, Rokossovsky and Meretskov were freed . . .

The terror was necessary, and it couldn't have been completed without mistakes. The alternative was to carry the internal political debates into the war years . . .

Vlasov [a captured Soviet general who voluntarily organized an army from among fellow PWs to fight the USSR] would have been as nothing compared to what might have happened. Many people were wavering politically . . .

The 1920s and 1930s. I consider that period absolutely remarkable . . .

I don't consider it the bloody period.

Source: Felix Chuev, Molotov Remembers, *1993, pp. 183, 213, 254, 279.*

The telegram about the trial of Tukhachevsky would suggest that popular support for the terror was artificially manufactured from above. However, it can also be argued that the terror was in part a populist strategy to deflect hostility away from the regime to various scapegoats (S. Davies 1997a: 113). In the countryside, the show trials offered the chance for those disadvantaged and aggrieved by collectivisation to take their revenge on local party officials (Fitzpatrick 1994: 286–312).

There has been some dispute about the extent to which Stalin was directly involved in planning the terror. The debate can be compared to the discussions about the origins of the Holocaust: was there a straight or a twisted road to Auschwitz? Did Stalin intend the terror, or did it, for example, grow out of the attempts by the centre to impose its will on the regions? It has been suggested that 'there is no evidence of a planned straight line' to Stalin's terror (Getty 1993: 59). Others, following Conquest's original insights, suggest that it was directly planned from above, and that it was a result of systematic preparation (Werth 1997: 208; Rees 1998a: 60). Certainly, archival discoveries confirm that Stalin was directly involved in planning the executions, although that does not in itself resolve the questions of long-term intentions. Lists of people to be shot were usually reviewed and signed by him and Molotov. However, the fact that Stalin so clearly approved the terror does not itself mean that all the events associated with it were initiated by him, or were carried out as the party wanted. It has been suggested that the lists of people selected for arrest were often drawn up on the basis of local hearsay and accusation as well as input from above (Manning 1993a: 192), and that while the party and NKVD leadership could stop and start the process of eliminating opponents, it was very difficult to control primary party organisations (Reese 1993: 212).

The following document, for example, illustrates the way in which local party bosses might apply for permission to increase the execution rates in their region. The Secretary of the Irkutsk oblast party committee (in the Eastern Siberia krai) here asks for permission to convict an additional 5,000 people according to the first category.

His reason would likely be a desire to impress his superiors with his political vigilance. Nevertheless, the document indicates how a process which started from above could acquire a momentum of its own.

Document 5.11   Initiative from Regional Party Leadership
25/8/1938

To TsK VKP(b) Com. STALIN,
NKVD Com. YEZHOV

In view of the as yet unfinished purge of the oblast of right-Trotskyite white-guardist panmongol counter-revolutionary hostile elements, residents of Kharbin, SRs, kulaks of the first category, we request the TsK VKP(b) to extend the limit by 5 thousand people in the first category for the Irkutsk oblast.

SECRETARY OF THE IRKUTSK OBKOM VKP(b) FILIPPOV
HEAD OF UNKVD MALYSHEV

Source: 'Rasstrel po 1'i Kategorii, Izvestiia, *3 April, 1996, p. 5.*

It can be difficult to interpret these documents, because the text does not reveal the motives behind them. An example of a similarly complex document is the following Central Committee directive of January 1938, calling for greater carefulness in the process of elimination of enemies. It is possible to interpret this as a prelude to the approach taken after Yezhov's fall, in which the party sought to dissociate itself from the excesses of the terror. At the same time, it can be argued that the terror did indeed acquire a momentum of its own, and thus that the document can be taken at face value. In arguing that the whole process had contradictory elements; one historian suggests that terror and anti-terror 'proceeded simultaneously' (Getty 1993: 51).

Document 5.12   Restraining the Terror

The VKP(b) Central Committee plenum considers it necessary to direct the attention of party organizations and their leaders to the fact that while carrying out their major effort to purge their ranks of trotskyite-rightist agents of fascism they are committing serious errors and perversions which interfere with the business of purging the party of double-dealers, spies, and wreckers. Despite the frequent directives and warnings of the VKP(b) Central Committee, in many cases the party organizations adopt a completely incorrect approach and expel Communists from the party in a criminally frivolous way . . .

There have been many instances of party organizations, without any verification and thus without any basis, expelling Communists from the party, depriving them of their jobs, frequently even declaring them enemies of the people without any foundation, acting lawlessly and arbitrarily toward party members.

Source: Robert McNeal, Resolutions and Decisions of the Communist Party of the Soviet Union, Vol. 3, The Stalin Years: 1929–1953, *1974, pp. 188–9.*

It is unlikely that terror was ever seriously out of control (see Khlevniuk 1995a: 167). Where terror and anti-terror did sometimes go together, it was partly the result of the logic of the government's own policies. It has been argued that the government wanted a regulated system in which local parties took appropriate decisions. However, it was unprepared to countenance a real devolution of power; when things got out of control, the government had to reassert its authority, provoking further problems (Rittersporn 1993: 103).

The post-war era saw no let-up in the use of political terror. There was nothing as dramatic as the Yezhovshchina but the same techniques of government continued to be used. There is a lot of evidence to suggest that before he died, Stalin had been planning a new series of purges. His last years in power saw an attack on what was called 'cosmopolitanism', which meant a lack of respect for all things Russian. This Soviet Russian nationalism contained a powerful stream of anti-semitism. On 13 January 1953 TASS announced the discovery of a 'doctor's plot', in which Jewish doctors were accused of deliberately killing certain government officials. *Pravda*'s report of the discovery contains a call for widespread vigilance, in effect a new process of denunciation and purge:

Document 5.13   The 'Doctor's Plot'

Today TASS announces the arrest of a group of doctor-saboteurs . . .

It was discovered during investigation, that participants of this terrorist group, using their medical position and misusing the trust of patients, intentionally and maliciously undermined their health, made incorrect diagnoses and then killed them with incorrect treatment. Under the cover of the high and honourable calling of doctor, of man of science, these monsters and murderers trampled on the sacred banner of science. Engaging in these monstrous crimes, they defiled the honour of scientists.

Comrades A.A. Zhdanov and A.S. Shcherbakov fell victim to this band of anthropomorphous beasts . . .

It has been established that all the participants of the terrorist group of doctors were in the service of foreign intelligence services, sold their souls and bodies to them, were their hired and paid agents.

The majority of participants of the terrorist group – Vovsi, B. Kogan, Feldman, Grinshtein, Etinger, were bought by American intelligence. They were recruited by a branch of American intelligence – an international Jewish bourgeois-nationalist organisation, 'Joint'. The dirty face of this Zionist espionage organisation, which masked its real activity as charitable work, has been completely uncovered . . .

Soviet people should not for a moment forget the need to increase in all ways their vigilance, to alertly watch for all the intrigues of these instigators of war and their agents, to tirelessly strengthen the armed forces and organs of intelligence of our state . . .

We still have not a few idlers in our country. Specifically this idle loafishness of our people is fertile soil for malicious sabotage.

Source: Pravda, *13 January 1953, p. 1.*

Arrest was a sudden and terrible experience. The night-time knock at the door from the NKVD became an infamous feature of the Stalin regime. For those whose relatives were arrested, it was equally traumatic, especially when there were no clear explanations for it. Lydia Chukovskaya, close friend of the poet Anna Akhmatova, in a novella written in the winter of 1939–40 which was only published in the 1960s, tells the story of the psychological breakdown of a mother, Olga Petrovna, whose son, Kolya, is arrested for no apparent reason. Olga Petrovna is unable to accept what has happened and is prey to unrealistic hopes. In the following extract, 'Alik' is a friend of Kolya.

Document 5.14 Mother and Son

Olga Petrovna lay awake all night without even closing her eyes. How many nights ago was it since Kolya's arrest? It seemed an eternity.

She knew it all by heart already: the summer sound of feet under the window, the shouts from the beer-house along the street, the rumble of trams in the distance – then a short silence, and darkness – and then again the pale light filtering into the room, and another day beginning, a day without Kolya.

Where was Kolya now? What was he sleeping on? What was he thinking about? Where was he, and with whom? Olga Petrovna never for a moment doubted his innocence: terrorist activity? Raving nonsense – as Alik said. He must have come up against an investigator who was over-zealous, made him lose his head. And Kolya wasn't able to justify himself, he was still very young, after all.

Towards morning, when it was beginning to get light again, Olga Petrovna at last remembered the word she had been trying to think of all night: alibi. She had read about it somewhere. He had simply been unable to produce an alibi . . .

She wouldn't see Kolya for ten years. But why? What hideous nonsense. It simply couldn't be. One fine day – very soon – things would return to normal again: Kolya would be at home, arguing with Alik, as he used to, about cars and locomotives, drawing plans again . . .

At the office, she no longer spoke to anyone. Even the papers brought to her for typing she handed to the typists without a word. And no one spoke to her either.

Source: Lydia Chukovskaya, The Deserted House, *1967, pp. 97–98, 101.*

The remarkable literary talent of women like Lydia Chukovskaya, Evgenia Ginzburg, and Anna Akhmatova (see Document 12.15) has influenced scholars to assume that fear was an all-pervasive phenomenon during the purges. Recently, historians have started to question that view, noting Stalin's apparent popularity and the many memoirs where people write fond memories of the 1930s. It has been suggested that 'terror was not the central factor of Soviet existence' in the 1930s (Thurston 1996: 164). It is certainly true that many people did have fond memories of the 1930s, although it is also possible that for those unaffected by the arrests, fear was suppressed and frequently unrecognised.

Certainly, terror was not the only thing on people's minds, even when it played a part. Andrei Arzhilovsky worked at the Tiumen woodworking factory. He was from a peasant family, and had been imprisoned during collectivisation but released in 1936 for health reasons. His diary entry of 19 June 1937, at the time of the trial of the military, reveals a lucid understanding of the purges, but it appears alongside a description of the beauties of nature and references to his family that suggests a man relatively detached from the atmosphere of repression. There is no sense of self-censorship about the writing. He was subsequently rearrested and shot in September 1937 for involvement in a 'counterrevolutionary kulak sabotage organisation'. His diary was used against him, and the italicised lines in the extract represent what an NKVD official, in searching for incriminating material, had underlined in red.

Document 5.15   Terror and Ordinary Life

6/19. At last we've gotten our rain. The land, which had gotten so parched, now makes squelching noises under my feet. All nature rejoices at the rain: the seeds are well rested and all they need now is a few sunny days to bring them up out of the ground and make them bloom. The birds have fallen silent, but at the first sign of sun they'll come to life and start their joyful chirping and singing. The kids have finished their exams. They got good marks. Now we want to pile up some working days . . . Today I dreamed I went fishing and caught a carp with silver scales and a bird's tail. *An interesting dream. The GPU has uncovered a whole group of high-ranking secret agents, including Marshall Tukhachevsky. The usual executions. A replay of the French revolution. More suspicion than fact. They have learned from the French how to kill one's own.*

Source: Véronique Garros et al. (eds), Intimacy and Terror, *1995, p. 162.*

Peasants and workers evidently developed subtle strategies of resistance in dealing with the regime. In the labour camps, however, a whole alternative culture developed. Alexander Solzhenitsyn observed in his *The Gulag Archipelago*, an account of the labour camps based on 220 oral histories, that to be arrested meant to be transferred into another 'clandestine' world of prisons and labour camps, which most citizens had little idea of. He describes the labour camps as 'a continent – an almost invisible, almost imperceptible country inhabited by the zek people', and suggests that its inhabitants developed a culture and mentality of their own (Solzhenitsyn 1974: 3, x;

1975, 502–33). The word 'zek', an abbreviated form of the word *zakliuchennyi*, meaning 'prisoner', was the term generally used to describe labour camp inmates. An extensive prison vocabulary emerged in the labour camps, traces of which can still be found in contemporary Russian.

Document 5.16   Labour Camp Language

Zek: A prisoner
Zechka: A female prisoner

Source: Slovar' tiuremno-lagerno-blatnogo zhargona, *1992, p. 93.*

The labour camps have given rise to some great memoirs and literature. Frequently, their power is due to stories of human survival (see Document 11.14). For most people, however, the camps were a place of cruelty and degradation. Varlam Shalamov's collection of short stories, *Kolyma Tales*, offers an insight into the brutalising effect of camp life on ordinary people in the infamous Kolyma region. One dimension which he describes is the criminal community. The criminals operated like independent brotherhoods in the camps, frequently avoiding the penalties applied to political prisoners. They had their own ethical system and had a profound impact on the culture of the inmates.

Document 5.17   The Criminal World and the Camps

The evil acts committed by criminals in camp are innumerable. The unfortunates are those from whom the thief steals their last rags, confiscates their last coin. The working man is afraid to complain, for he sees that the criminals are stronger than the camp authorities. The thief beats the working man and forces him to work. Tens of thousands of people have been beaten to death by thieves. Hundreds of thousands of people who have been in the camps are permanently seduced by the ideology of these criminals and have ceased to be people. Something criminal has entered their souls for ever. Thieves and their morality have left an indelible mark on the soul of each . . .

The influence of their morality on camp life is boundless and many-sided. The camps are in every way schools of the negative . . .

Every minute of camp life is a poisoned minute . . .

There a convict learns to hate work. He does not and cannot learn anything else. He learns flattery, lying, petty acts and major villainies. He becomes totally engrossed in himself.

When he return to 'freedom', he sees that he has not only failed to grow during his years in camp but his interests have narrowed, become impoverished and crude. Moral barriers have somehow been pushed aside . . .

According to his own ethics, the criminal's attitude to the female sex is a combination of vicious contempt for women in general and a religious cult of motherhood . . .

At first glance, the only human emotion that seems to have been preserved in the criminal's obscene and distorted mind is his feeling for his mother. The criminal always claims to be a respectful son, and any crude talk about anyone's mother is always nipped in the bud. Motherhood represents a high ideal and at the same time something very real to everyone . . .

But even this one supposed ray of life is false – like every other feeling in the criminal soul. The glorification of one's mother is camouflage, a means of deceit – at best, a more or less bright expression of sentimentality in prison . . .

The mother cult is a peculiar smokescreen used to conceal the hideous criminal world. The attitude towards women is the litmus test of any ethical system. Let us note here that it was the coexistence of the cult of motherhood with contempt for women that made the Russian poet Esenin so popular in the criminal world.

Source: Varlam Shalamov, Kolyma Tales, *1994, pp. 411–12, 428–9.*

Strikes in the labour camps in 1952–53 posed a considerable danger to the regime (see Graziosi 1992). In general, just as collectivisation ultimately proved a millstone around the neck of Soviet leaders, so the labour camps too would prove a mixed blessing. For after Stalin's death, the release of millions of prisoners meant the introduction of an embittered community back into ordinary life. The experience of that community profoundly influenced the late Soviet intelligentsia and its attitude to the Soviet state.

Government | 6

According to traditional Marxist doctrine, the state was supposed to wither away under socialism. In theory, the state and the law were part of the so-called 'superstructure', i.e. they grew out of the social and economic structure – the 'base' – of a particular society. It was argued that in a bourgeois-capitalist society, the state was used by the ruling middle class to maintain its power and privileges; with socialism, however, class divisions would be abolished and the state would disappear, leaving just a few basic administrative tasks to be done. In his *State and Revolution* (1917), Lenin qualified this by noting that, in taking power, the proletariat would need first to use the bourgeois state to crush the counter-revolution before the state would finally begin to wither away (Lenin 1947 vol. 2: 201–2, 208).

Stalin developed his own theory for why there was a need for a strong and repressive state in the USSR. He argued that, with the approach of socialism, there would be an intensification of the class struggle and the proletariat would have to use all possible means to fight the class enemy. Thus, a strong state was in no way incompatible with the general idea of the withering away of the state. In a report to the 16th Party Congress in June 1930, Stalin suggested that the apparent contradiction between the theory of a shrinking state and the reality of strong government, was a contradiction which was true to the principles of Marxian dialectics.

Document 6.1   Stalin on the State

We stand for the withering away of the state. At the same time we stand for the strengthening of the dictatorship of the proletariat, which is the mightiest and strongest state power that has ever existed. The highest development of state power with the object of preparing the conditions *for* the withering away of state power – such is the Marxist formula. Is this 'contradictory'? Yes, it is 'contradictory'. But this contradiction is bound up with life, and it fully reflects Marx's dialectics.

Source: J. Stalin, Works, *vol. 12, 1955, p. 381.*

With the advent of socialism, therefore, classes were supposed to disappear. Using the same theoretical framework, Stalin could dispense with the need for political parties: parties were supposed to represent class interests; where there were no classes, no parties would be needed. This was a point that Stalin made in a speech on a draft of the constitution in November 1936. The idea that socialism had been achieved in the Soviet Union by the mid-1930s was used to justify the need for the constitution and it was formally accepted in December 1936.

Document 6.2   Stalin on Freedom and Democracy

A party is a part of a class, its most advanced part. Several parties, and consequently, freedom for parties, can exist only in a society in which there are antagonistic classes whose interests are mutually hostile and irreconcilable – in which there are, say, capitalists and workers, landlords and peasants, kulaks and poor peasants, etc. But in the U.S.S.R. there are no longer such classes as the capitalists, the landlords, the kulaks, etc. In the U.S.S.R. there are only two classes, workers and peasants, whose interests – far from being mutually hostile – are, on the contrary, friendly. Hence there is no ground in the U.S.S.R. for the existence of several parties, and consequently, for freedom for these parties . . . In the U.S.S.R. only one party can exist, the Communist Party, which courageously defends the interests of the workers and peasants to the very end . . .

Source: Merle Fainsod, How Russia is Ruled, *1963, p. 139.*

The most prominent Soviet legal theorist of the 1920s was the Marxist E.B. Pashukanis, who was the director of the Institute of Soviet Construction and Law. He developed an argument that at a time of transition from capitalism to socialism, law should be understood as dependent on politics. No static system of law should be allowed to impede the dynamic process of social development. This certainly fitted the traditional Marxist approach, wherein law was considered to be part of the superstructure. The following extract is taken from his book *The Soviet State and the Revolution in Law* (1930).

Document 6.3   The Relationship between Law and Politics

The relationship of law to policy and economics is utterly different among us from what it is in bourgeois society. In bourgeois-capitalist society, the legal superstructure should have the maximum immobility – maximum stability – because it represents a firm framework for the movement of the economic forces whose bearers are capitalist entrepreneurs. Accordingly, the aspiration to create final and integrated systems of law, free from inner contradictions, is characteristic of bourgeois jurists. Among us it is different. We require that our legislation possess maximum elasticity. We cannot fetter ourselves by any sort of system, because every day we are demolishing the structure of production relationships and replacing them by new production relationships . . .

   We have a system of proletarian policy and upon it law should be orientated . . . We are against law . . . absorbing policy. We are in favor of policy occupying the first place in law, of policy being sufficient above law because it leads forward . . .

I may say that for us revolutionary legality is a problem that is 99 per cent political . . . we must not put in the place of a movement forward . . . any system that has been frozen into immobility, even though it be dubbed proletarian law.

Source, E.B. Pashukanis, 'The Soviet State and the Revolution in Law', in V.I. Lenin et al., Soviet Legal Philosophy, *1951, pp. 279–80.*

In practice, Pashukanis's argument offered an intellectual justification for party dictatorship: at a time of transition, the leaders of the proletarian party should not be restricted by law. It is thus surprising that in the 1930s, Pashukanis' school of law should lose favour. It is one of many Stalinist paradoxes, that Stalin's rule witnessed the rehabilitation of the idea of law at the very time when legal and political institutions were at their least powerful. Vyshinsky, as well as presiding over the show trials, had from the spring of 1934 spearheaded a move towards justifying the idea of law as the foundation for politics and society (Solomon 1996: 156–73). In 1938 in Moscow, Vyshinsky addressing the First Congress of the Sciences of Soviet State and Law, attacked Pashukanis' school of legal theory and noted that the Soviet constitution of 1936 should be understood as providing a firm legal foundation for Soviet power.

Document 6.4   Vyshinsky and Soviet Law

The Pashukanises thus rejected the very possibility of constructing a soviet socialist theory of law . . .

In asserting that law is nothing but a form of capitalist relationships, and that law can develop only in the conditions of capitalism . . . , the wreckers who have been busying themselves on our legal front were striving towards a single objective: to prove that law is not necessary to the soviet state – and that law is superfluous, as a survival of capitalism, in the conditions of socialism . . .

In reducing law to policy, these gentlemen have depersonalized law as the totality of statutes – undermining the stability and authoritativeness of statutes, and suggesting the false idea that the application of the statute is defined in the socialist state by political considerations, and not by force and authority of the soviet statute. Such an idea means bringing soviet legality and soviet law into substantial discredit . . . If law is merely a form of policy, then how is article 112 of the Stalin Constitution – which says that among us judges are independent and subordinate only to the statute – to be explained? Article 112 solves the problem of the independence of the judges in their court work perfectly, clearly, and distinctly: that work is subordinate to the statute and nothing else. The incorrectness of mechanically reducing law to policy is thereby emphasized once again . . .

The tasks confronting us at the present time require work which is directed at making the soviet law and the soviet state strong.

Source: Andrei Vyshinsky, 'The Fundamental Tasks of the Science of Soviet Socialist Law', in V.I. Lenin et al., Soviet Legal Philosophy, *1951, pp. 325, 328–9, 331.*

In one way, Vyshinsky's comments are a piece of sophistry. He argues that law is not just a form of policy, and that in the USSR, judges are answerable only to the state. Yet he makes no mention of the fact that in a system where both government and state bodies are dependent on the party, the distinction between the two is effectively lost. At the same time, the move to rehabilitate the idea of law was rooted in a genuine desire on Stalin's part to see the emergence of a powerful state (Solomon 1996: 158). Here there was a contradictory dimension to his own aspirations. For the personalised system of rule which he established could only operate freely when the legal framework was bypassed. But at the same time he wanted to establish such a framework for the smooth running of the state (see Kershaw and Lewin 1997b: 356).

The updated version of the party rules of 1934 (which replaced the rules of 1925), which was accepted at the 17th Party Congress, offers a good illustration of the way the Stalinist party formally adhered to certain formalised procedures, which were in practice set aside. According to the rules, the principle of democratic centralism, which the party subscribed to, involved the election of all party members, and the 'subordination of the minority to the majority'. In theory, for example, the Secretariat was answerable to the Central Committee. In practice, Stalin, as General Secretary, ran the party and built up a personalised dictatorship. This tension between formal institutions and arbitrary rule was typical of the Soviet Union: there was 'a multiplicity of institutions operating in an uninstitutionalized framework' (Sakwa 1989: 194).

Document 6.5   Updated Version of Party Rules

The party leads all the organs of the proletarian dictatorship and secures the successful construction of socialist society . . .

IV THE ORGANIZATIONAL STRUCTURE OF THE PARTY

18. The guiding principle of the organizational structure of the party is democratic centralism, which signifies:
   a Election of all leading party organs from the highest to the lowest ranks;
   b Periodic reports of party organs before the party organization;
   c Strict party discipline and subordination of the minority to the majority;
   d Unconditional adherence by the lower party ranks and all party members to the decision of the higher party organs . . .
23. The organizational structure of the party is as follows:
   a. USSR: all-union congress – Central Committee of the VKP(b);
   b. Oblast, krai or republic: oblast or krai conferences or national party

congresses – oblast committees, krai committees, central committees of national communist parties.

c. Cities, raions: city or raion conferences – city or raion committees.

d. Enterprises, hamlets, kolkhozes, MTSs, Red Army units, institutions: general meetings, conferences of primary party organizations – primary party committees (factory and plant party committees, party bureaus of Red Army units, etc.).

24. The order of subordination, accountability, of proceedings and debate of party decisions (from the highest instance to the lowest): all-union congress; Central Committee of the VKP(b); oblast/krai conference; conference or congress of national communist party; oblast/krai committee, central committee of a national communist party; city/raion conference; city/raion committee; and so forth . . .

27. The party congress is the highest organ of the party. Regular congresses are convened at least once every three years. Extraordinary congresses are convened by the Central Committee on its own initiative or on the demand of at least one-third of the party members represented at the preceding party congress. The convocation of a party congress and its agenda are announced at least a month and a half before the congress. Extraordinary congresses are convened on two months' notice . . .

29. The congress:

a) hears and approves reports by the Central Committee, Commission of Party Control, Central Revision Commission and other central organizations;

b) reviews and revises the party Programme and Rules;

c) defines the tactical line of the party on basic questions of current policy;

d) elects the Central Committee, the Commission of Party Control, Central Revision Commission . . .

32. The Central Committee organizes: for political work – a Political Bureau; for general leadership organization work – an Organizational Bureau; and for current work of an organizational and executive character – a Secretariat.

Source: Robert McNeal, Resolutions and Decisions of the Communist Party of the Soviet Union. Vol. 3, The Stalin Years: 1929–1953, *1974, pp. 140, 143–6.*

The Soviet constitution of 1936 is a further example of a document which is filled with ambiguity. Superficially, the constitution established a coherent separation of powers. The legislature, the Supreme Council (Soviet), was the highest organ of state, and it passed laws and made policy. The government, the Council of People's Commissars, carried out policy. This was replicated in the union-republics, in what was a federal system from which the constituent parts could at any time secede. However, Article 25 noted that such rights as freedom of speech were given 'for the purpose of strengthening the socialist system', and article 26 observed that the Communist Party was the 'leading nucleus of all organisations'. In practice, the so-called 'nomenklatura' system of appointments – nomination to posts from party lists – ensured that all power rested in the hands of those appointed by the party elite.

The Soviet constitution can thus be read as a piece of Stalinist propaganda. Certainly, the regime used the constitution to try to draw the population's attention away from the growing reality of terror. Furthermore, the constitution offered sympathetic observers in the West encouragement to believe that democracy was already establishing deep roots in the USSR. Propaganda it doubtless was. On the other hand, the constitution created at least a formal regulatory framework, and its hypocrisies gave critics of the regime a stick with which to beat it. Furthermore, it could be considered puzzling that a regime so anxious to centralise power, should devote so much media space in 1936 to public discussion of the constitution, even to the point of widely raising the issue of electoral rights. Indeed, certain electoral procedures were introduced in May 1937 which had the effect of removing low level party officials. Although the issue of electoral rights was soon shelved, the fact that it was raised at all, and then quietly forgotten, has led at least one historian to suggest that the regime did not know its own mind, and was making up policy as it went along (Getty 1991: 32).

Document 6.6   The Constitution of 1936

1. The Union of Soviet Socialist Republics is a socialist state of workers and peasants . . .

4. The economic foundation of the U.S.S.R. consists in the socialist system of economy and socialist ownership of the implements and means of production, firmly established as a result of the liquidation of the capitalist system of economy, the abolition of private ownership of the instruments and means of production and the abolition of exploitation of man by man.

5. Socialist ownership in the U.S.S.R. has either the form of state ownership (public property) or the form of co-operative and collective farm ownership (property of individual collective farms, property of co-operative associations) . . .

9. Alongside the socialist system of economy, which is the dominant form of economy in the U.S.S.R., the law allows small private economy of individual peasants and handicraftsmen based on individual labour and excluding the exploitation of the labour of others . . .

13. The Union of Soviet Socialist Republics is a federal state, formed on the basis of the voluntary association of the Soviet Socialist Republics with equal rights:–

> Russian Soviet Federated Socialist Republic
> Ukrainian Soviet Socialist Republic [S.S.R.]
> Belorussian [S.S.R.]

Azerbaijan [S.S.R.]
Georgian [S.S.R.]
Armenian [S.S.R.]
Turkmenian [S.S.R.]
Uzbek [S.S.R.]
Tajik [S.S.R.]
Kazakh [S.S.R.]
Kirghiz [S.S.R.] . . .

16. Every Union republic has its own constitution, which takes into account the specific features of the republic and is drawn up in full conformity with the Constitution of the U.S.S.R.

17. Each Union republic retains its right freely to secede from the U.S.S.R. . . .

30. The supreme organ of state power of the U.S.S.R. is the Supreme Council [or Soviet] of the U.S.S.R. . . .

64. The supreme executive and administrative organ of state power in the U.S.S.R. is the Council of People's Commissars of the U.S.S.R. . . .

79. The supreme executive and administrative organ of state power of a Union republic is the Council of People's Commissars of the Union Republic . . .

102. Justice in the U.S.S.R. is administered by the Supreme Court of the U.S.S.R., the supreme courts of the Union republics, territories and province courts, courts of the autonomous republics and autonomous provinces, special courts of the U.S.S.R. which are created by decisions of the Supreme Council of the U.S.S.R. and People's Courts . . .

105. The Supreme Court of the U.S.S.R. and special courts of the U.S.S.R. are elected by the Supreme Council of the U.S.S.R. for a period of five years . . .

112. Judges are independent and subject only to the law. . .

118. Citizens of the U.S.S.R. have the right to work – the right to receive guaranteed work with payment for their work in accordance with its quantity and quality . . .

122. Women in the U.S.S.R. are accorded equal rights with men in all fields of economic, state, cultural, social and political life . . .

124. To ensure to citizens freedom of conscience the church in the U.S.S.R. is separated from the state and the school from the church. Freedom to perform religious rights and freedom for anti-religious propaganda is recognised for all citizens.

125. In accordance with the interests of the toilers, for the purpose of strengthening the socialist system, the citizens of the U.S.S.R. are guaranteed:-

    a) Freedom of speech
    b) Freedom of the press
    c) Freedom of assembly and meetings.
    d) Freedom of street processions and demonstrations . . .

126. In accordance with the interests of the toilers and for the purpose of developing the organisational self-expression and political activity of the masses of the people, citizens of the U.S.S.R. are ensured the right of combining in public organisations: trade unions, co-operative associations, youth organisations, sport and defence organisations, cultural, technical and scientific societies, and for the most active and conscientious citizens from the ranks of the working class and other strata of the toilers, of uniting in the Communist Party of the U.S.S.R., which is the vanguard of the toilers in their struggle for strengthening and developing the socialist system and which represents the leading nucleus of all organisations of the toilers, both public and state . . .

134. Deputies to all soviets of toilers' deputies, the Supreme Council of the U.S.S.R., Supreme Councils of the Union republics, territorial and province soviets of toilers' deputies, Supreme Councils of autonomous republics, soviets of toilers' deputies of autonomous provinces, regional, district, city, and village soviets of toilers' deputies . . . are elected by the electors on the basis of universal, equal and direct suffrage by secret ballot . . .

141. Candidates are put forward for election according to electoral districts. The right to put forward candidates is granted to social organisations and societies of the toilers: communist Party organisations, trade unions, co-operatives, youth organisations and cultural societies . . .

Source: The New Soviet Constitution, *1936.*

Since Stalin was General Secretary of the party, he could conveniently portray any opposition to him as 'anti-party'. It would be wrong to believe that there was no opposition to Stalin during the 1930s. Indeed, during the years of collectivisation, there was a lot of dissatisfaction. The most serious manifestation of unease in the early 1930s was the so-called 'Ruitin Group', which belonged to the 'Union of Marxist-Leninists'. Its members, who included former members of the Right Opposition and some academics, produced a document entitled 'Stalin and the Crisis of Proletarian Dictatorship' which called for Stalin to be overthrown. The document was circulated in the Central Committee in 1932. When it was uncovered, the GPU and Stalin recommended that Riutin be executed, but the Politburo voted instead that he be exiled. It was not until 1936 that Stalin could move freely against his enemies in the party.

Document 6.7 'Stalin and the Crisis of Proletarian Dictatorship'

The measures necessary for the party and the country to exit this crisis and deadend are essentially as follows:

1. The liquidation of the dictatorship of Stalin and his clique.
2. The immediate overthrow of the whole leadership of the party apparatus and new elections of party organs on the basis of genuine democracy within the party and the creation of strong organisational guarantees against the usurpation of the rights of the party by the party apparatus.
3. An immediate extraordinary congress of the party.
4. A decisive and immediate return of the party on all issues to the ground of Leninist principles.

Source: 'Stalin i krizis proletarskoi diktatury', Izvestiia TsK KPSS, 1990, no. 12, p. 198.

Stalin's private secretariat, headed by A.N. Poskrebyshev, was an important mechanism for his control over the bureaucracy and the decision-making process. It has even been suggested that it was through Poskrebyshev that Stalin ruled (Tucker 1992: 272). The secretariat was neither a state nor a party institution. Stalin used it to avoid, where possible, the formal mechanisms of decision-making. Another mechanism under Stalin's control was the Special Sector. A resolution of the Central Committee Secretariat on 13 November 1933 made the Secret Department of the Central Committee answerable directly to Stalin himself. The Secret Department was renamed the 'Special Sector' at the beginning of 1934. One of the tasks of the Special Sector, where Stalin's secretary was again Poskrebyshev, was administrative: it supervised the distribution of documentation to Central Committee Secretaries, Politburo members and other party leaders. This gave Stalin complete control of information. If he wanted to isolate someone, he could simply withhold documentation from them. Furthermore, Poskrebyshev was the head of all the assistants to other members of the Politburo, and thus through them could keep a close watch on them.

The Central Committee Secretariat was reorganised in 1934. The new structure reflected an attempt by the Secretariat to keep control of the rapidly growing economy. The following document is a Politburo resolution of 4 June 1934, in which the duties of the Central Committee Secretaries were allocated. Stalin's responsibility for the Special Sector and the Politburo, as well as Culture and Propaganda, illustrates his hold on the central levers of power. The sections concerned with transport, industry, agriculture, planning-finance-trade and political administration each had subsections that were concerned with more specialised branches of industry and administration. In general within their own sectors, they were responsible for cadres, party organisational work, mass agitation, and checking up on the fulfilment of party and government decrees. The Section on Leading Party Organs supervised the party apparatus. The Section on Culture and Propaganda in 1935 dissolved into five new sections: Party Propaganda and Agitation, Press and Publishing, Schools, Cultural-Instruction Work, and Science (see Fainsod 1963: 194).

Document 6.8   Distribution of Central Committee Duties

Com. Stalin:
1) Culture and Propaganda,
2) The Special Sector,
3) The Politburo of the CC,

Com. Kaganovich:
1) The Orgburo of the CC,
2) The Industrial Section,
3) The Transport Section,
4) Komsomol,
5) Party Control,

Com. Zhdanov
1) The Agricultural Section,
2) The Planning-Finance-Trade Section,
3) The Political-Administrative Section,
4) The Section of Leading Party Organs,
5) The Chancellery,
6) The CC Secretariat.

Source: Oleg Khlevniuk et al. (eds), Stalinskoe Politbiuro, 1995, pp. 141–2.

Wherever possible, Stalin bypassed the formal mechanisms of decision-making altogether. From early 1933, the Politburo went into decline. The total number of Politburo meetings fell rapidly through the 1930s: there were 43 meetings in 1932, 24 in 1933, 18 in 1934, 15 in 1935, 9 in 1936, 6 in 1937, and just 2 in 1940. Furthermore, while there were 32 meetings of the Secretariat in 1932, there were none between 1936–40, and the number of Orgburo meetings also declined considerably from the levels of the late 1920s. In addition, the number of meetings of Sovnarkom (the Council of People's Commissars) also declined considerably (Rees 1995a: 106–8; Watson 1996: 55). Increasingly, policy-making took place in Stalin's office. The Politburo, when it met, came to be a rubber-stamp for decisions made by Stalin in the company of small groups of selected party leaders.

The following document gives an insight into this process. It is taken from the lists of visitors to Stalin's office which have been recently published for all of his years in power. This extract covers the final days of the third major show trial in March 1938. On 11 March 1938, Vyshinsky summed up his testimony. His presence in Stalin's office that evening, along with V.V. Ulrikh, who presided over the trial, illustrates how closely Stalin was involved in monitoring the events of the trial. The court retired to consider the verdict on the evening of 12 March, and announced its verdict in the early hours of 13 March (Conquest 1992: 395). Subsequently, Stalin met his closest colleagues on the evening of the 13 March:

Document 6.9 Visitors to Stalin's Office

11 March 1938	Entrance	Exit
1. com. Molotov	18.50	22.45
2. com. Voroshilov	19.15	22.45
3. com. Kaganovich	19.20	22.45
4. com. Beria	19.20	22.45
5. com. Smirnov	19.20	20.20
6. com. Vyshinsky	19.30	19.45
7. com. Ulrikh	19.30	19.45
8. com. Mikoian	20.15	22.45
9. com. Eikhe	20.30	22.10
10. com. Bulganin	20.30	22.10
11. com. Shestiakov	20.30	21.55
12. com. Popov	20.30	22.10

The last left at 22.45

13 March 1938	
1. c. Molotov	17.15–22.30
2. c. Yezhov N.I.	18.00–22.30
3. c. Kaganovich	18.15–22.30
4. c. Voroshilov	18.55–22.30
5. c. Zhdanov	19.00–22.30
6. c. Kalinin	20.35–21.00
7. c. Gorkin	20.40–20.50

The last left at 22.30

Source: A.V. Korotkov et al. (eds), 'Posetiteli kremlevskogo kabineta I.V. Stalina 1938–1939', Istoricheskii arkhiv, 1995, nos 5–6, p. 10.

This kind of source cannot, of course, reveal what was discussed at these meetings. However, that such meetings took place throughout Stalin's rule, coupled with the declining importance of the formal institutions of power, illustrates the fact that Stalin's regime was founded on a highly personalised system of decision-making. The Politburo and the party Secretariat were divided into fragmented small groups, which were answerable to Stalin alone, and he began to dominate the decision-making process completely (Bialer 1980: 33). In his Secret Speech in 1956, Khrushchev noted the way that party institutions were thus downgraded.

Document 6.10   Stalin's Small Groups

Many decisions were taken either by one person or in a roundabout fashion, without collective discussions . . .

The importance of the Central Committee's Political Bureau [Politburo] was reduced and its work was disorganized by the creation within the Political Bureau of various commissions – the so-called 'quintets', 'sextets', 'septets', and 'novenaries' . . .

The result of this was that some members of the Politburo were in this way kept away from participation in reaching the most important state matters.

One of the oldest members of our Party, Kliment Yefremovich Voroshilov, found himself in an almost impossible situation. For several years he was actually deprived of the right of participation in Political Bureau sessions. Stalin forbade him to attend the Political Bureau to receive documents. When the Political Bureau was in session and Comrade Voroshilov heard about it, he telephoned each time and asked whether he would be allowed to attend. Sometimes Stalin permitted it, but always showed his dissatisfaction. Because of his extreme suspicion, Stalin toyed also with the absurd and ridiculous suspicion that Voroshilov was an English agent . . . A special tapping device was installed in his home to listen to what was said there.

By unilateral action Stalin had also separated one other man from the work of the Political Bureau – Andrei Andreyevich Andreyev. This was one of the most unbridled acts of willfulness.

Source: Nikita Khrushchev, Khrushchev Remembers, *1971, pp. 558–9.*

Dinner parties also became a venue for the discussion of policy. In the last decade of his life, Stalin would meet with cronies such as Malenkov, Molotov, Khrushchev and Beria for long night-time sessions of eating, drinking and joking. Milovan Djilas, vice-President of Yugoslavia, who witnessed such dinners, has left an account of them, going so far as to suggest that they occupied a central political role.

Document 6.11   Dinner Parties

In a spacious and unadorned, though tasteful, dining room, the front half of a long table was covered with all kinds of foods on warmed heavy silver platters as well as beverages and plates and other utensils. Everyone served himself and sat where he wished around the free half of the table. Stalin never sat at the head, but he always sat in the same chair – the first to the left of the head of the table.

The variety of food and drink was enormous – with meats and hard liquor predominating. But everything else was simple and unostentatious . . .

Such a dinner usually lasted six or more hours – from ten at night till four or five in the morning. One ate and drank slowly, during a rambling con-versation which ranged from stories and anecdotes to the most serious political and even philosophical subjects. Unofficially and in actual fact a significant part of Soviet policy was shaped at these dinners. Besides they were the most frequent and most convenient entertainment in Stalin's otherwise monotonous and sombre life.

Source: Milovan Djilas, Conversations with Stalin, *1962, pp. 72–4.*

In 1952, Stalin decided to abolish the Politburo and replace it with a Presidium of twenty-five members. In his Secret Speech, Khrushchev suggested that the change was designed to bring about the removal of Mikoian and Molotov, who had fallen from favour. Indeed, he argued that Stalin was preparing to replace the older Politburo members with a new and younger leadership. In his memoirs, Khrushchev describes the introduction of the Presidium in scornful terms, portraying Stalin as an arbitrary and even incompetent tyrant. The episode illustrates very clearly the tension between Stalin's desire to set up formal procedures, and the personalised nature of his dictatorship.

Document 6.12   The Presidium

Stalin himself opened the first Central Committee Plenum after the [Nineteenth Party] Congress and proposed the creation of a Presidium of twenty-five members. He took some papers out of his pocket and read a list of names to us – the new membership. The proposal and the nominations were accepted without discussion. We were all too accustomed to such undemocratic procedures . . .

When the plenum session was over, we all exchanged glances. What had happened? Who had put this list together? Stalin himself couldn't possibly have known most of the people whom he had just appointed . . . I confess that at first I thought Malenkov was behind the new Presidium and wasn't telling the rest of us . . .

I now guess on the basis of certain indications that Stalin bypassed Malenkov and made use of Kaganovich's assistance. Some of the names were little known in the Party, and Stalin certainly had no idea who the people were. But Kaganovich knew them . . .

You see what sort of leadership we had? Stalin was supposedly running the Congress, putting together a new Central Committee, and creating a new Presidium, but in fact he had very little idea of what he was doing . . .

After Stalin proposed the twenty-five names, he said that because a group of that size would be cumbersome, we had to select a Bureau from the Presidium membership. Now, this was a non-statutory proposal. We had just adopted new Party Statutes at the Nineteenth Party Congress, and we had made no provision for a Presidium Bureau. We were violating the Statutes already! Stalin said that the Bureau would meet more often than the full Presidium and would make decisions on all operational matters that might come up. He proposed a Bureau of nine men and straightway appointed the staff: himself, Malenkov, Beria, Khrushchev, Voroshilov, Kaganovich, Saburov, Pervukhin, and Bulganin. Molotov and Mikoian were left out . . .

Out of the nine members in the Bureau, Stalin selected an inner circle of five
. . . The usual five were Stalin himself, Malenkov, Beria, Bulganin, and
Khrushchev.

Source: Nikita Khrushchev, Khrushchev Remembers, *1971, pp. 246–8.*

The totalitarian interpretation of the Stalin regime suggested a system of centralised
control which was so thorough that there was no room for political infighting. Stalin
was ultimately in complete control. In a revisionist critique of this approach, it has been
argued that in practice a significant measure of the decision-making was left to Stalin's
subordinates, and that beneath the monolithic façade of Stalinist government, there
was some real elite politics going: Ordzhonikidze and Molotov had disagreements;
Malenkov and Zhdanov were at odds. Furthermore, these personalised rivalries
were the symptoms of deeper bureaucratic struggles (Getty 1985: 199). The collapse
of the Soviet Union, and the release of valuable archival material have not led to a
radical reassessment of the totalitarian argument. It is clear that there was an
extraordinary centralisation of power under Stalin; the mechanisms of decision-
making, and the way Stalin used them, point away from the idea that there were
significant elements of plurality in his regime. Nevertheless, tight control over the
central levers of power is not incompatible with certain revisionist perspectives.
Complete institutional control, as far as that is practically possible, is not in itself
incompatible with the idea that policy decisions were taken on the spur of the
moment. Furthermore, particularly in the later years, there is considerable evidence
to suggest that issues were dealt with in a haphazard way. In his memoirs, for example,
Molotov notes that in Stalin's later years many resolutions were issued in Stalin's name
without him being aware of them.

Document 6.13 'Packages would Lie Unopened'

It's worth remembering how [Stalin] handled resolutions of the Council of
Ministers and the Central Committee. The Council of Ministers sometimes
passed a hundred resolutions a week. Poskrebyshev had all of them sent
in a big package to the dacha for Stalin to sign. Packages would lie unopened
at the dacha for months. But then they'd all be published over Stalin's
signature. In our meetings he would inquire about these resolutions, what the
problems had been. We'd have dinner, talk, argue, and compare notes. If they
were not clear, the problems got sorted out. It was senseless for him to read
all those resolutions. He simply would have become a bureaucrat. He wasn't
in a position to read all that. And you know what questions were discussed
– economic, military, political, cultural, and the devil knows what else . . . All
this came out in the name of the Council of Ministers, of which he was
chairman. Everything was promulgated over his signature, yet all these packages
of resolutions were thrown in a corner, unopened. You would go to the
dacha and they would have been lying there for a month, and now there is a
new pile. Lenin used to say, 'This is published' – and he said this when there

was ten times less paperwork. He would sign resolutions that he had not yet managed to read. 'I don't read everything I sign. You must have confidence in your staff.'

Stalin would ask, 'Is it an important question?' 'Yes, it's important.' Then he would pore over it to the last comma. But it was, of course, impossible to know everything in order to approve a resolution on how much to give whom for this or that. So he had to trust his deputies, or the people's commissars and members of the Central Committee.

Source: Felix Chuev, Molotov Remembers, *1993, pp. 179–80.*

The reality is that for all his power, Stalin's system was very inefficient. During the first Five Year Plan, there was a massive expansion in the state bureaucracy. Centralised ministries – People's Commissariats – were set up to administer the different branches of industry. There were three such ministries in 1932, twenty in 1939, and thirty-two in 1948. In 1928, white-collar workers made up 4.8 per cent of the workforce; by 1939 they had expanded to 15.5 per cent. This meant an increase from just under 4 million to almost 14 million personnel (Lewin 1997: 63). The influx of new workers without administrative experience was not the only reason for the inefficiency. The 'nomenklatura' system meant that the party was unaccountable to anything outside itself. Following Lenin's suggestion, in 1923 the Central Control Commission-Workers' and Peasants' Inspectorate (1923–34) had been formed to supervise party and state institutions and provide a democratic check on party organs. In practice, this simply became an instrument in Stalin's hands, as indeed were the Commissions of Party and Soviet Control which replaced it (see Rees 1987: 225–32). These factors set the scene for the stagnation and 'bureaucratisation' of the system.

Stalin was critical of bureaucratic hindrances to his policies, but in many ways he was the creator of the bureaucracy. The idea that the Stalinist system involved a corruption and bureaucratisation of the Soviet system owes much to Trotsky. Trotsky had to account for the fact that leadership of the party had fallen into the hands of Stalin, a 'mediocrity' in his eyes. In *The Revolution Betrayed* (1937), which presented a version of a Menshevik interpretation of Soviet history, Trotsky suggested that since the socialist revolution had occurred in a country without a powerful industrial working class, it had fallen on the shoulders of the party itself to modernise the country and by political means to create the conditions for socialism. However, this had led to the emergence of a bureaucracy keen to protect its own interests. Stalin, in Trotsky's view, was the personification of that bureaucracy. Thus, by this interpretation, Stalin rose to power not through any skills of his own. Just as the French Revolution had degenerated into Bonapartism, Trotsky suggested, so the Bolshevik revolution had degenerated into Stalinism.

Document 6.14 Trotsky on Bureaucracy

The inner regime of the Bolshevik party was characterized by the method of *democratic centralism*. The combination of these two concepts, democracy and centralism, is not in the least contradictory . . .

In March 1921, in the days of the Kronstadt revolt . . . , the tenth party congress of the party thought it necessary to resort to a prohibition of factions . . . This forbidding of factions was . . . regarded as an exceptional measure to be abandoned at the first serious improvement in the situation . . .

However, what was in its original design merely a necessary concession to a difficult situation, proved perfectly suited to the taste of the bureaucracy, which had then begun to approach the inner life of the party exclusively from the viewpoint of convenience in administration . . .

Democratic centralism gave place to bureaucratic centralism. In the party apparatus itself there now took place a radical reshuffling of personnel from top to bottom. The chief merit of a Bolshevik was declared to be obedience. Under the guise of a struggle with the Opposition, there occurred a sweeping replacement of revolutionists with *chinovniks* [professional functionaries]. The history of the Bolshevik party became a history of its rapid degeneration . . .

The increasingly insistent deification of Stalin is, with all its elements of caricature, a necessary element of the regime. The bureaucracy has need of an inviolable super-arbiter, a first consul if not an emperor, and it raises upon its shoulders him who best responds to its claim for lordship. That 'strength of character' of the leader which so enraptures the literary dilettantes of the West, is in reality the sum total of the collective pressure of a caste which will stop at nothing in defense of its position. Each one of them at his post is thinking: *l'état – c'est moi.*' In Stalin each one easily finds himself. But Stalin also finds in each one a small part of his own spirit. Stalin is the personification of the bureaucracy. That is the substance of his political personality . . .

The Stalin regime, rising above a politically atomized society, resting upon a police and officers' corps, and allowing of no control whatever, is obviously a variant of Bonapartism – a Bonapartism of a new type not before seen in history . . .

In the last analysis, Soviet Bonapartism owes its birth to the belatedness of the world revolution.

Source: Leon Trotsky, The Revolution Betrayed, *1972, pp. 94, 96–7, 98, 277.*

The state over which Stalin ruled expanded between 1939 and 1945. The Baltic states and Moldavia, both annexed in 1940, were incorporated into the Soviet Union. Towards the end of the war, Stalin annexed the Western Ukrainian regions of Galicia and Volhynia, which had previously belonged to Poland. Galicia had been part of the Austro-Hungarian empire prior to 1914. Simmering unrest in Western Ukraine would prove a headache for Soviet leaders in subsequent years. In particular the Organisation of Ukrainian Nationalists, headed by Stepan Bandera, and the associated Ukrainian

Insurgent Army, were responsible for conducting a guerrilla campaign for Ukrainian independence which lasted until 1953. The following party resolution of 1944 illustrates the concerns of the Soviet leadership about the mood in Western Ukraine towards the end of the war.

Document 6.15   Deficiencies in Party Work in Western Ukraine

A major inadequacy in the work of party organizations of the western oblasts of the Ukraine is their poor development of work concerning the measures that the Soviet state has taken to re-establish Soviet order and law in the territories that have been liberated from the fascist brigands. In their political work with the populace party organizations inadequately utilize the fact that the land has been returned to the toiling peasantry – land that the Soviet state had allotted to them before the war and the German brigands had taken from the peasants . . .

A serious omission of party organizations of the western oblasts of the Ukraine is their inadequate work in denouncing fascist ideology and the activity of agents of the German brigands, the Ukrainian-German nationalists who are hostile to the people and who in recent times were active in distributing significant numbers of anti-Soviet newspapers, brochures, and leaflets, and in spreading provocational rumours . . .

Work on the marxist education of the intelligentsia, a significant part of which was educated in German, Austro-Hungarian, Polish, and Rumanian schools in the spirit of bourgeois ideology, is poorly organized.

Source: Robert McNeal (ed.), Resolutions and Decisions of the Communist Party of the Soviet Union, vol. 3, The Stalin Years, 1929–1953, *1974, pp. 228–9.*

Although the federal system was in some ways a fiction under Stalin, since most important decisions were taken in Moscow, the existence of national territories within the Soviet Union was potentially destabilising. In the crisis of the Gorbachev era, national grievances which had been suppressed for decades turned out to be fatal to the Soviet Union's very existence.

7 | Stalin: the man and the cult

Stalin is an elusive personality. Certainly, he dominated his country for almost three decades, and had a profound effect on the wider world. But was this because he was a very capable, if also merciless leader? From one angle, he can be seen as a kind of evil genius, what one writer calls the 'the arch-intimidator, arch-prodder and the arch-cajoler' (Deutscher 1967: 331). On the other hand, Trotsky saw in Stalin a mediocrity. E.H. Carr, writing on the 1920s, suggested that 'more than any other great man in history, Stalin illustrates the thesis that circumstances make the man, not the man the circumstances . . . He had no creed of his own' (Carr 1958: 176–7). Which is the true Stalin? Was he a man who shaped things according to his will, or beneath his mask was there another, less secure figure, with his own moments of weakness and self-doubt?

Stalin was born Iosif Vissarionovich Djugashvili in Georgia to a semi-literate artisan family, and he grew up in the small town of Gori. Officially, his birthday was 21 December 1879, although there is evidence to suggest that he was born just over a year earlier on 6 December 1878 (Radzinsky 1996: 20). His father, a cobbler, was a violent heavy-drinking man, who used to beat both the young Iosif and his mother, and who eventually died in a bar-room brawl. His mother was strict, hard-working and deeply religious. Keen that her son enter the priesthood, she arranged for him to study at the Tiflis theological seminary, starting in August 1894. However, Stalin was quickly drawn away from religion towards Marxism. In an interview in 1931 with the German author, Emil Ludwig, Stalin explained his reasons.

Document 7.1   Stalin Embraces Marxism

I cannot assert that I was already drawn to socialism at the age of six. Not even at the age of ten or twelve. I joined the revolutionary movement when fifteen years old, when I became connected with underground groups of Russian Marxists then living in Transcaucasia. These groups exerted great influence on me and instilled in me a taste for underground Marxist literature . . . It was a different matter at the Orthodox theological seminary which I was then attending. In protest against the outrageous regime and jesuitical methods prevalent in the seminary, I was ready to become, and actually did become, a revolutionary, a believer in Marxism as a really revolutionary teaching.

Source: Edward Ellis Smith, The Young Stalin, *1967, p. 35.*

While at the seminary, Stalin gained a reputation as a troublesome student. The following extracts from his conduct books for November 1896 and the year 1898–99 while he was at the seminary, indicate that he borrowed radical books from a library outside the seminary, and that he openly expressed contempt for some of his teachers.

Documents 7.2 Extracts from Stalin's Conduct Books

[November 1896, Inspector Germogen]
Djugashvili, it transpired, has a card for the 'Cheap Library' and is checking books out. Today I confiscated from him V. Hugo's *Toilers from the Sea*, in which I found the aforementioned card.

Punish by lengthy confinement in the cell – I had already issued him a warning in connection with the outside book *Ninety-Three* by V. Hugo.

[1898–1899]
Djugashvili, Iosif (V,I), during a search of the belongings of certain fifth class pupils, several times spoke up to the inspectors, giving voice in his remarks to discontent over the searches carried out from time to time among the seminary students. In one of them he asserted that in not a single seminary were such searches made. In general pupil Djugashvili is rude and disrespectful towards persons in authority and systematically fails to bow to one of the teachers (A.A. Murakhovsky), as the latter has repeatedly informed the inspectors.

Reprimanded. Confined to the cell for five hours by order of Father Rector.

Source: Robert Tucker, Stalin as Revolutionary, 1879–1929, *1974, pp. 86, 90.*

While he was at seminary, Stalin gained the reputation of being a 'touchy' character. He certainly took himself very seriously. Before entering the seminary, while at Gori school, Stalin had been influenced by the writings of the Georgian romantic novelist, Alexander Kazbegi, and in particular his novel *The Patricide* which tells the story of an outlaw named Koba who avenges the death of his close friends during the Russian invasion of Georgia in the mid-nineteenth century. When Stalin quit the seminary to become a professional revolutionary in May 1899, 'Koba' became one of his revolutionary cover-names, and it was used throughout his life. It has been argued that Stalin's whole political life was an attempt to live up to this idealised self-image (Tucker 1974: 428, 462–77).

Stalin was made a member of the Tiflis Social-Democratic Committee in November 1901, and was subsequently involved in revolutionary activities in Batum. He was soon drawn to Lenin's more radical version of social democracy. He spent most of the years 1902–13 either in prison or in exile or on the run. There is unconfirmed evidence that at one point he acted as a police informer. He was made a member of the Bolshevik Central Committee in 1912, and after exile in Siberia from 1913–17, returned in March to St Petersburg, where he played a leading role in the Bolshevik party prior to Lenin's arrival in April.

The dominant traits of Stalin's early life continued, it seems, to play a central role in his life as a politician. Bukharin once suggested that he was fiercely jealous of anyone who was superior to him in any way (Tucker 1974: 423). Certainly, he was known in party circles for having a vengeful character. The following anecdote is one of many stories told about Stalin that suggest that he had a sadistic nature.

Document 7.3   Stalin's Vengeful Character

On a summer night in 1923, opening his heart to Dzerzhinsky and Kamenev, Stalin is supposed to have said: 'To choose one's victim, to prepare one's plans minutely, to slake an implacable vengeance, and then to go to bed . . . There is nothing sweeter in the world.'

Source: Boris Souvarine, Stalin, *1939, p. 485.*

This evidence of Stalin's vengeful character from his student years and from the 1920s suggests that certain traits of his character were formed in his earlier life; these qualities were reinforced rather than forged by his years in power. Yet Stalin was also a man affected by his decisions and experiences. Perhaps it was not inevitable that he turned out the way he did. He was certainly influenced by the Bolshevik political culture which was itself cruel and hard, if at times also idealistic. Another approach is to explain Stalin's ambition and careerism as containing a class content: Stalin had the 'character traits of a petty-bourgeois revolutionary and careerest inclined toward degeneration' (Medvedev 1989: 689).

Politburo member Lazar Kaganovich, who remained an admirer of Stalin until his death in 1991, suggested that the Stalin of the early 1920s was a genuinely humble person, and that certain features of his character were part of the Georgian temperament. He disputes Volkogonov's view that Stalin was cruel from his earliest years.

Document 7.4   Kaganovich on Stalin

Stalin was not the kind of man he is made out to be. And he was not, when he became Generalissimus. I have known Stalin since the first period of his work, when he was a humble man, very humble. He not only lived humbly, but behaved humbly with all of us.

We used to go to dinner with him . . . Sometimes he would invite me to dinner, we ate very simply, he, I, his wife. In his last years, it was different. I know him from the earlier period.

It is wrong to take Stalin from Volkogonov. Volkogonov depicts Stalin as cruel from childhood. Because his father was a cobbler and he out of want lived in a seminary, then in Siberia, in exile – this made him a cruel person. Instead of concluding from a class point of view that a revolutionary and a real fighter came out of this bad life . . ., Volkogonov says that it made him a crueller person.

But this is not a Marxist approach, surely it is not serious, it is stupid! It is idiotic! Furthermore, the character of a person changes. In childhood, it is one thing, then another, then a third thing. Moreover, Stalin, he says, was silent . . . [In Georgia] there are characters that are slow and silent . . .

It is important to take the characters of people into account. But in Stalin this is taken for cunning. And what leader is not cunning? He must be cunning . . . Everyone has his own particular cunning . . .

He changed, but he remained the same. Nowadays, people say that he was something of an artist, having a dual personality . . .

He was iron, hard, calm, I would say. An inwardly self-possessed, always mobilised person. He never uttered a word without thinking about it first . . . He would talk with you, but would be thinking at the same time. And focused. Focused. He was like that throughout his life . . . But depending on circumstances, his moods, relationships and actions would change. For me, for example, the most pleasant time of our relationship was the period of my work from 1922–1925. At that time, I was often with him, would often drop in on him. He was working hard on organisational work. I was his right hand, you could say.

Source: Felix Chuev, Tak govoril Kaganovich, *1992, pp. 81–2, 190.*

Clearly, in spite of his paranoia and cruelty, Stalin had the ability to inspire devotion in his colleagues and in the wider population. Men like Molotov and Kaganovich defended Stalin vigorously until their deaths many decades later (see also Document 5.10). It could be that for these members of the party elite, to defend Stalin meant in fact to defend themselves, but that does not preclude the possibility of genuine admiration.

Stalin's family life offers further clues as to his character. He was married twice. He married his first wife, Ekaterina Svanidze around 1902. She had a son, Yakov in 1908, and then died a year or so later. In 1919, he married Nadezhda Alliluyeva, the daughter of a prominent Bolshevik, who was twenty-two years younger than he. She bore him a son, Vasily (1921), and a daughter, Svetlana (1926). However, she committed suicide in November 1932. The memoirs of Stalin's daughter, Svetlana Alliluyeva, are unusual in revealing a warmer side to his character. His brief letters, of which the following is typical, reveal a tender and affectionate quality.

Document 7.5   Stalin to Svetlana Alliluyeva

Little Housekeeper!

I got your letter and postcard. I'm glad you haven't forgotten your little papa. I'm sending you a few red apples. In a few days I'll send tangerines. Eat them and enjoy yourself. I'm not sending Vasya any because he's doing badly at school. The weather is nice here. Only, I'm lonely because my Housekeeper isn't with me. All the best, then, my little housekeeper. I give you a big kiss.

(October 8, 1935)

Source: Svetlana Alliluyeva, 20 Letters to a Friend, *1967, p. 160.*

The playful relationship between Stalin and his daughter is confirmed by the recently published diary of Maria Svanidze, who was the sister-in-law of Stalin's first wife, and who in the 1930s was part of the family circle which visited Stalin on social occasions. Her diary entries also indicate that Stalin (at least outwardly) regarded Kirov as a friend.

Document 7.6   Stalin and Svetlana

4/11/34 . . . Svetlana hung around her father the whole time. He petted her, kissed her, admired her, lovingly gave her the choicest morsels from his plate. She wrote him 'Order No. 4': he must allow her to spend holidays at Lipki – one of his dachas was there.

14/11/34 . . . Svetlana wrote an order: 'I order you to allow me to go to the theater or the cinema with you.' And signed it 'Svetlana, Mistress of the House.' She handed it to him, and J. said: 'Oh well. I must obey.' They've been playing that game for a year now. Svetlana is the Mistress of the House, and she has several secretaries. Papa is No. 1 secretary, then come Molotov, Kaganovich, Ordzhonikidze, Kirov and a few others. She is great friends with Kirov, because J. is on very good and close terms with him. Svetlana writes orders and pins them on the wall with drawing pins.

Source: Edvard Radzinsky, Stalin, 1996, p. 294; also Iuriia Murina (ed.), 'Iosif Beskonechno Dobr, Dnevnik Marii Anisomovny Svanidze', Istochnik, 1, 1993b, no. 1, pp. 9–10.

Stalin's relationship with Svetlana when she grew up was much more complex. He did not like her boyfriends and the men she chose to marry, and there was much tension between them. Maria Svanidze and her husband Alexander were later repressed, shot in March 1942 and August 1941, respectively.

The circumstances of Nadezhda Alliluyeva's suicide remain mysterious. There was even a rumour that Stalin had killed her, although the evidence for it is not substantial. They had quarrelled at a private dinner party, after Stalin had made some crude remarks, and she was found dead the following morning with a pistol beside her. However, Nadezhda Alliluyeva had felt isolated from people by her life in the Kremlin and had probably been unhappy for some time. Furthermore, while studying at an industrial technical school, Nadezhda had discovered something of the reality of collectivisation through fellow students, and was uncomfortable with it. Stalin did not like her interest and occasional interference in politics. The following letter reveals her concern at the arbitrary way in which certain party officials behaved. She refers to an episode in which the secretary of the party cell of *Pravda*, Kovalev, was accused of being a Zinovievite, and was attacked for failing to prevent the publication of an article which had revealed the occurrence of suicides among Leningrad party workers who had been subject to criticism. Stalin subsequently took measures to prevent Kovalev taking all the blame and he remained in post for the present. However, writing to Molotov in December 1929, Stalin stated that Kovalev was a former Trotskyist, and a 'shadowy figure' who would have to be dismissed (see Lih 1995 *et al.*: 185). Although the episode was not in itself very important, Nadezhda's letter indicates that she reacted to things very differently from her husband, and suggests a certain tension between them on political matters.

Document 7.7 Nadezhda Alliluyeva to Stalin

Between 16 and 22 September 1929

Dear Iosif,
I received your note. I am very glad that your affairs are working out. For me also all is well for the present, except for today which troubled me very much. I will now tell you all about it. Today I was at the [party] cell of *Pravda* . . . and of course Kovalev told me about all his sad news. It relates to the Leningrad matter. You of course know about it, that *Pravda* featured the material without prior authorisation from the TsK, although N.N. Popov and Yaroslavsky had seen the material and neither of them thought it necessary to inform the party section of *Pravda* about the need for authorisation from the TsK (i.e. Molotov). Now . . . all the blame has fallen on Kovalev . . . [At a Party meeting] Kovalev explained his perspective, and Sergo [Ordzhonikidze] did not let him finish, hit his fist on the table 'in the traditional way' and began to shout that Kovalevshchina in *Pravda* would lead only so far . . . In a word it is possible that Kovalev made a mistake, which Yaroslavsky and Popov also made, but that does not mean that the matter should be dealt with in this kind of tone and turn. Don't get angry with me, but seriously, I have become very unhappy for Kovalev. I know what a colossal work he has done and suddenly . . . the editorial board makes a decision to 'free Koval[ev] from being the leader of the party section, as an undisciplined party worker', it is simply monstrous . . . I personally advised Kov[alev] to go directly to Molotov, and to raise the question from the point of view of principle, and that it must be done without the accusation of party indiscipline, Kovalevshchina, Zinovievshchina etc . . .

In a word, I didn't expect that everything would end so sadly. He gives the impression of being a man who has been killed . . .

I know that you very much dislike my interferences, but all the same it seems to me that you ought to interfere in this very unjust matter.

I am well. I am studying . . .

The children are well . . .

Goodbye, a very big kiss. Please reply to this letter.

Yours, Nadya

Source: Iu. Murina (ed.), 'Nadezhde Sergeevne Alliluevoi Lichno ot STALINa,' (correspondence 1928–1931), Istochnik, 1993a, no. 0, p. 12.

Nadezhda Alliluyeva's death had a profound impact on Stalin's life. The domestic environment which previously had surrounded him ceased to play a role in his life.

Politics became even more dominant than it was before. 'He had nothing but work' (Volkogonov 1991: 70). Certainly, Svetlana Alliluyeva suggests that her mother's death was a turning point in her father's life. The emotional side of life thereafter had little opportunity to express itself.

Document 7.8   Human Feelings

Human feelings in him were replaced by political considerations. He knew and sensed the political game, its shades, its nuances. He was completely absorbed by it. And since, for many years, his sole concern had been to seize, hold and strengthen his power in the Party – and in the country – everything else in him had given way to this one aim.

I believe that my mother's death, which he had taken as a personal betrayal, deprived his soul of the last vestiges of human warmth. He was now free of her moderating and, by the same token, impeding presence. His sceptical, harsh judgment of men only hardened; this came naturally to his unsentimental nature.

Source: Svetlana Alliluyeva, Only One Year, 1969, p. 351.

Stalin was not close to his sons. When Yakov at one point tried unsuccessfully to shoot himself because of his father's coldness, Stalin said to him: 'Ha! You missed!' Eventually Yakov died in a Nazi prison camp in 1943. Vasily commanded various air regiments during the war, but this was solely due to his father's influence. In fact he was a degenerate figure, who was destroyed by alcoholism and died in March 1962. Faced with news of his son's unreliability as a regimental commander, Stalin dictated the following order to Marshal of the Air Force Novikov on 26 May 1943.

Document 7.9   Stalin and his Son Vasily

1. V.I. Stalin is to be removed at once from the post of commanding officer of his air regiment and be given no other command post without my orders.
2. Both the regiment and its former commander, Colonel Stalin, are to be told that Colonel Stalin is being removed from his post as regimental commander for drunkenness and debauchery and because he is ruining and perverting the regiment.
3. You are to inform me that these orders have been carried out.

Source: Dmitri Volkogonov, Stalin, 1991, p. 468.

The dismissal did not have a major impact on Vasily's career. He apparently recognised his mistakes, and at the end of 1943 was promoted to be commander of an air division.

Much has been made of Stalin's supposed paranoia. There seems little doubt that 'quasi-paranoic behaviour was inherent in the logic of the great purges' (Deutscher 1967: 611). At the same time, Stalin was also mentally very competent (Medvedev

1989: 542). Conceivably he became more paranoid while in power, as a consequence of the number of people whose deaths he was responsible for. Anecdotal evidence has it that Stalin once said to Yagoda that he preferred people to follow him out of fear rather than conviction, because convictions can change (see Conquest 1992: 13). Whether he said that or not, there is no doubt that he found it almost impossible to trust anyone. The wives of some of his closest colleagues – Molotov, Kalinin, Poskrebyshev – were at different points arrested and imprisoned, while their husbands were working for Stalin. It was a subtle way of keeping them under control. In her memoirs, Svetlana Alliluyeva suggested that suspiciousness was a key component of her father's character. She also argued that in some ways her father, far from being a strong man, was 'broken': he was prey to the flattery and deviousness of Beria. Her comments about Beria must be treated with a certain scepticism, for they suggest a desire on her part to find some excuse for her father's crimes. At the same time, they indicate that on occasions, Stalin's subordinates could play on his character weaknesses to gain their own ends.

Document 7.10   Stalin's Suspiciousness

When the 'facts' convinced my father that someone he knew well had turned out 'badly' after all, a psychological metamorphosis came over him. Maybe in his heart of hearts he still had his doubts, and wondered and suffered over it. But he was in the grip of an iron logic whereby once you've said A, then B and C have to follow. Once he accepted the premise that X was his enemy, the premise became a hypothesis and no matter what the facts might be, they had to be made to fit. My father was unable ever to go pyschologically to believing that X wasn't an enemy but an honest man after all.

Source: Svetlana Alliluyeva, 20 Letters to a Friend, *1967, p. 86.*

Document 7.11   The Influence of Beria

I speak advisedly of [Beria's] influence on my father and not the other way round. Beria was more treacherous, more practised in perfidy and cunning, more insolent and single-minded than my father. In a word, he was a stronger character. My father has his weaker sides. He was capable of self-doubt. He was cruder and more direct than Beria, and not so suspicious. He was simpler and could be led up the garden path by someone of Beria's craftiness. Beria was aware of my father's weaknesses. He knew the hurt pride and the inner loneliness. He was aware that my father's spirit, in a sense, was broken. And so he poured oil on the flames and fanned them as only he knew how. He flattered my father with a shamelessness that was nothing if not Oriental. He extolled and flattered him in a way that caused old friends, accustomed to looking on my father as an equal, to wince with embarrassment . . .

I have said already that in a good many things Beria and my father were guilty together. I am not trying to shift the blame from one to the other. At some point, unfortunately, they became spiritually inseparable. The spell cast by this terrifying evil genius on my father was extremely powerful and it never failed to work.

Source: Svetlana Alliluyeva, 20 Letters to a Friend, 1967, pp. 148–9.

Although this assessment of Beria's influence may be exaggerated, it suggests that Stalin was not just a strong man. It has been observed that Stalin was not just a 'master planner', but also a fallible human being who sometimes reacted to events. Svetlana Alliluyeva's perspective supports this. To take such an approach does not mean to minimise Stalin's evil behaviour; it is simply to observe that there was something very ordinary as well as monstrous about it. As Getty writes, comparing Stalin to Eichmann: 'His evil, like Eichmann's, was ordinary and of this world; it was banally human and is more horrifying for being so' (1993: 62).

The suggestion that Stalin was in the grip of certain inner compulsions suggests a weak man, and that his hardness compensated in some way for some unrecognised inner problems. Certainly a pyschological approach to the study of Stalin can only lead to the conclusion that key aspects of the political system were products of his own psychological needs (Tucker 1992: 171). The Stalin cult is an example of that. The cult, even if it developed a life of its own and had wider social causes, had roots in Stalin's character.

The origins of the personality cult can in part be found in the Lenin cult, of which Stalin had made himself chief guardian, and which set a precedent for things to come. The Stalin cult itself began to gather momentum at the time of Stalin's 50th birthday in December 1929, when workers throughout the USSR issued resolutions extending their birthday greetings to Stalin, and he was proclaimed supreme leader (*vozhd'*). *Pravda*, over five days, listed hundreds of organisations which had sent him messages, and continued to print messages of congratulation for the next twelve months. In the first edition of *Pravda* in 1934, Karl Radek, the Bolshevik journalist who had supported Trotsky and been in active opposition to Stalin for many years, wrote a eulogistic article on Stalin as the 'architect of socialist society', which was reissued as a pamphlet. This set the scene for the extraordinary cult of the subsequent years.

Western intellectuals also contributed to the Stalin cult. The following document is an extract from a book about Stalin by the French communist, Henri Barbusse. During a visit to Moscow in 1932 to celebrate the life and achievements of the writer Maxim Gorky, Barbusse met and was very impressed by Stalin. His subsequent book on Stalin was uncritical in the extreme.

Document 7.12   Barbusse on Stalin

[Stalin's] power lies in his formidable intelligence, the breadth of his knowledge, the amazing orderliness of his mind, his passion for precision, his inexorable spirit of progress, the rapidity, sureness and intensity of his decisions, and his constant care to choose the right men . . .

[O]ne may also say that it is in Stalin more than anyone else that the thoughts and words of Lenin are to be found. He is the Lenin of today.

In many ways, as we have seen, he is extraordinarily like Vladimir Ilitch: he has the same knowledge of theory, the same practical common sense, the same firmness. In what way do they differ? Here are two opinions of Soviet workers: 'Lenin was the leader: Stalin is the master.' And also: 'Lenin is a greater man, Stalin is a stronger.' . . .

Stalin is not, nowadays, the man of great tempestuous meetings. However, he has never made use of that tumultuous force of eloquence which is the great asset of upstart tyrants and the only one, very often, of successful apostles: this is a point which should be considered carefully by historians who attempt to gauge him. It is by other paths that he came into and remains in contact with the working, peasant, and intellectual population of the USSR . . .

We have caught the glimpse of some of the secrets of his greatness. Among all the sources of his genius, which is the principal one? Bela Kun said, in a fine phrase: 'He knows how not to go too quickly. *He knows how to weigh the right moment.*' . . . Is it not this power that had made Stalin, of all the Revolutionaries of history, the man who has most practically enriched the spirit of Revolution, and who has committed the fewest faults? He weighs the pros and cons and reflects a great deal before proposing anything (a great deal does not mean a long time). He is extremely circumspect and does not easily give his confidence. He said to one of his close associates, who distrusted a third party: 'A reasonable amount of distrust is a good basis for collective work.' He is as prudent as a lion.

Source: Henri Barbusse, Stalin: A New World Seen Through One Man, *1935, pp. 275–7.*

Barbusse was one of a number of Western intellectuals who visited the Soviet Union in the 1930s and returned with enthusiastic accounts of what they saw. They included the founders of British Fabianism, Sidney and Beatrice Webb, the English novelist and futurologist H.G. Wells, and the German novelist Leon Furchtwänger, who, like Barbusse, wrote an uncritical biography of Stalin.

The mid-1930s saw an explosion of the cult not only in politics but also in the arts. Socialist realism was an extremely flexible artistic trend, which was essentially designed to encourage artists and writers to support the state in their work (see Documents 12.2 and 12.3). After 1934, there was a move away from an emphasis on class and general social forces to a focus on heroes. In this climate, Stalin's own heroism was particularly emphasised. Paintings designed to draw out Stalin's humanity flourished. For example, the following painting of 1937 by Grigory Shegal portrays Stalin at the Presidium of the 2nd Congress of Collective Farm and Shock Workers in February 1935. Stalin, beneath a statue of Lenin, is shown as a father figure dealing with the problems of ordinary people of diverse backgrounds and races.

Document 7.13 'Leader, Teacher, Friend'

Source: D. Ades et al. (eds), Art and Power: Europe under the Dictators, *1930–1945, 1995, p. 239.*

Film-makers made an important contribution to the Stalin cult, reinforcing the idea of the individual leader in a variety of ways. One historian talks of three rough categories to classify cult films: first, 'proto-cultic' films presented the moral transformation of a hero(ine) in a traditional narrative plot-structure, and were frequently set in the factory or collective farm; second, in 'quasi-cultic' films, which generally were more political and often featured historical events like the October

Revolution or the Civil War, the leading figure did not change in the course of the film, but was from the beginning imbued with the right kind of political commitment; finally, in 'cultic' films, Lenin or Stalin themselves were the heroes (Taylor and Spring 1993: 83–9). Of course, many films contained a mixture of these elements, but a struggle between good and evil in which a heroic personality wins out was a common feature of all of them.

An example of a film with 'proto-cultic' qualities was *The Circus* (1936). The director of the film was Grigory Alexandrov, who made many of the most famous musical comedies of the pre-war era, including *The Happy Fellows* (1934), *Volga Volga* (1938) and *Shining Path* (1941). *The Circus* tells the story of a white American actress, Marion Dixon, who has caused a scandal at home by having a black child outside wedlock. Ostracised in 'racist' America, she comes to the Soviet Union with her baby, where she is welcomed, starts to discover a socialist worldview and finds a handsome Soviet husband. The part of Marion Dixon was played by Liubov' Orlova, who was the most popular actress of the 1930s. Although the main part of the film is set in a circus top, at the very end the focus shifts to a marching scene on Red Square, which includes Marion Dixon. In the crowd, people are carrying banners of Marx, Engels, Lenin and Stalin. What had previously been a light film, full of romance and music, is thus rounded off with the appropriate political statement. The Stalinist project is linked with Marion Dixon's personal journey towards happiness and acceptance. In the following two shots, Marion Dixon and her Soviet husband are in the centre of the picture, and the baby is on the right.

Document 7.14   Screen Shots from the Marching Scene in
The Circus

[See page 112]

Source: The Circus, *1936.*

The marching scene in *The Circus* was accompanied by Vasily Lebedev-Kumach's famous poem 'Song about our Motherland,' set to music by I.O. Dunaevsky. The melody was so popular that it became the broadcasting signal for Radio Moscow in the 1930s. Dunaevsky wrote the music for all the musical comedies of both Alexandrov and Pyriev (see also Document 3.15). Lebedev-Kumach was a court poet of the time, and the song, from which the following verses and chorus are extracts, became something of an unofficial national anthem.

Document 7.15   'Song about our Motherland'

All the way from Moscow to the border,
Southern peaks to northern oceans' foam

[Document 7.14]

Man can walk and feel he's the owner
Of this boundless motherland and home . . .

But we'll frown our eyebrows most severely
If a foe should want to cause our fall –
Like our bride, we love our homeland dearly;
Like our mother we'll save her from all.

O, my homeland is a spacious country:
Streams and fields and forests full and fair.
I don't know of any other country
Where a man can breathe a freer air.

Source: Vladimir Markov and Merrill Sparks (eds), Modern Russian Poetry, *1966, pp. 739–41.*

There is some evidence to suggest that films like The Circus were very successful. They encouraged the 'feel-good' factor, and at the same time passed on the right political messages. For example, Leonid Potemkin, vice-minister of geology of the USSR 1965–75, went to see The Circus as a student and wrote the following in his diary. However, it is interesting to observe how Potemkin, even writing in the privacy of his diary, appears to be framing his reactions to the film in the kind of rhetoric which would be acceptable to the regime. The recent study of another contemporary diary, the diary of Stepan Podlubnyi, suggests that Soviet citizens would often to try to refashion their identities to fit in with the state's requirements (see Document 13.13).

Document 7.16 Potemkin on *The Circus*

August. [. . .] On my day off I came to Sverdlovsk. I saw the film *Circus*. The ideological-emotional contents of that film are beautiful. It fascinates the viewer and fills him with a sensation of good cheer. The psychological resurrection of Mary Dixon in the country of the new mankind, growing and blooming together with the triumph of rising socialism. Her first free and confident joy in life filled my eyes with tears of sympathy and an excess of our common joy. And at that moment of renewal, living clarity and sincere purity you involuntarily cast a glance at your own life before the image of creative wise simplicity, the charm of sincere purity, persistent energetic creators of a happy world.

Source: Véronique Garros et al. (eds), Intimacy and Terror, *1995, pp. 288–9.*

Lenin, with Stalin as his closest colleague, featured in the 'cultic' films, Lenin in October (1937) and Lenin in 1918 (1938) (see Documents 13.6 and 13.7). After the Second World War, Stalin himself became the focus of attention in such films as The Oath (1946) and The Fall of Berlin (1949). In both these films, which were directed by Georgian Mikhail Chiaureli, the Georgian actor, Mikhail Gelovani, played the part of Stalin. Stalin was in effect presented as an earthly God, a man set apart from the rest of humanity. *The Oath* was built around Stalin's oath to Lenin of January 1924. In *The Fall of Berlin*, which was Mosfilm's gift to Stalin on his 70th birthday, the deification of Stalin reached extraordinary proportions: the film climaxed with Stalin, dressed in white, arriving in Berlin to celebrate the victory of the Soviet forces in the war. In reality, Stalin never visited Berlin.

Document 7.17   Screen Shot from *The Fall of Berlin*

Source: The Fall of Berlin, *1949*.

The Stalin cult came to serve a definite political purpose. It provided a focus of loyalty and patriotic feeling and a means of mobilising the population. It became an essential feature of the Stalinist system of rule. Participation in the cult was a passport to participation in Soviet public life. It was one of the 'rules of the game'. The following local Leningrad party report of August 1936 illustrates the way in which the party and NKVD were involved in encouraging the proliferation of the cult.

Document 7.18   Fostering the Cult

During agitation and propaganda in the press there must be more popularisation of the *vozhdi*, and love for them must be fostered and inculcated in the masses, and unlimited loyalty, especially by cultivating the utmost love for comrade Stalin and the other leaders amongst children and young people, inculcating Soviet patriotism, bringing them to fanaticism in love and defence of comrade Stalin and our socialist motherland.

Source: Sarah Davies, Popular Opinion in Stalin's Russia, *1997a, p. 150.*

The Stalin cult was used to encourage certain policies. For example, at Stakhanovite national conferences and congresses, ritual celebrations of Stalin's achievements were at the same time opportunities for promoting policies like collectivisation.

Document 7.19   Stakhanovite Ovations

Thank you, Comrade Stalin, our leader, our father for a happy merry kolkhoz life!

He, our Stalin, put the steering wheel of the tractor in our hand . . . He, the great Stalin, carefully listens to all of us in this meeting, loves us with a great Stalinist love (*tumultuous applause*), day and night thinks of our prosperity, of our culture, of our work . . .

Long live our friend, our teacher, the beloved leader of the world proletariat, comrade Stalin! (*Tumultuous applause, rising to an ovation. Shouts of 'hurrah!'*)

Source: Sheila Fitzpatrick, Stalin's Peasants, *1994, p. 277.*

Even those who were repressed did not always lose their faith in Stalin or the Stalinist system. It would thus appear that the cult was relatively successful in establishing the popularity of Stalin and his regime. However, that does not by itself reveal the depth or the nature of that belief. Fear can be subconscious. Even contemporary diaries do not fully clarify such things. For example, Galina Shtange, the wife of a professor at the Moscow Electromechanical Institute of Railroad Engineers, identified whole-heartedly with the regime. On 11 December 1937, while she was looking after her son Sasha, she heard Stalin speaking on the radio and she recorded in her diary the impact his words had on her. It appears that she was a true believer. On the other hand, is there is a hint of forced enthusiasm here as well?

Document 7.20   Enthusiasm for Stalin

[T]he 11th, evening. I tried to listen to Stalin's speech on the radio just now. He was speaking to voters about the election for the Supreme Soviet. Unfortunately Sashenka wouldn't let me hear the whole speech and I caught only individual phrases, which I wrote down:

. . . *I would like to assure you, comrades, that you may most confidently place your trust in Com. Stalin . . . You can count on Com. Stalin fulfilling his mission before the working class . . . before the intelligentsia . . . You yourselves know every family has a black sheep . . . Uncommitted people are of no use to anyone . . . People need to instill in their deputies the idea of emulating the Great Lenin . . .*

Stalin speaks very slowly and distinctly – extremely simply, so simply that each word penetrates into your consciousness and you think that the man cannot be found who would not be able to understand what he says.

I really love that, I don't like highfaluting bombastic speeches that are aimed at creating an acoustic effect.

Source: Véronique Garros et al. (eds), Intimacy and Terror, *1995, p. 205.*

Another 'believer' was Vladimir Bukovsky, later one of the leaders of the dissident movement. In his memoirs, he wrote of how deeply upset he had been when, as a boy of 10 in 1952, he learned of the 'discovery' of the 'doctor's plot' to kill Stalin. He also recalled the mass outpourings of grief at Stalin's death, and his growing disillusionment when he saw the illusory nature of his earlier beliefs.

Document 7.21   Belief and Disillusionment

In 1952 we heard about the 'doctor's plot', which coincided with a wave of anti-semitism . . . For every single one of us Stalin was greater than a God, a reality in which it was impossible not to believe . . . It was impossible to imagine an act of greater barbarism than killing Stalin.

I took these developments very hard. Several times I dreamed the same persistent dream: I was sitting in an enormous auditorium, full of people who were clapping and shouting; Stalin was on the platform, giving a speech and being interrupted by the applause. He reached for a pitcher of water, poured some into a glass, and was about to drink it. I was the only one there who knew that the water was poisoned, but I could do nothing. I cried out: 'Don't drink it, don't drink it!' But my voice was drowned by the ovations and shouting. I wanted to run to the platform, but there were so many people that I couldn't get through. The nightmare of Stalin being killed haunted me and made me literally ill . . .

Stalin's death shook our life to its foundations. Lessons in school virtually came to a halt, the teachers wept openly . . .

[E]normous unorganised crowds streamed through the streets to the Hall of Columns, where Stalin sat in state. There was something awe-inspiring about these immense, silent, gloomy masses of people. The authorities hesitated to try and curb them and simply blocked up some of the sidestreets with buses and lorries . . . The crowd below us surged forwards and backwards, like waves in the sea, and then suddenly, in one of the sidestreets, a bus shivered, toppled over and fell, like an elephant rolling on its side. This vast procession continued for several days and thousands of people perished in the crush . . .

But the years passed . . . Stalin was mentioned less and less. And I was bewildered: hadn't God died, without whom nothing was supposed to take place? . . .

[A]nother rumour spread like an obscure muttering: 'The biggest enemy of the people of them all was – Stalin!'

It was amazing how quickly people believed this, people who two years before had stampeded to his funeral and been ready to die for him . . .

All those people whose business it had been to praise Stalin for so many years now assured us that they had known nothing about this Terror or, if they had, had been afraid to say so. I didn't believe the ones who said they had never known: how could you fail to notice the death of millions of people, the deaths of your neighbours and friends? Nor did I believe the ones who said they had been afraid – their fear had brought them too many promotions.

Source: Vladimir Bukovsky, To Build a Castle, *1978, pp. 81–3.*

Bukovsky's comments highlight the pervasiveness of the Stalin cult. At the same time, they illustrate its lack of depth. Although devotion to Stalin was not necessarily insincere, it was also in some way artificial, and could easily be dispensed with when it was necessary. Bukovsky's comments also point to the generational tensions which would emerge in later years, as young people asked their parents what they had been doing during the Stalin era.

Following a stroke, Stalin died on 5 March 1953. He had been deteriorating for some time. No longer the confident tyrant of earlier years, he had become an unpredictable man, 'raging, like Lear, against failure and mortality' (Ward 1999: 226). The extraordinary outpouring of grief at his death is testimony to his widespread popularity. Yet, he died alone, feared rather than loved by those closest to him. It might indeed be said that his desire for adulation was the very thing which prevented him developing any lasting relationships. In the end, he too had come to believe in aspects of the cult. Just as his regime's propaganda offered a world of fantasy and illusion for the population to believe in, so he was himself a participant in and victim of that fantasy.

8 | The Second World War

The rise of Hitler in Germany had provoked Stalin to change his foreign policy. In the years prior to Hitler's rise, the Comintern chose to dissociate itself from the German social democrats, arguing that social democracy was objectively a kind of 'social fascism'. Throughout Europe, social democrats and communists often disagreed more violently amongst themselves than they did with their right-wing opponents. However, when Hitler came to power and so openly expressed an interest in acquiring *Lebensraum* for the German people in the east, Stalin changed Comintern policy, advocating instead the creation of 'popular fronts' which would bring together progressive and left-wing movements of different persuasions. Nevertheless, in spite of this, there is evidence that throughout the 1930s, Stalin was interested in coming to some agreement with Hitler. It has been argued, for example, that Stalin had long wished to see a war between the Western imperial powers, and sought an agreement with Germany to encourage that possibility (Tucker 1992: 232). Although after the Munich conference in 1938, he continued to explore the possibility of an anti-Hitler collective security pact with Britain and France, he suspected that the Western governments had similar motives to his own: Western appeasement of Hitler was designed to turn Hitler's attention to the east.

On 23 August 1939, the foreign ministers of the USSR and Germany, Molotov and Ribbentrop, signed a treaty of non-aggression. Furthermore, they added certain secret protocols demarcating the future spheres of influence of the two countries. This permitted Stalin, after Hitler's invasion of Poland, to occupy the Baltic states, substantial parts of Poland, and Bessarabia, which became the Moldavian Soviet Socialist Republic.

Document 8.1   The Nazi–Soviet Pact

23 August 1939

Guided by the desire to strengthen the cause of peace between the USSR and Germany, and proceeding from the fundamental stipulations of the neutrality treaty concluded in April 1926, the Government of the USSR and the Government of Germany have come to the following agreement:

Article 1. The two contracting parties undertake to refrain from any act of force, any aggressive act, or any attack against each other, either individually or in conjunction with other Powers . . .

Article 4. Neither of the contracting parties will join any group of Powers which directly or indirectly is directed against the other party . . .
Article 6. The present treaty shall remain in force for ten years; unless one of the contracting parties gives notice to terminate it one year before its expiration, it will be regarded as automatically prolonged for a further five years.

Secret Additional Protocol
[T]he two parties discussed in strictly confidential conversation the question of the delimitation of their respective spheres of interest in Eastern Europe. These conversations led to the following result:

1. In the event of a territorial and political transformation in the territories belonging to the Baltic States (Finland, Estonia, Latvia, Lithuania) the northern frontier of Lithuania shall represent the frontier of the spheres of interest both of Germany and the USSR . . .
2. In the event of a territorial and political transformation of the territories belonging to the Polish state, the spheres of interest of both Germany and the USSR shall be bounded approximately by the line of the rivers Narev, Vistula and San . . .
3. With regard to South-Eastern Europe, the Soviet side emphasizes its interest in Bessarabia. The German side declares complete political *désintéressement* in these territories.

Source: Jane Degras (ed.), Soviet Documents on Foreign Policy, vol. III, 1933–1941, *1953, pp. 359–61.*

A further secret protocol of 28 September 1939 brought Lithuania into the Soviet sphere of influence.

Prior to the annexation of the Baltic states in June 1940, the Soviet government tried to encourage the Finns to move their border away from Leningrad in return for some territorial compensation. When the Finns did not prove forthcoming, the two countries found themselves at war. The Finnish war was a humiliation for Stalin. The purges of the military had affected the quality of the command. The Soviet forces in the Leningrad military district were tactically unprepared for long-drawn-out battles against well-prepared and mobile Finnish units. Although they made gains, their losses were high, and a peace treaty was signed in March 1940. In December 1939, the USSR was expelled from the League of Nations. On the positive side, the war had revealed the inadequacies of the Soviet army, and gave it time to make improvements before the war with Hitler. Voroshilov's weaknesses as Defence Commissar were recognised and he was replaced in May 1940 by S.K. Timoshenko.

On 5 March 1940, the Politburo, following a memorandum from Beria, passed a resolution to execute 25,700 Poles, Belorussians and Western Ukrainians then in prisons and prisoner-of-war camps, who were deemed to be potentially hostile to the Soviet state. It was to be one of the more infamous episodes in Soviet history. Stalin, Molotov, Voroshilov and Mikoian were directly involved in the decision, and

Kalinin and Kaganovich also agreed to the action (see Sakwa 1999: 250). The subsequent massacre of 4,421 Polish officers in the Katyn forest was denied for many years by the Soviet government and it was only in April 1990 that the Soviet government admitted its responsibility.

Document 8.2   The Order for the Execution of Poles, Belorussians and Western Ukrainians

I. To direct the USSR NKVD:

1. [To look at] the cases on the 14,700 former Polish officers, officials, landowners, police-officers, intelligence agents, gendarmes, guards and jailors, who are in prisoner-of-war camps,

2. and also the cases concerning the 11,000 arrested and now in the prisons of the Western regions of Ukraine and Belorussia – members of various counter-revolutionary espionage and diversionary organisations, former landowners, factory-owners and deserters – to examine them under special procedure, with the highest measure of punishment to be applied – shooting.

II. Examination of cases should proceed without calling the arrested and without declaring the charges, or the decision to end the investigation and its conclusion . . .

III. The examination of the cases and the pronouncement of judgment is to be entrusted to a troika consisting of c[omrades] Merkulov, Kobulov and Bashtakov (the head of the First Special Department of the USSR NKVD).

Source: A.G. Koloskov and E.A. Gevurkova (eds), Istoriia otechestva v dokumentakh 1917–1991, vol. 3, 1939–1945, *1995, p. 31.*

In the months up to the Nazi attack on the USSR on 22 June 1941, Stalin frequently received intelligence reports suggesting that Hitler was preparing to attack. However, he stubbornly refused to countenance the idea that Hitler would try to fight a war on two fronts. Just before the attack, the evidence was overwhelming. It seems that Stalin simply refused to come to grips with the reports. The following letter, for example, sent by V.N. Merkulov to Stalin, Molotov and Beria, contained information coming originally from an intelligence source in the German Ministry of Economy. On receiving this information, however, Stalin simply asked for a new and conclusive summary of all intelligence reports. However, the summary which was produced did not reach him before the German attack (Gorodetsky 1999: 297) Stalin's refusal to take advice and permit forces to assume battle readiness was a crucial reason for the huge losses which the Soviet forces suffered in the months following the invasion. The letter includes a reference to a TASS announcement of 6 June to the effect that there was no basis to doubt the reliability of the Nazi–Soviet pact. Between 3 February 1941 and 20 July 1941, the NKVD was divided into two sections: the NKGB, dealing with security; and the NKVD, dealing with internal affairs.

Document 8.3 NKGB Informs Stalin of Forthcoming German Strike

17 June 1941
Absolutely Secret

We present intelligence received from the USSR NKGB in Berlin
People's Commissar of State Security – Merkulov . . .

Information from Berlin

The source, working in the headquarters of the German airforce, states:

1. All military preparations by Germany for an armed action against the USSR have been fully completed, and the blow can be expected at any moment.

2. At airforce headquarters the TASS announcement of 6 June was perceived in a very ironic manner. It is emphasised that this declaration cannot have any possible significance.

3. The flight targets of the German airforce in the first place are: the 'Svir 3' electric power station, Moscow factories producing parts for aeroplanes . . . , and also motor repair services.

4. Hungary will play an active part in military actions on the side of Germany. Some German planes, mainly fighters, are at Hungarian airfields . . .

The source, working in Germany's Ministry of Economy, states that the appointment has taken place of the heads of military-economic administration of the 'future areas' of the occupied territory of the USSR: for the Caucasus, Amonn has been appointed, one of the leading workers of the National Socialist Party of Dusseldorf; for Kiev – Burandt, a former official of the Ministry of Economy, who until recently worked in the economic administration in France; for Moscow – Burger, leader of the chamber of finance in Stuttgart. These persons have all been seconded to military service and have departed for Dresden, which is the assembly point.

For the general leadership of the economic administration of the 'occupied territories of the USSR' Shloterer has been appointed – the head of the foreign section of the Ministry of Economy, which is still situated in Berlin.

In the Ministry of Economy they are saying that at a gathering of economic managers, who are intended for the 'occupied territories of the USSR,' Rosenberg also spoke and declared that the 'concept of the "Soviet Union" must be erased from the geographical map.'

Head of the First Directorate of the NKGB USSR Nitin

Source: V.K. Vinogradov et al. (eds), Sekrety Gitlera na Stole u Stalina, *1995, pp. 161–2.*

There is evidence that Stalin suffered some kind of breakdown after the German invasion. German advances and Soviet casualties were so huge that the situation looked nearly hopeless. Stalin became depressed and refused to see people for a couple of days at the end of June (Volkogonov 1991: 409). The announcement of the outbreak of hostilities fell to Molotov instead of Stalin. It was not until 3 July that Stalin made his first speech to the Soviet people, admitting that the German forces had achieved some major initial successes. His tone, referring to the Soviet people as his 'friends', was unusually warm.

Document 8.4   Radio Broadcast, 3 July 1941

Comrades, citizens, brothers and sisters, men of our Army and Navy! My words are addressed to you, my friends!

The perfidious military attack by Hitlerite Germany on our Fatherland, begun on June 22, is continuing. In spite of the heroic resistance of the Red Army, and although the enemy's finest divisions and finest air force units have already been smashed . . . , the enemy continues to push forward, hurling fresh forces to the front. Hitler's troops have succeeded in capturing Lithuania, a considerable part of Latvia, the western part of Byelorussia and part of Western Ukraine. The fascist aircraft are extending the range of their operations, bombing Murmansk, Orsha, Moghilev, Smolensk, Kiev, Odessa, Sevastopol. Grave danger overhangs our country . . .

Is it really true that the German-fascist troops are invincible, as the braggart fascist propagandists are ceaselessly blaring forth?

Of course not! History shows that there are no invincible armies and there never have been . . . [The German-fascist army] can be smashed and will be smashed, as were the armies of Napoleon and Wilhelm . . .

The aim of this national patriotic war is . . . to aid all the European peoples groaning under the yoke of German fascism . . . In this great war we shall have true allies in the peoples of Europe and America . . . In this connection, the historic utterance of the British Prime Minister, Mr Churchill, regarding aid to the Soviet Union, and the declaration of the United States Government signifying readiness to render aid to our country, which can only evoke a feeling of gratitude in the hearts of the peoples of the Soviet Union, are fully comprehensible and symptomatic . . .

All the forces of the people for the destruction of the enemy!

Forward to victory!

Source: Generalissimo Stalin, War Speeches, *n.d., pp. 7, 11.*

The central government institution of the war was the State Defence Committee, which was set up on 30 June, and was headed by Stalin. It had 5–8 members, and included Molotov, Stalin's deputy, Malenkov, as senior party secretary, Beria, head of security, Mikoian and Kaganovich, as senior Politburo members, Voznesensky, head of Gosplan and Voroshilov. Stalin also presided over the Stavka, or Supreme Command, which coordinated military strategy and included the Soviet Marshals, the Chief of the General Staff, and the heads of various services. Stalin's presence on both bodies ensured proper coordination between the two bodies, as well as preserving his control over all decision-making:

Document 8.5   Formation of State Defence Committee

The Presidium of the Supreme Soviet of the USSR, the Central Committee of the VKP(b) and the Council of People's Commissars of the USSR, in view of the extraordinary situation which has been created, and with the aim of mobilising all the forces of the peoples of the USSR . . . , have recognised the necessity of creating a State Defence Committee under the leadership of c. Stalin I.V.

All the fullness of the power of the state is concentrated in the hands of the State Defence Committee. All citizens, and all party, soviet, komsomol and military organs must unconditionally fulfil the decisions and instructions of the State Defence Committee.

Source: A.G. Koloskov and E.A. Gevurkova (eds), Istoriia otechestva v dokumentakh 1917–1991, vol. 3, 1939–1945, *1995, p. 53.*

One of the great Soviet achievements of the early years of the war was the mass evacuation eastwards of industries and qualified personnel. A large percentage of Soviet industry had been located in areas now occupied by Germany. Significant resources were lost to the Germans immediately, but in the second half of 1941 a monthly average of 165,000 railway truckloads of industrial equipment rolled eastwards. The transportation of industries to the east was a feat which the party's highly centralised structures were well suited for (Lieberman 1985: 71). It was nevertheless not a smooth operation, and was largely improvised. Sometimes, evacuated goods were simply dumped to permit empty trucks to return to the front. It could not prevent the country's slide into economic crisis in 1942 (Barber and Harrison 1991: 129–30).

An insight into the magnitude of the evacuation operation can be gained from the following report by deputy chairman of the evacuation council of Sovnarkom A.N. Kosygin to the First Secretary of the Moscow party A.S. Shcherbakov about the evacuations from Moscow. The extract concerns the aviation industry alone, and thus concerns just a fraction of the evacuation process.

Document 8.6   Transportation from Moscow

30 November 1941

1. In Narkomaviaprom [People's Commissariat of the Aviation Industry] 53 industrial enterprises are being evacuated. As of the 25 November 1941 the following factories had been completely evacuated – Nos 84, 241, 482, 293, 468, 476, OKB-28, 279 and 479; equipment from the following factories has been completely evacuated – Nos 1, 22, 207, 445, 51, 240, 294, 289, 219, 20, 33, 132, 161, 34, 119, 120, 145, 261, 469, 213, 214 . . .

In factory No. 24 23 units of equipment remain to be dispatched. Out of all the enterprises under Narkomaviaprom, 26,281 units of metal-cutting and pressing equipment, and 111, 826 working people, not considering members of families, have been evacuated; also 11,414 tons of non-ferrous metal and 7,700 tonnes of ferrous metal. 18,000 wagons have been used for the evacuation of the enterprises.

Source: M. Gorinov et al. (eds), Moskva voennaia 1941–1945, *1995, p. 366.*

Initial German advances were spectacular. Smolensk was captured by mid-July, and by the end of August Leningrad was threatened. However, instead of pressing on towards Moscow and Leningrad, Hitler veered south to try and capture the industrial heartlands of Ukraine and the oil wealth of the Caspian. It was autumn before Moscow was really threatened, and the Germans got bogged down in the deteriorating weather conditions. Marshal Zhukov was brought in to organise the defence of Moscow, and in his memoirs he recalled the importance of the Soviet victory at the subsequent battle.

Document 8.7 Zhukov on the Battle of Moscow

The rout of the German troops on the approaches to Moscow was of great significance for the world . . .

The German setbacks near Leningrad, Rostov, Tikhvin and in the Battle of Moscow had a sobering effect on the reactionary circles in Japan and Turkey . . .

The German troops were now on the defensive. To restore their fighting efficiency the Nazi military and political leadership had to take a number of extreme measures as well as lift from France and other occupied lands a considerable part of the forces and fling them to the Eastern Theatre. Germany had to resort to pressure on the Governments of the satellite countries so that they would send more troops and materials to the East. And this served to aggravate the political situation in those countries . . .

Stalin was in Moscow, in control of the troops and weapons, preparing the enemy's defeat. He must be given credit for the enormous work in organizing necessary strategic, material and technical resources which he did as head of the State Committee for Defence with the help of the executive staff of the People's Commissariats. With strictness and exactness Stalin achieved the near-impossible.

When I am asked what event in the last war impressed me most, I always say: the Battle of Moscow.

In severe, often unbelievably difficult, conditions our troops matured, accumulating battle wisdom and experience, and as soon as they received the minimum necessary technical means they turned from a retreating defensive force into a powerful offensive one.

Source: Marshal G.K. Zhukov, The Memoirs of Marshal Zhukov, *1971, pp. 360–61.*

It is not clear how sincere Zhukov was in his appreciation of Stalin's contribution to the defence of Moscow and the war effort in general. Stalin, especially in the early months, made a number of mistakes. For example, in September 1941, his refusal to permit forces in Ukraine led by Colonel General Kirponos to make a tactical retreat was responsible for the loss of Kiev and large numbers of men.

There is clearly much evidence to suggest that it was Stalin's incompetence that lay behind the early Nazi successes and other wartime blunders. At the same time, there is also testimony to suggest that Stalin could be an effective war-leader. For example, Churchill visited Moscow in August 1942 to report to Stalin that plans to open a second front in Europe were being postponed. At the same time, he outlined the proposed alternative Anglo-American operation in North Africa, which was entitled 'Torch'. Churchill's report of the conversation in his memoirs is revealing of Stalin's mentality. Stalin was very impatient with the delay in opening up a second front in Europe. At the same time, as Churchill observes, his understanding of the implications of 'Torch' was impressive.

Document 8.8   Churchill on Stalin

The first two hours were bleak and sombre. I began at once with the question of the Second Front, saying that I wished to speak frankly and would like to invite complete frankness from Stalin . . . Stalin, whose glumness had by now much increased, said that as he understood it, we were unable to create a second front with any large force and unwilling even to land six divisions. I said that this was so. We could land six divisions, but the landing of them would be more harmful than helpful, for it would greatly injure the big operation planned for next year. War was war but not folly, and it would be folly to invite a disaster which would help nobody . . . Stalin, who had become restless, said that his views about war were different. A man who was not prepared to take risks could not win a war. Why were we so afraid of the Germans? He could not understand. His experience showed that troops must be bloodied in battle . . .

The moment had come to bring 'Torch' into action . . . As I told the whole story Stalin became intensely interested . . . I then described the military advantages of freeing the Mediterranean, whence still another front could be opened . . .

I emphasised that we wanted to take the strain off the Russians . . . If North Africa were won this year we could make a deadly attack upon Hitler next year. This marked the turning point in our conversation. At this point Stalin seemed suddenly to grasp the strategic advantages of 'Torch'. He recounted four main reasons for it: first, it would hit Rommel in the back; second, it would overawe Spain; third, it would produce fighting between Germans and Frenchmen in France; and fourth, it would expose Italy to the whole brunt of the war.

I was deeply impressed with this remarkable statement. It showed the Russian Dictator's swift and complete mastery of a problem hitherto novel to him. Very few people alive could have comprehended in so few minutes the reasons which we had all so long been wrestling with for months. He saw it all in a flash.

Source: T.H. Rigby (ed.), Stalin, 1966, pp. 83–4.

On 16 August 1941, in his Staff Order No. 270, Stalin introduced orders to the effect that no soldier should surrender to the enemy and that families of soldiers who surrendered or deserted would lose their state allowances. In July, the NKVD and NKGB had been reunited as one in order to better deal with retreating forces, and according to a letter from Beria after he was arrested in 1953, tens of thousands of deserters were shot (Beria 1994: 8). However, Stalin was so frustrated by continuing military setbacks in the summer of 1942 that on 28 July he signed another disciplinary order. This was Order No. 227 of the USSR Defence Commissariat. It called for special units to go behind Soviet forces and shoot any soldiers discovered deserting. It was decided that these units would contain soldiers who had spent time for some reason in enemy-occupied territory, and who therefore had something to prove about their loyalty. The tone and substance of the order are typical of Stalin's approach to leadership, in peacetime as in war. Victory in the war, it could be argued, was achieved with the same methods that were used in peacetime (Bonwetsch 1997: 207).

Document 8.9   Order No. 227

The enemy is throwing more and more fresh forces into the fight and, regardless of his losses, he is creeping forward and breaking into the depths of the Soviet Union, seizing new districts, laying waste to our towns and villages, raping, looting and murdering the population. Part of the Southern front forces followed the panic-mongers and left Rostov and Novocherkassk without serious resistance, covering their colours with disgrace.

Some unwise people at the front console themselves by saying we can retreat still further to the east, as we have so much territory, so much land, so much population, that we have no shortage of grain, and they use this to justify their shameful behaviour at the front . . .

After the loss of the Ukraine, Belorussia, the Baltic, the Donbass and other regions, we have a lot less territory than we had. So it follows that there must be far fewer people, less grain, less metal, less factories and mills. We have lost more than 70 million of the population, more than 12 million tons of grain and 10 millions tons of metal a year. We have even lost our superiority over the Germans in human resources and grain reserves. To retreat further would mean to destroy ourselves and with us our Motherland.

Not one more step backwards! That has to be our main slogan from now on.

We will no longer tolerate officers and commissars, political personnel, units and detachments abandoning their battle positions of their own free will. We will no longer tolerate officers, commissars and political personnel allowing a few panic-mongers to determine the position on the field of battle and to induce other fighters to retreat and open the front to the enemy. Panic-mongers and cowards must be destroyed on the spot.

a) the retreat mentality must be decisively eliminated.

b) army commanders who have allowed voluntary abandonment of positions must be removed and sent to Staff HQ for immediate trial by military tribunal.

c) one to three punitive batallions (of 800 men each) should be formed within the limits of the front to which middle-ranking and senior officers and political officers of corresponding rank are to be sent . . .

Three to five well-armed detachments (up to 200 men each) should be formed within an army and placed directly behind unreliable divisions and they must be made to shoot the panic-mongers and cowards on the spot in the event of panic and disorderly retreat. Depending on circumstance, from five to ten penal companies (of 150 to 200 men each) should be formed within the army and posted to difficult spots so as to give them a chance to atone with their blood for the crimes they have committed before the Motherland.

This order is to be read to all companies, squadrons, batteries, crews and headquarters.

Source: Dmitri Volkogonov, Stalin, *1991, pp. 459–60.*

Order No. 227 was an important factor in disciplining the Soviet forces during the crucial autumn months of the Battle of Stalingrad in 1942. The German forces were in a very strong position when on 13 September Zhukov and Chief of General Staff, A.M. Vasilevsky, proposed a plan, involving forces from the Stalingrad, Southwestern and Don fronts, which entailed surrounding and trapping the German forces. The plan, entitled 'Operation Uranus' and put into operation on 19 November, proved very successful (Beevor 1998: 239–65; see also Erickson 1975: 394–472). Some 330,000 German soldiers, largely from General Von Paulus' Sixth Army, were caught in the trap. Vasilevsky, in his memoirs, recalled the successful operation as follows.

Document 8.10   Germans Encircled at Stalingrad

During 21 November, the forces of the Southwestern, Stalingrad and Don fronts, inflicting on the enemy huge losses, advancing into the deep rear of its main force and disrupting the administration of the fascist forces, continued to fulfil its battle plan. On 23 November, as a result of some skilfully completed thrusts converging in the direction of Kalach, the Southwestern and Stalingrad fronts with the active help of the right wing of the Don front closed the ring of encirclement around the main group of Germans stationed in the Stalingrad region.

This was the first large-scale encirclement in which the German-fascist forces had found themselves since the beginning of the war. In the second half of the day, military action on all three fronts to implement the operation, in spite of the desperate, gradually increasing opposition of the stunned and surprised enemy, continued to unfold extremely successfully for us. Infantry divisions, advancing behind the mobile forces increasingly made the circle tighter, creating a continuous inner front of encirclement. At the same time, the command of the South-Western and Stalingrad fronts took measures to as quickly and as far as possible move aside the outer front of advance so as to further isolate the surrounded enemy group from its main army. In this way, the first and most crucial stage of the advance operation was brilliantly completed. The strategic initiative at the Soviet-German front passed once more to the Red Army.

Source: A.M. Vasilevsky, Delo moei zhizni, *1975, pp. 251–2.*

Victory at Stalingrad was the turning point of the war. The subsequent victory at the battle of Kursk in July 1943 consolidated the Soviet position, and thereafter, the Red Army moved steadily forward into central Europe.

Although the expression 'Great Fatherland War', as it came to be called, suggests mass support for the Stalin regime, it was frequently very difficult to mobilise the population. In the first months of the war in particular, when the country was facing catastrophe and when the nature of German atrocities was not yet clear, there were some who hoped for a Nazi victory. This was particularly so in border areas like Ukraine or the Baltic states. However, such sentiments were also expressed in the big cities.

The tension in Leningrad in late summer 1941 was accentuated by the arrival of thousands of deserters and people fleeing the front, whom the government made periodic attempts to arrest and send way (Lomagin 1995: 213). There were similar problems in Moscow. The following agitprop report, for example, illustrates the mood of panic that existed in Moscow in October 1941, and the measures taken by the party to try and combat a defeatist mood (see Overy 1997: 97).

Document 8.11   Agitprop Work in Moscow

From a report of the agitprop department of the Pervomaisky raikom party of the Moscow City Party Committee of the VKP(b) (no earlier than 20 November 1941)

During the especially tense days of 15, 16, 17, 18 of October, when longer queues were accumulating at the shops, all manner of false provocative rumours were spread, anti-semitic moods were manifest etc., all the attention of the department of propaganda and agitation was concentrated on putting a revolutionary order into place, both in the factories and on the streets. There was created a special section of agitator-communists consisting of 45 persons, on which fell the task of carrying forward a mass explanatory work in queues, bombshelters, tram stops to destroy the false provocative rumours and to fish out provocateurs, panic-mongers, hooligans. During those days a brigade of agitators worked literally day and night, doing an enormous work. Many suspicious elements were with the help of the agitators delivered over to the organs of the police.

For example, on one such occasion, one evening, during an air-raid warning, a group of young people standing by the gates of a house on Volochaevsky Street was approached by a man in a red-army uniform. A conversation began. This 'red-army man' tried to persuade them that the front was near and that Moscow would inevitably fall, and that Stalin and Molotov were arguing over how to surrender Moscow – with or without a fight. Stalin was for a battle, and therefore there would inevitably be bombings . . .

Listening to this conversation the agitator Anisimov, pretending to be a simpleton, advised him to go out into the entrance of the house, where a lamp was burning, and at that very moment he contacted the organs of the police, and the Hitlerite spy was arrested at that very place.

Head of Department of Agitation and Propaganda
Pervomaisky RK VKP(b) *Zhidkova*

Source: Izvestiia TsK KPSS, *1991, No. 1, p. 217.*

Stalin was extremely suspicious of potentially hostile opinion at home. He regarded certain national groups as essentially subversive and ordered their deportation. Already on 28 August 1941, the Presidium of the Supreme Soviet issued the following directive, ordering the deportation of the Volga Germans.

Document 8.12   Deportation of Volga Germans

According to reliable data received by the military authorities, there are among the German population living in the Volga area, tens of thousands of saboteurs and spies who at a given signal from Germany are going to set off explosions in the Volga regions inhabited by Germans . . .

In order to avoid such undesirable occurrences . . . the Presidium of the Supreme Soviet of the USSR considers it necessary to resettle the whole German population, living in the Volga region . . .

Rich arable land has been set aside for the settlement in Novosibirsk and Omsk oblasts, the Altai, Kazakhstan and other neighbouring areas.

In this connection, the State Defence Committee has been instructed to immediately resettle all Volga Germans and to provide them with land in the new regions.

Source: A.G. Koloskov and E.A. Gevurkova (eds), Istoriia otechestva v dokumentakh 1917–1991, vol. 3, 1939–1945, *1995, pp. 120–1.*

Following the order, 400,000 Volga Germans were deported in August 1941, and this was the prelude to numerous mass deportations in the following years. A total of 1.1 million Soviet Germans, 1.2 million Western Ukrainians and Western Belorussians, and a substantial proportion of the Balkar, Chechen, Crimean Tatar, Ingush, Kalmyk, Karachai, Meskhetian and Soviet Greek populations, were deported. Furthermore, during post-war collectivisation, substantial numbers of Baltic 'kulaks' were also sent into exile. It is estimated that nearly 3.3 million people were exiled or resettled between 1941 and 1948 (R.W. Davies *et al.* 1994: 79; Ward 1999: 196). The deportations, often by cattle truck, took place in appalling conditions, and hundreds of thousands died en route.

The party was well aware of the need to raise public morale. This was one of the reasons why Stalin chose to talk of a 'national patriotic war' in his speech of 3 July 1941. It was unclear whether the Russian population's loyalty lay with the Soviet system or the Russian nation. Wartime propaganda stressed the 'national patriotic' theme. The following poster by Irakly Toidze, which employs the emotionally powerful idea of the 'motherland' and invites comparison with the famous Kitchener poster of the First World War, was released in the summer of 1941. The mother in the poster invites the audience to make the oath of commitment which she is holding up and which is translated below.

Document 8.13 'The Mother Country Calls'

[See opposite]

Source: Russian State Library Collection.

Military Oath

I, a citizen of the Union of Soviet Socialist Republics, entering the ranks of the Worker-Peasant Army, take an oath and solemnly swear to be an honest, brave, disciplined and vigilant fighter, to strictly protect military and state secrecy, unquestioningly to fulfil all military regulations and orders of commanders and bosses.

I swear to honestly learn my military task, to use all means to guard military and people's property and to my last breath to be true to my people, to my Soviet homeland and my Worker-Peasant government.

At the order of the Worker-Peasant government I am always ready to go to the defence of my homeland, the Union of Soviet Socialist Republics and, as a warrior of the Worker-Peasant Red Army, I swear to defend her manfully, skilfully, worthily and honourably, not sparing my life or blood for the purpose of achieving a total victory over our enemies.

If, by malicious intent, I break this solemn vow, then let the severe punishment of the Soviet law overtake me: the universal hatred and contempt of the toilers.

Although the idea of the 'motherland' was designed to appeal to Russian patriotic sentiments, the military oath on Toidze's poster suggests a Soviet patriotism. Russian patriotic themes are more clearly evident in the following collection of stamps issued in 1944. They are commemoratives of war medals: the Order of the Patriotic War (top left); the Order of Alexander Nevsky (top right); the Order of Field Marshal Suvorov (bottom left); and the Order of Field Marshal Kutuzov (bottom right). The

[Document 8.13]

reference to pre-revolutionary Russian war heroes illustrates the way in which the regime made use of patriotic 'Russian' themes in its propaganda (see also Document 9.7).

Document 8.14   Stamps Commemorate Russia's Military Past

[See page 132]

Source: Anthony Rhodes, Propaganda, The Art of Persuasion: World War II, *1993, p. 237.*

[Document 8.14]

Russian patriotic sentiments are also evident in Stalin's speech at a victory banquet in honour of Red Army Commanders on 24 May 1945. Indeed, the speech is often cited as an example of Stalin's enthusiasm for a certain kind of militaristic Russian nationalism. The speech also contains an admission by Stalin that mistakes were made in the early years of the war.

Document 8.15 Stalin's Toast to the Russian People

Comrades, permit me to propose one more, last toast.

I would like to propose a toast to the health of our Soviet people, and in the first place, the Russian people. (*Loud and prolonged applause and shouts of 'Hurrah'.*)

I drink in the first place to the health of the Russian people because it is the most outstanding nation of all the nations which make up the Soviet Union . . .

I propose a toast to the Russian people not only because it is the leading people, but also because of its clear mind, stable character and patience.

I raise a toast to the health of the Russian people because in this war it deserves to be recognised as the leading force of the Soviet Union out of all the peoples of our country.

Our government made not a few errors. We went through desperate times in 1941–1942, when our army was retreating, abandoning our own villages and cities of Ukraine, Belorussia, Moldavia, the Leningrad oblast, the Baltic area and the Karelo-Finnish Republic, abandoning them because there was no other way out. A different people could have said to the Government: 'You have failed to justify our expectations. Go away. We shall install another government which will conclude peace with Germany and assure us a quiet life.' But the Russian people did not do this because it trusted the correctness of the policy of its government, and it made sacrifices to ensure the rout of Germany. This confidence of the Russian people in the Soviet Government proved to be that decisive force which ensured the historic victory over the enemy of humanity – over fascism.

Thanks to it, to the Russian people, for this confidence!

To the health of the Russian people! (*Stormy and prolonged applause.*)

Source: Pravda, *25 May 1945, p. 1.*

Throughout the war, writers and artists of all kinds were harnessed to support the war effort. The war produced an outburst of creative activity and a distinctive wartime culture (see Stites 1995). One of the most widely known writers of the time was Konstantin Simonov. His poem 'Wait for Me', written in the summer of 1941, became a very popular wartime ballad. Soldiers would send copies of it home, and it provoked replies which were then republished in frontline newspapers. At least ten composers set it to music (Rothstein 1995: 84–5).

Document 8.16 Simonov's 'Wait for Me'

Wait for me, and I'll come back,
But wait with might and main.
Wait through the gloom and rack
Of autumn's yellow rain.
Wait when snowstorms fill the way,
Wait in summer's heat,
Wait when, false to yesterday,
Others do not wait . . .

Wait for me and I'll come back,
Defying death. When he
Who could not wait shall call it luck
Only, let it be.
They cannot know, who did not wait,
How in the midst of fire
Your waiting saved me from my fate.
Your waiting and desire.
Why I still am living, we
Shall know, just I and you:
You knew how to wait for me
As no other knew.

Source: James von Geldern and Richard Stites (eds), Mass Culture in Soviet Russia, *1995, pp. 335–6.*

The siege of Leningrad, known as 'the 1,000 day siege', began in September 1941 and lasted until January 1944. The only link between the city and the outside world was across the frozen Lake Ladoga, and conditions within the city were extremely difficult. The suffering of the siege, however, also brought people together and provoked some of the most memorable writing of the war. For example, the work of the poet and prose-writer, Vera Inber, captured the atmosphere of the time very effectively. Her collection of poems *The Soul of Leningrad* (1942) was followed after the war by the publication of her wartime diary. The following extract from the diary illustrates the sense of civic responsibility which pervaded Leningrad during the siege, as well as the resourcefulness of the population.

Document 8.17   The Siege of Leningrad

29th March, 1942. Sunday, Evening

We have just learned that in the morning trucks loaded with shells were set on fire by German bombs on the line near Rzhevka.

I am now doing very little work and this torments me. The poem has been pushed aside, scattered irretrievably. On top of this, the stove drives me mad. It is cold and it smokes, and where we shall find anyone to repair it and sweep the chimney, God only knows. It seems that there was a chimney sweep but he died a few days ago . . .

The entire population of the city, everyone who is capable of holding a spade or a crowbar, cleans the streets. And that is rather like putting a soiled North Pole in order. All is chaos – blocks of ice, frozen hummocks of rubbish, stalactites of sewage. There are many volunteers. The *Leningrad Pravda* published an interview with eleven-year-old Fima Ozerkin from Ligovskaya Street. Fima said:

'Nobody ordered us to clean up the courtyard, we did it of our own free will. Have you noticed the large snow mound in our yard is no more? That is because Tolya and I cleared it up. Tomorrow we shall do some more clearing.'

We are moved when we see a piece of clear pavement on the quayside or on the bridge. To us it seems as beautiful as a flower-strewn glade.

And a yellow-faced bloated-up woman, wearing a smoke-blackened fur coat – she can't have taken it off all winter – leaned on a crowbar, gazing at a scrap of asphalt, cleaned by her. And then she went back to work.

A new idea in the city – everyone is carrying pine and fir branches. They contain vitamins, and we drink an extract of pine needles. The bark is sliced off oak trees, particularly the young ones, up to the height of a human adult. It is boiled and drunk in order to prevent stomach disorders. There is a lot of tannin in the bark, and this is a binding substance. But the stripped trees look like a human being without skin . . .

Anything I do makes me terribly tired. What am I afraid of? Not the bombing, not the shells, not the hunger, but a spiritual exhaustion – the limit of tiredness, when one begins to hate things, sounds and objects.

Source: Vera Inber, Leningrad Diary, *1971, pp. 73–4.*

The war experience was one that many people recalled with some fondness. The atmosphere was freer. There was a sense that people were truly engaged in fighting an enemy rather than artificially created 'enemies of the people'. The wartime spirit did not last long after 1945, although it can be argued that the sense of community that it engendered prepared the ground for the thaw of the 1950s (Mandelstam 1976: 391). The party re-established its control, and the victory of the 'Great Fatherland War' became a central theme of its post-war propaganda. The defeat of fascism, it was argued, was primarily due to the leadership of Stalin and the party. The Soviet system itself was declared to be the winner (see also Document 4.16).

Yet the Soviet victory in the Second World War came at a terrible price. It has been estimated that total losses due to premature death amounted to a total of 26 million, one in eight of the pre-war population and including at least 8.7 million soldiers. Of the 15 million or more civilians who died, over 2.5 million were Jews exterminated by Nazis, and 800,000 died in the Leningrad siege. Most of the losses were due to malnourishment and ill-treatment in occupied territory, and in the harsh conditions within the country itself where food was scarce and sickness widespread. According to official statistics, some 622,000 died in the labour camps in 1941–45 (R.W. Davies et al.: 1994: 79). In addition to the loss of population, the country lost about a third of its pre-war wealth.

9 | Education and science

Soviet ideology stressed two dimensions of Marxism: historical materialism, a theory of social development; and dialectical materialism, a philosophy of science. Dialectical materialism did not argue for the crude reduction of all things to physical particles; rather, it suggested, matter has evolved through various stages and qualitative transformations to produce different levels of being. By this argument, physics, biology, and the social sciences, representing different spheres of being, have their own distinct laws. Thus the distinctive nature of human society was preserved without destroying the materialist worldview (Graham 1993: 100–3).

The 1920s saw a concerted attempt by Soviet intellectuals to create a Marxist philosophy of mind based on dialectical principles. One of the foremost thinkers in this process was the psychologist, L.S. Vygotsky. Much influenced by Marxist thought, Vygotsky argued in his *Thought and Language* (1934) that the human mind has its origins in the biological and socio-historical levels of being. Although rooted in the biological, 'animal' level of being, the mind of the child is qualitatively transformed into a higher state by the dialectical interaction of thought and language. This argument was in direct contrast to the thinking of French psychologist Jean Piaget who suggested that individual thought patterns precede the social dimension (see also Bakhurst 1991: 59–90).

Document 9.1   Vygotsky on the Development of Thought and Language

The development of thought is, to Piaget, a story of the gradual socialization of deeply intimate, personal, autistic mental states. Even social speech is represented as following, not preceding, egocentric speech.

The hypothesis we propose reversed this course . . . We consider that the total development runs as follows: The primary function of speech, in both children and adults, is communication, social contact. The earliest speech of the child is therefore essentially social. At first it is global and multifunctional; later its functions become differentiated. At a certain age the social speech of the child is quite sharply divided into egocentric and communicative speech. (We prefer to use the term *communicative* for the form of speech that Piaget calls *socialized* as though it had been something else before becoming social. From our point of view, the two forms, communicative and egocentric, are both social, though their functions differ.) Egocentric speech emerges when the child transfers social, collaborative forms of behavior to the sphere of inter-personal psychic functions . . . In our conception, the true direction of the development of thinking is not from the individual to the socialized, but from the social to the individual . . .

The nature of the development itself changes from biological to socio-historical. Verbal thought is not an innate natural form of behavior but is determined by a historical-cultural process and has specific properties and laws that cannot be found in the natural forms of thought and speech. Once we acknowledge the historical character of verbal thought, we must consider it subject to all the premises of historical materialism, which are valid for any historical phenomenon in human society. It is only to be expected that on this level the development of behavior will be governed essentially by the general laws of the historical development of human society.

Source: Loren Graham, Science in Russia and the Soviet Union, *1993, pp. 105, 106. (For whole text, see Vygotsky, 1962.)*

Vygotsky's thinking, although it went out of fashion in the mid-1930s, was part of a broader psychological and educational attempt to place the development of mind in a social context. The dominant educational theory of the 1920s was the idea of 'polytechnical' education. This was an attempt to break down the barriers between the school and the workplace. Schools were to be equipped with workshops, and children would combine academic study with the experience of productive labour. Teachers were supposed to embrace an interdisciplinary 'complex' method of education, which involved selecting themes which could be embraced by a variety of disciplines. A related idea was 'pedology', a discipline combining pedagogy and psychology which attempted to systematically analyse the range of influences on the young child and which also sought an end to the division between the classroom and the outside world.

A yet more radical idea, put forward by the theorist V.N. Shulgin, was the 'withering away of the school' and the complete removal of the artificial division between school and life. This kind of radicalism became popular in the winter of 1929–30, when there were severe labour shortages. By the end of 1930, all schools were required to be linked to an enterprise, in order to prepare their students for life in the workplace. Teachers were encouraged to use the 'project method': to send pupils out of the classroom to do project work in the community. In practice, however, many teachers did not adopt these innovations. The atmosphere became very politicised, and many of the older teachers left to be replaced by a new generation of 'Red Specialists'.

The following poster by Elizaveta Ignatovich illustrates the emphasis on poly-technical education during the first Five Year Plan. The text in the top right-hand corner of the poster says: 'The link between education and productive work is a powerful weapon in the hands of the proletariat for the creation of the new man.' The text at the bottom of the poster reads: 'The struggle for the polytechnical school is a struggle for the Five Year Plan, for cadres, for a class communist education.' The design of the poster reflects the tradition of constructivism in Russian and Soviet art, in which emphasis was placed on the aesthetic depiction of materials and technology.

Document 9.2 'The Struggle for the Polytechnical School is the Struggle for the Five Year Plan' (1931)

Борьба за политехническую школу есть борьба за пятилетну, за кадры, за классовое коммунистическое воспитание

Source: The Merril C. Berman Collection.

Quantitatively, the primary and secondary education system expanded impressively during the first Five Year Plan. For example, between 1928 and 1930, the number of elementary schools in the Russian republic increased from 85,000 to over 102,000, and enrolment increased from 7.9 million to 11.3 million. There was a massive expansion in the Schools for Collective Farm Youth and Factory Apprenticeship Schools. At the same time, the educational experimentalism of 1929–30 was soon reversed. The successes masked considerable disorganisation and lack of quality (Holmes 1991: 129, 134–6). Already in 1931, the government became concerned by the lack of systematic education in primary and secondary schools, and decided to clamp down on educational radicalism. On 25 August 1931, the Central Committee passed a resolution condemning 'frivolous and hair-brained schemes'.

Document 9.3 The Basic Tasks of the School

The Central Committee considers the *fundamental inadequacy* of the schools at the present moment to be their inability to provide general education in sufficient volume and their unsatisfactory solution of the problem of producing fully educated people, with knowledge of the basic sciences (physics, chemistry, mathematics, one's native language, geography, etc.), for the technical colleges and for higher education generally. Because of this the polytechnical transformation of the schools in many instances takes on a formal character and fails to prepare children as comprehensively developed builders of socialism who combine theory and practice and have a mastery of technical knowledge . . .

While introducing in the Soviet schools various new teaching methods that can advance the education of active participants in socialist construction, it is necessary to struggle resolutely against frivolous and hair-brained schemes in teaching methods which have not previously been tested in practice, as has been especially vividly manifested in the application of the so-called 'project method'. The attempts, deduced from the anti-Leninist theory of the 'dying out of the school', to put the so-called 'project method' at the basis of all school work have in fact led to the destruction of the school.

Source: Robert McNeal (ed.), Resolutions and Decisions of the CPSU. Vol. 3, The Stalin Years: 1929–1953, *1974, p. 110.*

In February 1933, a regulation for elementary schools reinstated the textbook as the principal teaching aid. The new 'stable textbooks' were a reaction to the so-called 'journal-textbooks', in which the curriculum could be added to or changed with the addition or removal of new pages. 'Stable textbooks' were a valuable means of controlling the information passed to pupils, and also keeping control of the teachers. It became much harder for those who disagreed with the official line to depart from the formal curriculum.

The pedagogical dilemmas of the new system are described in the following extract from an interview with Tatiana Khodorovich, a teacher who became a human rights activist in the Brezhnev era. Khodorovich grew up in a family of noble background and taught Russian language and literature at high school from 1948–51. However, she reacted against the political nature of the education, and eventually left the profession. She disliked the requirement to teach and sing the praises of Stalinist poets like Vasily Lebedev-Kumach (see Document 7.15). In general, the value of oral history is that it takes one beyond the written record into events as they are actually experienced. In regard to Soviet education, this can give an insight into what can be called the 'hidden curriculum': what actually happened in the classroom (Holmes 1997: 283).

Document 9.4 The Teacher's Dilemma

I saw with horror what I was teaching them. One would think that there can be no politics in the Russian language. But it turned out to be pure politics . . . because all the exercises, all the examples which were demanded from the pupils for them to illustrate some grammatical rule, all this was full of words like 'communists', 'socialism', . . . 'we invented everything', . . . 'all this is the achievement of the Soviet state', . . . 'our Soviet state is one family of nations' . . . The textbooks were full of all this. The teacher only had the right to use so-called 'stable textbooks' . . . I could not avoid this for various reasons. Firstly, no one would have given me the chance, because teachers' lessons were inspected. People would come into classes – methodologists, the director of the school. The director had to be a member of the party – that was strictly the case. There was nothing I could change, and I did not know how to do it. I could only, as they say now, tell them something 'on the side', say something to the pupils which was not in the textbook. But at the same time, I had to say to them: 'I am going to tell you something, say about Tsvetaeva or Pushkin, but not as it is written in your textbook but how it was in reality, but just you be careful not to tell anyone about this, otherwise I will not be able to work with you.' . . . I understood that I was lying to them, telling them to study the poetry of, say, Lebedev-Kumach . . . , bad verse, badly written, with a disgusting idea; but one had to say that these verses were remarkable. Why did I have to say that? Not in order to save myself, i.e. to go on working at the school and to feed my children, but also because I understood very well that the pupils would soon finish their tenth class and go on further to the institutes and universities . . . And what would they answer in their exams to these academic institutions, if I told them that these were bad verses, if I told them the truth? . . . So I decided that I would leave the school.

Source: Interview between Tatiana Khodorovch and Philip Boobbyer, Paris, March 1997.

The radical education policies of the first Five Year Plan sometimes got out of control. For example, there was a purge of library stocks that were deemed potentially anti-Soviet. However, it was so extensive that at one point even top party leaders were having their books removed. For example, Emilian Yaroslavsky wrote the following letter to the Politburo on 15 September 1932 complaining that the process had got out of hand, and suggesting that the Central Committee should investigate the problem.

Document 9.5 The 'Purge' of the Libraries

It has become known to me that in almost all the libraries in the last two years the book collection has been devastated. It has taken place under the banner of the 'purge' from the book collection of any kind of ideologically uneven and harmful literature on the basis of the general instruction given out in 1930 by NKPros [the People's Commissariat of Enlightenment]. This instruction was concretised by separate ONO [Departments of Popular Education] lists and led to the following consequences.

The following material has been withdrawn: all anti-religious literature, exposing religion on the basis of natural science data (in spite of Lenin's directions to use such literature widely); all trade union literature released prior to the fifth plenum of the 8th convocation of the VTsSPS [All-Union Central Council of Trade Unions]; literature about unemployment and continuous service – on the move to the seven-hour working day; almost all mass literature on cooperatives, social insurance, protection of work, kolkhoz and sovkhoz construction, published prior to 1930–31; all idealistic philosophy, with the exception of Kant and Hegel; the works of Spenser, Simmel, Bukharin and others – on historical materialism and sociology.

Moreover, a 'secret section' has been created, where the books can only be used by members of the party *aktiv* and members of communist institutes of higher education. Such books as the following have been transferred into the secret section: Roza Luzemburg's *Accumulation of Capital*; Hilferding's *Finance Capital*; books on the history of the party by Nevsky, Kerzhentsev, Yaroslavsky . . .

In one Moscow region in 1930–32, 350,000 books were taken out of the trades union libraries . . .

Certain ONO, for example the Gudautskoe reached a point of issuing an instruction for the removal of works by Bebel, Lassalle, Plekhanov's *Our Disagreements*, the works of Marx and Engels, V.Il'ich's *The Development of Capitalism in Russia*, Stalin's *Booklet on the National Question*.

In certain libraries, particularly in Leningrad, the works of Marx and Engels in Riazanov's edition are being removed; and since in many libraries there are no other collections of Marx, that means that almost all the works of Marx and Engels are being removed.

To further illustrate the extent of this zeal, one can add a few facts: in the Siniavinsky peat-mining area of the Leningrad oblast they have removed the following from the libraries: Tolstoy, Turgenev, Goncharov, Korolenko . . . , M.I. Kalinin, *The Communist Manifesto*, Chernyshevsky, the works of Lenin etc.

Source: A.K. Sokolov (ed.), Obshchestvo i vlast', *1998, pp. 53–4.*

The early to mid-1930s mark what some historians have termed a 'great retreat' from the revolutionary experimentation of the cultural revolution (see Document 1.5). Certainly, at an ideological level, the regime moved towards a more conservative position on cultural matters. An example of this was in the teaching of history. In October 1931, a letter by Stalin to the journal *Proletarian Revolution* signalled the regime's intention to control historical research. Historians were henceforth to be required to defend Bolshevism rather than engage in independent scholarship (Barber 1981: 131). The Marxist school of historiography, led by M.N. Pokrovsky, subsequently fell from favour; emphasis was now to be placed on the role of heroic personalities in history and the importance of facts and dates. State control of the curriculum was tightened in 1934, when instructions were issued on the teaching of history and geography.

In 1938, the party produced an official version of its own history, which illustrates the extent to which the curriculum had become politicised. The following extracts from *History of the Communist Party of the Soviet Union/Bolsheviks/Short Course*, which came out in 1938, indicate the way in which the discipline of history had become a form of propaganda: the past was to be seen in the light of the Bolshevik seizure of power; the Marxist–Leninist theory of history was presented as scientifically proven; proletarian revolution was considered inevitable.

Document 9.6 History of the CPSU: Short Course

[From 'Introduction']

The history of the C.P.S.U. (B.) is the history of the overthrow of tsardom, of the overthrow of the power of the landlords and capitalists; it is the history of the rout of the armed foreign intervention during the Civil War; it is the history of the building of the Soviet state and of the Socialist society in our country . . . The study of the history of the C.P.S.U. (B.), the history of the struggle of our Party against all enemies of Marxism-Leninism, against all enemies of the working people, helps us to *master Bolshevism* and sharpens our political vigilance.

The study of the heroic history of the Bolshevik Party arms us with a knowledge of the laws of social development and of the political struggle, with a knowledge of the motive forces of revolution.

The study of the history of the C.P.S.U. (B.) strengthens our certainty of the ultimate victory of the great cause of the Party of Lenin-Stalin, the victory of Communism throughout the world . . .

[From 'Dialectical and Historical Materialism']

Dialectical materialism is the world outlook of the Marxist-Leninist party. It is called dialectical materialism because its approach to the phenomena of nature, its method of studying and apprehending them, is *dialectical*, while its interpretation of the phenomena of nature, its conception of these phenomena . . . is *materialistic*.

Historical materialism is the extension of the principles of dialectical materialism to the study of social life, an application of the principles of dialectical materialism to the phenomena of the life of society . . .

The dialectical method therefore holds that the process of development from the lower to the higher takes place not as a harmonious unfolding of phenomena, but as a disclosure of the contradictions inherent in things and phenomena, as a 'struggle' of opposite tendencies which operate on the basis of these contradictions . . .

Further, if the passing of slow quantitative changes into rapid and abrupt qualitative changes is a law of development, then it is clear that revolutions made by oppressed classes are a quite natural and inevitable phenomenon.

Hence the transition from capitalism to Socialism . . . cannot be effected by slow changes . . . , but only by a qualitative change of the capitalist system, by revolution . . .

Further, if development proceeds by way of the disclosure of internal contradictions, by way of collisions between opposite forces on the basis of these contradictions and so as to overcome these contradictions, then it is clear that the class struggle of the proletariat is a quite natural and inevitable phenomenon . . .

Hence, in order not to err in policy, one must pursue an uncompromising proletarian class policy, not a reformist policy of harmony of the interests of the proletariat and the bourgeoisie . . .

Such is the Marxist dialectical method when applied to social life, to the history of society.

Source: History of the Communist Party of the Soviet Union/Bolsheviks/ Short Course, *1939, pp. 2, 105, 109, 111.*

A good example of this politicised approach to history was the treatment of the tsars Ivan the Terrible and Peter the Great. Biographies and films of these men were written so as to present Stalin's ruthless leadership in a good light. A cult of Ivan the Terrible developed in which his power and military successes were celebrated. For example, a popular contemporary biography of Ivan, *Ivan Grozny*, by R.Iu. Wipper rejected sentimental criticisms of Ivan's cruelties and the behaviour of his secret police, the Oprichnina, noting instead his centralising achievement, and his military and diplomatic successes. The work was published in 1942, at a time when Stalin was anxious to compare himself with his powerful tsarist predecessors, was twice reissued, and also translated into English, German and Spanish. Wipper, who was a Senior Fellow at the Institute of History, was elected an Academician in 1943, following the publication of the biography (Perrie 1998: 118; see also Document 12.7; for contemporary interpretations of Peter the Great, see Riasanovsky 1985: Chapter iv).

Document 9.7 Ivan the Terrible

The enhanced attention to Ivan Grozny's cruelties, the stern and withering moral verdict on his personality, the proneness to regard him as a man of unbalanced mind, all belong to the age of sentimental enlightenment and high society liberalism . . .

[Historians of the nineteenth century] suffer from a defect which played a fatal role in establishing Grozny's reputation. They were absolutely indifferent to the growth of the Moscow State, its great unifying mission, Ivan IV's broad designs, his military innovations and his brilliant diplomacy. To some extent these judges of Ivan Grozny resemble Seneca, Tacitus and Juvenal who, in their sharp attacks [on] the Roman despots, concentrated their attention on Court and metropolitan affairs and remained indifferent to the vastness, the borderlands, the external security and the glory of the celebrated empire . . .

In their judgments, however, these writers lost sight of a very important circumstance, *viz.*, that Ivan Grozny's greatest social and administrative reforms – his struggle against the minor princes, his elevation of common people at the expense of the ancient boyars, his tightening up of military service and increasing of public burdens and the centralization of administration – were introduced not in peacetime, but amidst great military upheavals.

Source: R. Wipper, Ivan Grozny, 1947, pp. 234, 235, 240.

Education policy should not be seen outside the regime's wider modernisation drive. The renewed emphasis on traditional educational methods from the early 1930s onwards was just one dimension of a broader plan to create a new Soviet intelligentsia. Another aspect of this was the regime's plan to give people a technical education. Great emphasis was placed on engineering skills (see Bailes 1978: part III). During the first Five Year Plan, there was a massive influx into higher educational institutions of students from working-class and peasant backgrounds, and of ordinary communist party members. Student numbers jumped from 168,500 in 1927–28 to 458,000 in 1934. This was accompanied by the trials of the so-called 'bourgeois specialists' (see Document 4.5). However, in June 1931, at a conference of business executives, Stalin, while calling for the creation of a new Soviet intelligentsia, at the same time signalled a break with the attack on 'bourgeois specialists'. In the same speech, in addressing the problem of high rates of labour mobility, he signalled the abandonment of the idea of wage equalisation.

Document 9.8 Stalin on Creating a New Intelligentsia

What is the cause of the fluidity of manpower?

The cause is the wrong structure of wages, the wrong wage scales, the 'Leftist' practice of wage equalisation . . . The consequence of wage equalisation is that the unskilled worker lacks the incentive to become a skilled worker . . .

In order to put an end to this evil we must draw up wage scales that will take into account the difference between skilled and unskilled labour . . .

[O]ur country has entered a phase of development in which the *working class must create its own industrial and technical intelligentsia* . . .

No ruling class has managed without its own intelligentsia. There are no grounds for believing that the working class of the U.S.S.R. can manage without its own industrial and technical intelligentsia.

The Soviet Government has taken this circumstance into account and has opened wide the doors of all the higher educational institutions in every branch of the national economy to members of the working-class and labouring peasantry. You know that tens of thousands of working-class and peasant youths are now studying in higher educational institutions. Whereas formerly, under capitalism, the higher educational institutions were the monopoly of the scions of the rich – today, under the Soviet system, the working-class and peasant youth predominate there. There is no doubt that our educational institutions will soon be turning out thousands of new technicians and engineeers, new leaders for our industries.

But that is only one aspect of the matter. The other aspect is that the industrial and technical intelligentsia of the working class will be recruited not only from those who have had higher education, but also from practical workers in our factories, from the skilled workers, from the working-class cultural forces in the mills, factories and mines . . .

It would be stupid and unwise to regard practically every expert and engineer of the old school as an undetected criminal and wrecker . . .

[T]he task is *to change our attitude to the engineers and technicians of the old school, to show them greater attention and solicitude, to enlist their cooperation more boldly.*

Source: J. Stalin, Works, vol. 13, *1955, pp. 58–9, 68–9, 74–5.*

At the 18th Party Congress in March 1939, Stalin declared that the regime had been successful in dissolving the old intelligentsia and creating a 'new Soviet intelligentsia, the intelligentsia of the people' (Daniels 1985, vol. 1: 282).

Some people did well out of these policies and felt a corresponding sense of loyalty to the regime. Indeed, the purges themselves appear to have benefited the generation which was educated between 1928 and 1937 (Fitzpatrick 1979b: 398). In 1938, John Scott wrote an 'Addendum' to *Behind the Urals* for the American intelligence services, in which he gave examples of the *vydvizhentsy*, upwardly-mobile people who acquired a training in the early 1930s and benefited from the career opportunities which arose as a result of the purges (see also Document 4.11). The following document is a description of one of those *vydvizhentsy*.

Document 9.9 'The New People'

Sergei Vassilyevich Saltikov. The history of Saltikov is also typical of a new class of men who are rising as a result of the purge. This man is half Tartar, the son of a nomad. In 1930, he was taken by the scruff of the neck and sent to the Mining Institute in Moscow. Until then, his education had not equaled that of a fourth grade pupil in the United States. At that time the Institute was open to such men although I understand that the scholastic standards have now been raised to a certain extent. By 1934 Saltikov had received his diploma but little knowledge of engineering. However, he had joined the Party and had learned how to talk well at meetings.

At Magnitogorsk he became the managing foreman of the benzol shop of the chemical department. He received a room about nineteeen cubic meters and married a pretty Russian girl. Life seemed good to Saltikov; he attended all Party meetings, paid his dues regularly, and said everything a good Stalinist should say.

Then came the big purge which swept away almost the entire technical staff of the chemical plant. Saltikov found himself head of the whole department. By that time he had two years experience, but still little knowledge of chemistry. However, he tried hard to make up for his lack of training and the plant continued to work along more or less normally. Having risen from nomad to be head of a department, enjoying good living conditions judged from his standards, and possessing authority, Saltikov now represents the contented type of 'new man'. He does not know or care what goes on in the world outside, never reads any classical literature and is satisfied that the Soviet system is the best in the world since it has given him a chance to rise.

Source: John Scott, 'Addendum', Behind the Urals, 1989, pp. 299–300.

Educational theory of the mid-1930s onwards, exemplified in particular by the work of A.S. Makarenko (see Document 10.7), stressed will-power, discipline, duty, and the subordination of the individual to the collective. During the war years, there was increased concern about the lack of will-power and self-discipline in young people. This was one reason in July 1943 for the introduction of legislation introducing secondary single-sex schooling in republican capitals and regional centres. Also in 1943, the July issue of *Soviet Pedagogy* was devoted to the subject of discipline and this paved the way for the introduction in August of the 'Rules for Pupils'.

Document 9.10 Rules for Pupils

As a pupil you are obliged:

1. Tenaciously and persistently to acquire knowledge, and to become an educated and cultured citizen and to be of maximum use to the Soviet motherland.
2. To study hard, attend lessons regularly and not be late for them.
3. To obey absolutely the instructions of the director and teachers.
4. To come to school with all the necessary textbooks and writing materials; to get everything ready for the lesson before the teacher's arrival.
5. To appear at school clean, with hair brushed, and neatly dressed.
6. To keep your desk clean and tidy.
7. To come into the classroom promptly after the bell and take your place; to enter and leave the class during the lesson only with the teacher's permission.
8. To sit up straight during the lesson, not leaning on your elbows or lounging, to listen attentively to the teacher's explanations and pupils' answers, not to chat and not to do other things.
9. When a teacher or the director enters or leaves the class, to stand up and greet them.
10. When answering the teacher, to stand up straight, and sit down again only

with the teacher's permission; to raise your hand when wishing to answer or ask the teacher a question.

11. To note carefully in the daily record book or a special notebook the work set by the teacher for the next lesson, and show this note to your parents; to do all the homework yourself.

12. To be respectful to the director and teachers; when meeting teachers and the director in the street, to greet them with a polite bow, boys raising their caps.

13. To be polite to your elders; to conduct yourself modestly and decently at school, in the street and in public places.

14. Not to use coarse and abusive expressions and not to smoke; not to gamble for money or articles.

15. To look after school property; to have a careful attitude to your own things and those of comrades.

16. To be attentive and courteous to old people, small children, the weak and the ill; to give way to them, offer them your seat, and give them every assistance.

17. To obey your parents, help them, and take care of little brothers and sisters.

18. To keep your rooms tidy and keep your clothing, footwear and bed in order.

19. To keep your Pupil's Card on you, take good care of it, not to give it to others, and show it if required by the director and teachers.

20. To cherish the honour of your school and class as if it were your own. For infringement of the Rules the pupil is liable to punishment, up to expulsion from school.

Source: John Dunstan, Soviet Schooling in the Second World War, *1997, pp. 150–2.*

Much of the Stalinist state's power stemmed from its ability to utilise the Soviet intelligentsia. This was very much the case in science where in the early 1930s the regime had successfully taken over the Academy of Sciences (see Graham 1967). The most famous example of the contribution of scientists to the growth of Soviet state power was their work on the atomic bomb. At the end of the war, Stalin ordered Soviet scientists to produce an atomic bomb to match the one produced by the USA. It was the kind of high-profile project for which the Soviet command economy was well suited. Unlimited finances were available; slave labour in the camps was used to supply raw materials. Beria supervised the project. The first atomic bomb test took place in August 1949, and the first hydrogen bomb was exploded in 1953 (see Holloway 1994).

One of those who did crucial research on the project was Andrei Sakharov, who later became a well-known dissident. Initially Sakharov worked on theoretical questions in a group led by prominent physicist Igor Tamm. He was subsequently moved to work with Yuli Khariton, director of the bomb project at the 'Installation', a secret city, located in the settlement of Sarov, 400 kilometres to the east of Moscow, where those working on atomic and thermonuclear weapons lived. In the following extract from his memoirs, Sakharov describes an episode, when he was seconded to work with Yuli Khariton, that illustrates Beria's direct involvement in the project, and thus the extent to which scientific research had become subordinate to political considerations.

Document 9.11 Working on the Bomb

Early in 1949, Tamm and I were summoned to the office of Boris Vannikov, head of the First Main Directorate of the Soviet Council of Ministers . . .

Vannikov received Tamm and myself in his spacious office . . . Vannikov came to the point: 'Sakharov should be transferred to work on a permanent basis with Yuli Khariton [meaning to the Installation, where Khariton was director]. It's necessary for the project.'

Tamm became agitated and said I was a very talented theoretical physicist who could accomplish a great deal in key fields of science . . . ; to limit me to applied research would be a great mistake . . . The direct Kremlin line rang. Vannikov answered and then tensed up. 'Yes, they're here with me now,' he said. 'What are they doing? Talking, arguing.' There was a pause. 'Yes, I understand.' Another pause. 'Yes sir, I'll tell them.' Vannikov hung up and said: 'I have just been talking with Lavrenti Pavlovich [Beria]. He is *asking* you to accept our request.'

There was nothing left to say.

Source: Andrei Sakharov, Memoirs, *1990, pp. 96, 97, 103–5.*

In the field of genetics, political interference in science had disastrous consequences for research. In the late 1930s, the Soviet agricultural sciences came to be dominated by the biologist Trofim Lysenko. Lysenko argued that it would be possible to shorten the lifespan of winter wheat by soaking grain for a certain period of time before sowing – a process termed 'vernalisation'. He believed that useful traits in plants are not genetically transmitted but arise anew in each generation under the influence of the environment: environmental rather than genetic factors were the key to improved agricultural outputs. He called his own doctrine Michurinism, after an earlier Russian scientist. Lysenko clashed with the most prominent Soviet geneticist, N.I. Vavilov, who was the director of the Institute of Plant Breeding, and an admirer of Darwin and Mendel. Vavilov took the view that the genetic system of an organism provides the mechanism for transmission of traits from generation to generation. Lysenko became President of the Lenin Academy of Agricultural Sciences in 1938. The following document is from the stenographic report of a debate at a meeting of the presidium of the Lenin Academy of Agricultural Sciences on 23 May 1939, between Vavilov, Lysenko and Lukyanenko, Lysenko's Acting Vice-President, and it illustrates the way in which ideological judgments were being made about scientific research.

Document 9.12 Vavilov and Lysenko

Vavilov: . . . The Institute bases its selection work wholly on Darwin's evolutionary teaching . . .

Lukyanenko: Why do you speak of Darwin? Why don't you choose examples from Marx and Engels?

Vavilov: Darwin worked on evolution of species earlier. Engels and Marx held Darwin in high regard. Darwin is not all, but he is the greatest biologist, who proved the evolution of organisms.

Lukyanenko: It turns out that man originated in one place. I don't believe that he originated in one place.

Vavilov: I have already told you, not in one place but in the Old World, and contemporary biological science, Darwinian science, says that man appeared in the Old World, and that only 20 to 25 thousand years ago did man appear in the New World. Before then there was no man in America, and though this may be curious, it nevertheless is well known.

Lukyanenko: This is connected with your views on domesticated plants?

Vavilov: . . . my basic idea . . . is that . . . one and the same species of plant does not arise independently in different places, but spreads through the continents from some one region.

Lukyanenko: Everybody says that the potato came from America. I don't believe this. Do you know what Lenin said?

Vavilov: . . . we know very well that potatoes appeared in our country under Peter the First . . .

Lysenko: Potatoes were brought into the old Russia. This is a fact. One cannot go against facts. But that's not the point . . . Can new varieties [of potato] arise in Moscow, Leningrad, any place? I think they can. And, then, how does one view your theory of the centers of origin?

Vavilov: . . . We have worked out methods of studying plant life, but to understand each other we must first learn the vocabulary.

We Soviet geneticists . . . are doing much, but dumplings don't fall into one's mouth that easily. Perennial wheat is a fine thing, yet it was destroyed by frost this severe winter . . .

You can imagine how difficult and complex it is to guide graduate students, when all the time one is told that one does not share Lysenko's views . . .

Lysenko: I understood from what you wrote that you came to agree with your teacher, Bateson [English biologist], that evolution must be viewed as a process of simplification. Yet in chapter 4 of the history of the party it says evolution is increase in complexity . . .

Vavilov: . . . in short, there is also reduction . . .

Lukyanenko: Couldn't you learn from Marx? . . .

Vavilov: . . . I am a great lover of Marxist literature . . .

Lukyanenko: Marxism is the only science. Darwinism is only a part; the real theory of knowledge of the world was given by Marx, Engels, and Lenin . . .

Lysenko: I agree with you, Nikolay Ivanovich [Vavilov], it is somewhat difficult for you to carry on your work . . . But, you see, your being insubordinate toward me . . . We cannot go on in this way . . . We shall have to . . . take another line, a line of administrative subordination.

Source: Zhores Medvedev, The Rise and Fall of T.D. Lysenko, *1969, pp. 60–3.*

Vavilov lost his battle with Lysenko, and was arrested in July 1940. Sentenced to death for espionage, he died in a Saratov prison in 1943.

In July 1948, following an attack on his work by Zhdanov, Lysenko had a personal meeting with Stalin, in which he proposed that a new strain of wheat which promised great success should be called 'Stalin branched wheat' (Soifer 1994: 181). Stalin was impressed and decided to support him. In early August 1948, at a meeting of the Academy of Agricultural Sciences, Lysenko argued that his dispute with Mendelian genetics was ultimately a struggle between socialist and bourgeois approaches to science. Genetics was banned. On 16 August, the Orgburo adopted the following resolution, 'On Measures for Improvement of Biology Institutions of the Academy of Sciences'. Nikolai Dubinin was a prominent Soviet geneticist; August Weismann was one of the Western founders of genetics.

Document 9.13 Orgburo Resolution on Michurinism

To revise the research plans of biology institutions of the Academy of Sciences; to remove from the plans pseudo-scientific Weismannist topics and replace them with pressing problems that correspond to the tasks of socialist construction . . .

To strengthen the Bureau of the Biology Division and important biology institutions with Michurinist biologists . . .

To liquidate Dubinin's cytogenetics laboratory in the Institute of Cytology, Histology and Embryology . . .

To revise the plan of publications in the field of biology; to strengthen the editorial boards of biology periodicals with Michurinists . . .

To revise the syllabi and curricula for graduate studies in the institutions of the Biology Division . . .

Source: Nikolai Krementsov, Stalinist Science, *1997, p. 196.*

Although a purge of geneticists resulted, the structure of Soviet science limited its effects. By the early 1930s, there had emerged in Soviet science a strong division between research and teaching, a separation similar to that which existed in Germany (Graham 1993: 175–7). This meant that whereas the Michurinists were able to consolidate their hold in the university sector, where political and ideological considerations were always important, they were unable to do so to the same extent in the research institutes. Researchers mouthed the rhetoric of Michurinism, but in practice often continued as before. They simply got used to using politically-correct jargon to describe their work (Krementsov 1997: 45–6, 251). Indeed, Soviet science proved itself remarkably resilient. To some degree this was also because scholars had been educated at home and abroad prior to the advent of Stalinism (Graham 1993: 200).

Although the system was often ideologically rigid, informal practices flourished. In his memoirs, the Soviet dissident philosopher, Grigory Pomerants, notes that in his literature course at Moscow University, he assumed an anti-Marxist position in an exam presentation, and that he was openly critical of Chernyshevsky, the nineteenth-century Russian revolutionary novelist, in his exams. He preferred, instead, Ivan Goncharov, a more traditional writer and author of the famous novel *Oblomov*. This was in 1939. His examiner, Alexander Egolin, who was then professor of the Faculty of Russian Literature, became editor-in-chief of *Zvezda* in 1946, after it was attacked for publishing the supposedly 'alien' work of Zoshchenko and Akhmatova (see Document 12.16). Akhmatova was at the time proclaimed to be morally degenerate. However, according to Pomerants, Egolin was not an inquisitor by nature, but was himself playing the system for what he could get out of it. He was simply obeying orders; if there was no command to repress someone he would not do it.

Document 9.14 An Unpredictable Exam

The head of department, Alexander Mikhailovich Egolin, did not behave in a completely orthodox manner . . . I took his exam on literature of the second half of the 19th century. Of course, it did not fit the lectures: Egolin spoke in disconnected and insubstantial scrappy sentences . . . But there was no vengefulness in him . . . He gave me a '4' for my anti-marxist presentation. And now, when I prepared myself to choose a ticket, Alexander Mikhailovich dismissed me with his hand . . . and asked: 'Tell me, why do you not like Chernyshevsky's *What is to be Done?*?' I said that it was a very boring novel. 'But *Oblomov* is also boring,' objected Egolin. 'What a thing to say!' I exclaimed, and I recited a panygeric to Goncharov's epic style. Alexander Mikhailovich heard me out, took out my record book and gave me a '5'.

After that he worked in the Central Committee . . . and was appointed proconsul in Leningrad, assigned to persecute the semi-prostitute Akhmatova. Egolin fulfilled this task wholeheartedly, earned tens of thousands along the way, and eventually burned out . . . In another regime he would have been a bath-house attendant or a waiter in an inn and would have led a moderately honest life . . . Egolin did not *seem* to be good-natured, he really was good-natured.

Source: Grigory Pomerants, Zapiski gadkego utenka, *1998, p. 45.*

The example of Egolin illustrates once again the way in which people used the system to their own advantage. Egolin, apparently, had an essentially pragmatic approach to the ideological demands of the regime: he could be tolerant in certain circumstances, but was happy to play the role of inquisitor if his career was at stake.

10 | The family

Another way in which the party maintained its presence in the school was through the Pioneer organisations, for children of roughly 7–13, and the Komsomol, for pupils and students in their teens and early twenties. These groups offered a programme of social activities, as well as representing the voice of the party to their respective age groups. Most children belonged to these groups. There was considerable pressure to do so: for example, it became difficult to enter university without passing through the Komsomol.

On becoming a Pioneer, a new member would make the following pledge.

Document 10.1 Pledge of the Soviet Young Pioneer

I, a Young Pioneer of the Soviet Union, solemnly promise in the presence of my comrades
 – to warmly love my Soviet motherland
 – to live, to study, and to struggle as Lenin willed and as the Communist Party teaches.

Source: Allen Kassof, The Soviet Youth Program, *1965, p. 79.*

As well as reinforcing the political messages passed on in the education system, the Pioneers allowed the state to create a rival focus of loyalty for children to the family. Although the Stalin regime rehabilitated the institution of the family in the mid-1930s, it also developed a mythology which warned of the family's anti-Soviet potential. The central figure in this process was Pavlik Morozov, a young member of the Pioneers from the small town of Gerasimovka in Western Siberia, who in the early 1930s was supposed to have denounced his father to the police for kulak sympathies. Morozov's deed was heralded as the ultimate in loyalty to the regime, and in subsequent decades it inspired hundreds of artistic works, from poetry to opera. The following document is an extract from the entry on Pavlik Morozov in the second edition of the *Great Soviet Encyclopedia* of 1954, and reflects the official version of the myth. Morozov has now become a model youth, whose every action reflects official state policy. Morozov's denunciation of his father is dated as 1930, although this is an example of the way in which the Pavlik Morozov episode became as much myth as reality. Archival evidence suggests that the denunciation first took place in November 1931, and the trial of his father in March 1932 (Druzhnikov 1997: 35).

Document 10.2 Pavlik Morozov

MOROZOV, Pavlik (Pavel Trofimovich) (1918–1932) – a courageous pioneer selflessly fighting against the kulaks of his village at the time of collectivisation; brutally killed by a kulak brigade.

Pavlik Morozov was born in the remote village of Gerasimovka in the taiga in the northern Urals . . . in a poor peasant [*bedniatskoi*] family. In the rural school, M. was one of the best pupils, who had a well-earned authority among his comrades. He read a lot, and taught his mother to read and write. When the pioneer organisation was created in the school, M. was chosen as chairman of the section. The pioneers led an active struggle against the kulaks. M. denounced his own father, who was at that time (1930) the chairman of the village soviet, but who had fallen under the influence of kulak relatives. Telling the chairman of the regional committee of the party that his father had secretly sold false documents to exiled kulaks, M. then spoke at the trial of his father and branded him a traitor. When kulaks tried to frustrate the state grain procurements and incite the peasants to hide their grain, M. at a general meeting of the inhabitants of Gerasimovka addressed the peasants with an appeal to give the grain to the state and pointed out the kulaks who were hiding the grain and letting it rot; together with the poor peasants [*krestianami-bedniakami*] he participated in the taking of grain from the kulaks. Pioneers headed by M. actively aided the communists in carrying out explanatory work amongst the peasants, putting the case for the organisation of a kolkhoz in the village. The kulaks decided to be rid of M. On 3 Sept 1932. M., with his younger brother, was killed by bandit kulaks in a forest. The murderers were caught and shot according to the sentence of the court.

The heroic struggle which M. waged against the kulaks – is for the pioneer a model of fulfilment of duty and of devotion to the cause of the Communist party.

Source: Bol'shaia sovetskaia entiklopediia, *Vol. 28, 1954, p. 310.*

The Soviet state's attitude to the family and relations between the sexes was always ambiguous. There were two strains in Bolshevik thought: one stressed self-renunciation for the sake of the revolution; the other embraced a libertarian spirit and advocated freedom from 'bourgeois' norms of behaviour. At a theoretical level, both groups drew inspiration from Engels's critique of bourgeois marriage as an institution in which women were essentially commodities to be owned and exploited. The most famous exponent of the libertarian tendency was Alexandra Kollontai, a leader of the Workers' Opposition during the Civil War, and from 1920–22 head of the Women's Department of the Party, the *Zhenotdel*, which until its abolition in 1930 was at the forefront of pushing a radical women's agenda. In particular, Kollontai's short story, 'Love of the Three Generations' (1923), in which the heroine Zhenia has a number of sexual encounters and argues that sex need not take place in the context of a committed relationship, gained her a reputation as an advocate of promiscuity.

Kollontai's article of 1923, 'Make Way for the Winged Eros!', is a synthesis of her views (Stites: 1978: 352). She argues that a socialist society will itself lead to a different quality of relationship between the sexes. She also reveals a typically Bolshevik suspicion of private loyalties, and suggests that men and women should approach their mutual relations in the context of the collective good.

Document 10.3   Kollontai's Philosophy of Love

With the realisation of communist society love will acquire a transformed and unprecedented aspect. By that time the 'sympathetic ties' between all the members of the new society will have grown and strengthened. Love potential will have increased, and love-solidarity will have become the lever that competition and self-love were in the bourgeois system. Collectivism of spirit can then defeat individualist self-sufficiency, and the 'cold of inner loneliness', from which people in bourgeois society have attempted to escape through love and marriage, will disappear. The many threads bringing men and women into close emotional and intellectual contact will develop, and feelings will emerge from the private into the public sphere. Inequality between the sexes and the dependence of women on men will disappear without trace, leaving only a fading memory of past ages.

In the new and collective society . . . Eros will occupy an honourable place as an emotional experience multiplying human happiness . . . Modern love always sins, because it absorbs the thoughts and feelings of 'loving hearts' and isolates the loving pair from the collective . . . In the new world the accepted norm of sexual relations will probably be based on free, healthy and natural attraction (without distortions and excesses) and on 'transformed Eros' . . .

[At the present moment] the moral ideal defining relationships is not the unadorned sexual instinct but the many-faceted love experience of love-comradeship. In order to answer the demands formulated by the new proletarian morality, these experiences must conform to three basic principles: 1. Equality in relationships (an end to masculine egoism and slavish suppression of the female personality). 2. Mutual recognition of the rights of the other, of the fact that one does not own the heart and soul of the other (the sense of property, encouraged by bourgeois culture). 3. Comradely sensitivity, the ability to listen and understand the inner workings of the loved person (bourgeois culture demanded this only from the woman) . . . Bourgeois morality demanded all for the loved one. The morality of the proletariat demands all for the collective.

Source: Alix Holt (ed.), Selected Writings of Alexandra Kollontai, *1977, pp. 290–2.*

Soviet ideology stressed the importance of female emancipation, and the 1920s and 1930s saw a massive influx of women into the workforce. In 1922, there were 1,560,000 women in work, making up 25 per cent of the total industrial labour force.

That increased by 1940 to 13,190,000 at 39 per cent, and 19,180,000 at 47 per cent in 1950 (Heitlinger 1979: 97). Clearly, this was a revolutionary change, and one that had a profound impact on marriage and family life. Soviet propaganda and entertainment, in spite of the return in the mid-1930s to the concept of the traditional family unit, nevertheless continued to present the population with images of women as equal partners with men in labour, and as heroes of labour. In the age of Stakhanovism, in some light industries and rural areas, women Stakhanovites outnumbered their male counterparts (Buckley 1996: 200).

The 1918 Family Code introduced civil marriage, and made divorce easier. A marriage could be dissolved on the request of either party, and no grounds had to be cited. In the mid-1920s, when a new code was in discussion, a major issue was whether to permit *de facto* marriages, some taking the view that this would provoke chaos, others that it represented a more revolutionary approach. In January 1927, there was a new Code on Marriage, Family and Guardianship, which involved the recognition of *de facto* marriage, the establishment of joint property and a simplified divorce procedure.

The more liberal laws brought with them certain problems. The Soviet Union had the highest marriage and divorce rates of any European country in the mid-1920s. They were particularly high in urban areas. The high divorce rate was a factor in the appearance of large numbers of orphans, *bezprizorniki*, on the streets. In 1927, there were approximately 190,000 children in state institutions, and between 95,000 and 125,000 on the streets. The rapid social mobility of the Five Year Plans created further problems (Goldman 1993: 297–310).

In practice, these liberal laws often meant men abandoning their wives and children when they wanted to. The 1927 Code gave either spouse the right to register a divorce without the consent or knowledge of the partner. The process of claiming alimony was time-consuming, and cases were often undermined by bureaucratic delays. The following document is an eye-witness account of a case which came before a People's Tribunal in the summer of 1930 at Oranienbaum, a little town near Leningrad. The young woman involved in the episode has been abruptly abandoned by her husband, but in circumstances where alimony will be difficult to obtain.

Document 10.4 Divorce and Alimony

A scraggy, freckled girl with white eyelashes and reddish hair, shy and unhappy, muttered something incomprehensible, holding in her trembling hand a piece of paper with an official stamp on it. The judge conscientiously tried to listen and grasp what it was all about, but suddenly lost patience and stretched out his hand for the paper.

'Give me the paper, citizen. What document is this?'

She walked up to him overcome with confusion and ready to burst into tears.

'A copy . . . from the registry office at [K]habarovsk,' he read, omitting unnecessary words, 'dissolution of marriage . . . at the request of citizen

Nicolaev, Ivan Petrovitch, between him and his wife, citizen Anna Semyonovna Nicolaev . . . ' I see. Have you a child?' he asked the girl.

'A baby daughter,' she answered almost inaudibly. "Five months old." . . .

'I am a cashier at the "Peasant's House",' she said loudly, with hysterical notes in her voice. 'My salary is 65 roubles a month, I pay 20 a month to a nurse, I have no one to leave the baby with. I cannot feed her myself, I have nothing to live on and am in debt all round.'

'Don't get excited, citizen,' the judge, used to such stories, interrupted her. 'We'll get you the full amount of alimony, but . . . ' he threw up his hands, 'we'll send the verdict to [K]habarovsk where your husband had a post, and if meanwhile he has moved to another town . . . you can see for yourself how it is. It's not easy to find a man in the Far East, and perhaps he was there for a time only. In short, we'll look for him. The matter is clear.'

'Thank you,' she whispered, understanding very well that her case was hopeless. A man who had lived with her for a year while he was in charge of the 'Peasant House' at Oranienbaum and divorced her the moment he was transferred to a post in another town, would certainly not trouble about her and the child again. Soviet official bodies, slow, unwieldy and formalistic, were not likely to trace him – especially at a distance of nearly a fortnight's railway journey.

Source: T. Tchernavin, We Soviet Women, *1936, pp. 210–11.*

A 1920 decree permitted women to have free abortions in hospitals. By the late 1920s, the number of abortions had surpassed the number of births in a number of cities, and the early 1930s saw a massive increase in the abortion rate. Whereas in Russia in 1926, doctors performed 121,978 legal abortions, this figure had jumped by 1935 to 1,500,000. These rates were in part due to the migration of millions of women to the cities, where abortions were more easily available. At the same time, the birthrate fell dramatically, from 45 births per 1,000 in 1927 to 30.1 in 1935, in part because of increased abortions, but also because of the pressures of famine, rationing and new opportunities for women (Goldman 1993: 288–304).

The government's concern at these figures led in 1936 to a reversal of the previously liberal family laws, and to what amounted to the rehabilitation of marriage and the family. A widespread public debate led in June 1936 to a prohibition on abortion and measures to stabilise the family and encourage women to have more children. An article in *Pravda* on 9 June 1936 illustrated the ideological shift which had taken place in regard to the family. 'Free love', which had been widely promoted in the 1920s, was now condemned as 'bourgeois'.

Document 10.5   Strengthening the Soviet Family

In the eyes of bourgeois law the father is first of all the custodian and embodiment of private property. He is the owner of the family property . . . The wife and the children are included in this inventory . . .

The Soviet marriage in which husband and wife have equal rights is not built on private property. Nor is it simply a legal formality for satisfying sexual desires . . . The Soviet marriage opens up the truly spiritual side of marriage, its moral beauty which is beyond the reach of capitalist society. It reveals man striving for the development of the better sides of his personality. And without deep and serious love, without the bliss of motherhood and fatherhood, the personality of both individual and society is incomplete. Communism makes for whole and happy men.

To strengthen and develop the Soviet family is one of the main tasks of Soviet democracy. People who think that by relieving the father of his former slave-driving rights the Socialist Revolution has at the same time relieved him of his duties towards the family . . . are completely in the grip of bourgeois notions. The projected law on the prohibition of abortions, assistance to expectant mothers, development of the network of maternity homes . . . declares an irresponsible attitude towards the family and family duties to be incompatible with Soviet democracy and Soviet morals.

Source: Rudolf Schlesinger (ed.), The Family in the U.S.S.R., *1949, pp. 266–7.*

The actual law on the prohibition of abortion, which came out at the same time, was accompanied by various incentives to encourage women to have larger families, and new restrictions on divorce followed.

Document 10.6   Law on Prohibition of Abortion

Taking into consideration certain comments made by citizens during the discussion of the draft, the C.E.C. [Central Executive Committee] and the Council of People's Commissars of the USSR, decide:

1. In view of the proven harm of abortions, to forbid the performance of abortions whether in hospitals and special health institutions, or in the homes of doctors and private homes of pregnant women. The performance of abortions shall be allowed exclusively in those cases when the continuation of pregnancy endangers life or threatens serious injury to the health of the pregnant woman and likewise when a serious disease of the parents may be inherited, and only under hospital or maternity-home conditions . . .

10. To establish a State allowance for mothers of large families: for those having six children, an annual allowance of 2,000 rubles for five years for each subsequent child from the day of its birth, and for mothers having ten children one State allowance of 5,000 rubles on the birth of each subsequent child and an annual allowance of 3,000 rubles for a period of four years following the child's first birthday . . .

19. To triple the functioning network of permanent kindergartens in cities, factory settlements, and on railways within three years, bringing it up to 2,100,000 places by January 1 1939 . . .

27. To amend the existing laws on marriage, family, and guardianship, with the aim of combating light-minded attitudes towards the family and family obligations, and to introduce in divorce proceedings the personal attendance at the [Civil Registrar's Bureau] of both divorcees and the entry of the fact of divorce on the passports of the divorcees.

28. To increase the fees for registration of divorce as follows: 50 rubles for the first divorce, 150 rubles for the second, and 300 rubles each for the third and subsequent divorces.

Source: Rudolf Schlesinger (ed.), The Family in the U.S.S.R., *1949, pp. 271, 272, 275.*

The huge losses of men during the war led the government to pass further measures to encourage large families. Legislation introduced in 1944 brought in a tax on bachelors, introduced the 'Motherhood medal' for women who had five or six children, an Order of 'Motherhood Glory' for those with seven to nine children, and the title of 'Heroine Mother' with those of ten children and above. The new legislation also declared that *de facto* relationships would not be recognised, and introduced fees for divorce. The legislation was accompanied by efforts to brighten up the registration procedure and to give it something of the ritual significance of the traditional marriage ceremony.

An example of the way in which Soviet family policy changed in the 1930s is Makarenko's *Book for Parents* ([1937] 1954). The following extracts illustrate the new focus on self-discipline and strict codes of behaviour in relations between the sexes. Parental responsibility was now considered very important. There is a certain ambiguity in Makarenko's work: he emphasises the responsibility of parents towards the state, and at the same time their authority in the private sphere. This reflects a broader ambivolence in the state's attitude to the family from the mid-1930s onwards (Thurston 1991: 567).

Document 10.7   A Book for Parents

In this slipshod 'leftish' way of living there is nothing except poverty and nakedness. Some people even today . . . still despise accuracy and orderly movement, a mode of living that pays proper attention to details.

A slovenly attitude to life cannot fit in with the style of Soviet life. With all the means at our disposal we should exorcise that belated Bohemian spirit which only by great misunderstanding is considered by certain comrades as a token of poetic taste . . .

Slovenliness in the everyday life of the family, where no one is accustomed to keeping exact times . . . does great harm and more than anything else upsets the normal sexual experience of the young. How can one talk about upbringing if the son or daughter get up and go to bed when they think they will or just when they have to, if in the evening they 'go out walking' no one knows where, or spend the night 'at a girl friend's' or 'with a comrade', whose address and family circumstances are simply unknown . . .

A strict time-table for the child's day is an essential condition of upbringing. If you have no such time-table and you do not intend arranging one, your time is utterly wasted reading this book . . .

The habit of keeping exact hours is a habit of making an exact demand on yourself. An exact hour for rising is most essential for the training of the will, it is salvation from molly-coddling and from day-dreaming under the bedclothes. Punctual arrival at table is respect for mother, for the family, for other people, it is respect for oneself . . .

For a grown-up person a swear-word is simply an extremely insulting coarse word . . . But when a boy hears or speaks that word, it does not come to him as a relative term of abuse, it brings with it its inherent sexual meaning . . . The frequent uttering of such words trains him to pay exaggerated attention to sexual matters, to perverted day-dreaming . . . A woman appears to him not in the full splendour of her human charm and beauty . . . , but merely as a possible object of violence and utility, merely as a humiliated female. And such a youth sees love from the back yard, from the side where human history has long ago dumped its primitive physiological standards . . .

It is particularly important that a boy's or girl's feeling of solidarity should not be based only on the narrow pattern of the family; it should extend beyond the boundaries of the family into the broad sphere of Soviet life and the life of mankind in general.

Source: A.S. Makarenko, A Book for Parents, *1954, pp. 300–2, 305–6, 409.*

The revolutionary model of the family was certainly at an end. This, it has been argued, was part of a 'great retreat' away from revolutionary values towards middle-class conservatism in the 1930s and 1940s (see Document 1. 5). In explaining this, the historian, Vera Dunham, using Soviet literature as her main source in her book *In Stalin's Time*, suggested that the regime came to an agreement with the new Soviet middle class; in a so-called 'big deal', it agreed to reward its material and cultural aspirations in return for its political support (Dunham 1976: 4). Although it has been argued that the term 'middle class' is misleading here in that it implies a direct parallel between the Stalin regime and non-communist societies (Bonnell 1997: 245; see also Fitzpatrick 1992: 7–8), there is no doubt that the Stalin regime moved away from cultural radicalism after the First Five Year Plan. A popular concept of the time was *kultur'nost'*: the civilised quality of life which was to be obtained by dressing well, taking care of personal hygiene, cultivating one's environment, speaking correctly and avoiding 'dirty talk' (Volkov 2000: 217–28).

The following document contains a description from Yuri Trifonov's novel *The Students* ([1950] 1953), in which a student, Vadim, surveys the living room of a potential mother-in-law. The material culture of the family is comfortable and bourgeois; Lena's beauty and her attention to her dress point to a traditional image of a desirable woman. G.P. Danilevsky (1829–90) was a popular Russian-Ukrainian author of historical novels who in this context represents pre-revolutionary traditions. Here, the revolutionary family has become domesticated (see Dunham 1976: 45–6).

Document 10.8   The 'Bourgeois' Family

While Lena, aided by her mother, dressed in the next room, Vadim sat on the sofa, turning over the pages of a magazine, but he could not keep his mind on it, and soon put it down. He was agitated, but not by the thought that they would be late for the theatre, that by now they ought to be in the Metro, while Lena was not even dressed. He had forgotten all about the time, and was absorbed in a minute examination of the mauve wallpaper, the lampshade hovering like a rosy cloud over the table, the massive sideboard, the piano, on the top of which stood a host of knickknacks. His attention was caught by a book, also on the top of the piano, with an old-fashioned 'marbleized' binding, and a ribbon bookmarker. From where he sat he could just make out the name of the author – Danilevsky. Albina Trofimovna's probably reading it, he thought, remembering that Lena had told him that her mother was a great reader and adored historical novels . . .

Lena was standing in front of the mirror in a long dark-green dress, which brought out the delicate tan of her arms and neck. She seemed taller, slenderer, more feminine than usual. Vadim stopped in the doorway, amazed – he had had no idea that she was *so* beautiful.

'Quick, Vadim, give me your advice – which suits me better – the brooch or the necklace?' she cried, turning to face him, holding a round garnet brooch against her breast, her head held coquettishly on one side. 'Do you like it?'

Looking, not at the brooch, but at her serene and happy face, Vadim said with conviction:

'It's lovely, but we're late for the first act.'

Source: Yuri Trifonov, The Students, *1953, pp. 49–51.*

The law of 1936 marked a significant change in official attitudes to the family in the Stalin era. At the same time, the regime did not abandon its suspicion of the potentially subversive nature of private family loyalties. The underlying context for the change was a concern about birthrates and orphans as much as a profounder change of mind. This is indicated by the continuing official approval of the myth of Pavlik Morozov. There was certainly no sentimentality about children who indulged in delinquent or criminal behaviour. On 7 April 1935, the death penalty for children down to 12 years old was introduced. The reason for this decision was the growing hooligan element in Moscow. Writing to Stalin, Molotov and Kalinin, Voroshilov raised this issue. The article to which he refers in the following letter reported the case of two 16-year-old youths, who had committed two murders, been convicted to ten years in jail and then had their sentence reduced by half.

Document 10.9 Voroshilov Complains of Hooliganism

19 March 1935

Com[rade] Stalin.
Com[rade] Molotov.
Com[rade] Kalinin.

I am sending you an extract from the newspaper *Worker Moscow*, No. 61, 15.3.35, illustrating, on the one hand, the monstrous forms in which the hooliganism of our youth has expressed itself here in *Moscow* and, on the other, the almost complacent attitude of our judicial organs to these facts (the reduction of sentences by half etc.).

Com[rade] Vul', with whom I spoke on the phone about this, said that this matter was not unique, that he had registered up to 3000 malicious hooligan youths, of whom nearly 800 are indisputably bandits who are capable of anything . . .

I think that the TsK must require the NKVD to organise the accommodation not only of homeless but also of neglected children immediately and thus protect the capital from this growing 'child' hooliganism. In regard to this particular case I do not understand why these scoundrels should not be shot. Surely it is not necessary to allow them to grow up into greater thieves.

K. Voroshilov

Source: Oleg Khlevniuk et al. (eds), Stalinskoe Politbiuro, 1995, p. 144.

The law of 7 April 1935 was ostensibly designed to deal with the lawless orphan population, but it also allowed Stalin to threaten recalcitrant oppositionists with the death of their children (Conquest 1992: 75). Furthermore, a decree of 9 June 1935, later incorporated into article 58 of the Criminal Code (the section of the Code covering political crime), established that spouses and children of those who fled abroad were liable to a five-year term of exile, whether or not they knew anything about it. This was a clear attempt to increase the pressure on those who were considering seeking asylum abroad. During Yezhov's tenure at the head of the NKVD from 1936–38, the fate of children became an important bargaining tool.

The following document illustrates the impact of arrest on the families of the victim. It is a short family history by a Leningradian Vladimir Girshov, written at the end of the Soviet era. His father, Leonid Girshov, whose patronymic 'Naumovich' and surname 'Girshov' suggest that he came from a Jewish family, was arrested on 5 July 1937, sentenced under article 58 and shot on 29 November. His family was informed that he had received ten years without the right of correspondence: a formula which the authorities used when a person had been executed. His wife and baby were then also arrested for their association with him, and the rest of the family was split up.

Document 10.10 The Families of Those Arrested

I vaguely remember my father, Leonid Naumovich Girshov. I was not even five years old when he was arrested . . . [He] entered the communist party in 1919, fought at the front during the Civil War, later, in 1930 finished the Lensoviet Technical Institute and worked in the 'Elektrosila' and 'Russian Diesel' factories. Everyone who knew my father considered him an honest, principled person, who sincerely believed in communist ideals.

A lot of difficult things happened to our family after the arrest of my father. At the time of his arrest there were three children in the family who were from three to fifteen years old. In October 1937, mother gave birth to a daughter, but this did not save her from the persecution of the NKVD. In March 1938 she and her baby were arrested as members of the family of a traitor to the Fatherland and sentenced to 8 years in labour camps. Later the brother of my mother took our sister into his family and got her out of the camp, and I and my younger brother were taken to be brought up in the family of the sister of my father, with whom we lived through the Leningrad blockade.

In 1947 after finishing the 7th class of middle school I had to look for work because of the difficult material conditions of life. I couldn't get work because I was not yet 15. Then I approached the 'Russian Diesel' factory where many people remembered my father. I was treated with exceptional sympathy . . . , was made the apprentice of a plane-cutter, and helped materially. I never heard anything bad about my father at the factory, only good.

In 1944, due to bad health, my mother returned early from the camp. In 1956, she was rehabilitated. Mother repeatedly approached the NKVD, trying to discover the fate of my father. She had been told in 1937 that father had been sentenced to ten years in camps without the right of correspondence . . . [In] 1947, mother was called to the NKVD section . . . and informed that father had been given a further five years for another crime. In 1956, she was told of the death of my father, that it was supposed to have taken place on 8 February 1939. My mother died in 1977, not knowing the full truth about the death of her husband.

Vladimir Leonidovich Girshov, St Petersburg

Source: A.Ia. Razumov (ed.), Leningradsky martirolog, 1937–1938, vol. 3, November 1937, *1998, pp. 488–9.*

Family life was rarely easy for those growing up in Stalin's time. Even for those who escaped the terror, there were other problems to deal with. One of them was the housing problem. The huge influx of people to the cities ensured that people often lived in very cramped conditions. Many families were confined to one room in communal appartments. In theory, communal living was justified by the authorities on the grounds that it represented a new form of collectivism. However, it created many problems: for example, tensions between the generations and between families flourished (Fitzpatrick 1999: 47; see also Boym 1994: 121–67). The following extract from Sakharov's memoirs illustrates the cramped conditions which millions of people had to endure. Sakharov and his wife and daughter, however, seem to have coped well.

Document 10.11   The Communal Flat

In May 1948, I was assigned two rooms on Twenty-fifth of October Street, in the heart of Moscow. It was not a 'posh' place, despite its location: the rooms were off a long common corridor, and wood was still used for heating. At the last moment, a deputy director of the [Physics Institute of the Academy of Sciences] appropriated one of our two rooms for his mother . . . Our remaining room measured only 150 feet square, so we had no place for a dining table, and ate off stools or the windowsill. The ten families living on our corridor were served by a single small kitchen, and the toilet, which was located off the staircase landing, served two communal apartments. There was neither bath nor shower. But we were delighted . . . And so began four of the happiest years in our family life.

Source: Andrei Sakharov, Memoirs, *1990, p. 95.*

Contemporary propaganda presented Stalin as a perfect father-figure. In the following photograph of Stalin as 'Friend of the Little Children', Stalin is being embraced by a 6-year old girl, Galya Markizova, at a Kremlin reception in 1936. The photograph has been doctored. In the original, M.I. Erbanov, first secretary of the Buryat Mongol ASSR, stood to the right of Galya. However, he was subsequently purged, and was removed from the second version of the photograph when it was reproduced later. Galya Markizova's father, who was second secretary of the Buryat Mongol ASSR, was shot for spying for Japan in 1937, and her mother was murdered in mysterious circumstances a year later.

Document 10.12   'Friend of the Little Children'

[See page 164]

Source: David King, The Commissar Vanishes, *1997, pp. 152–3.*

A central theme of Soviet entertainment in the 1930s was 'happiness' (see Taylor 1996). In all the arts, fantasy and magic played an important role, and this had an important influence on later memories of childhood. Important children's work was written and produced. For example, the première of composer Sergei Prokoviev's symphonic poem 'Peter and the Wolf' took place on 5 May 1936. One of the first productions of the Central Children's Theatre, which opened in 1936, was the fairy story, *The Little Golden Key*, by Alexei Tolstoy, a novelist who was popular with Stalin for his novels about Peter the Great and Ivan the Terrible. The following document is the reminiscences of the producer, Natalia Sats, of the magical atmosphere of the opening night. It indicates that for young children, often unaware of political tensions, life in Stalin's time still offered enchanting experiences.

[Document 10.12]

Document 10.13 The Central Children's Theatre

At last we had the play in our hands. Rehearsals began on September 1 . . . The children were very proud that their theater was next to the Bolshoi, and for a long time they called it not the Central Children's but the 'Bolshoi theater for children' . . .

The curtain rose on December 10, 1936. On the stage was a huge town square in the kingdom of the Tatar monarch, showing luxurious houses and humble huts, to demonstrate how differently people lived. Then, suddenly, to strains of music, appears the Professor of the Science of Dolls, the bearded Karabas Barabas, with a crowd of his dolls at his heels – porcelain ones, wooden ones, rag dolls – every variety . . . In this first scene there were fifty players on the stage – on *this* stage it was possible to stretch one's wings! Our famous Coppelius of the children's theater, Vadim Ryndin, thought up all sorts of magic for this fairy tale, so many inventions that every new scene was applauded at the rise of the curtain.

The scene around the cottage of the doll Malvina, with the velvet butterflies, dancing beetles, moths, all flitting about tremendous flowers and leaves – it was a veritable fairyland – a feast of colors and marvels . . . The music's vivid symbolism, the expressiveness of its orchestration, the surprising turns of rhythm and harmony, blended with its melodic clarity and intelligibility. Everything devised by the composer pleased the children . . . The humor in the music was distinctive and articulate. The greatest favorite was the polka music for the dancing bird and the refrain of the hero, Buratino. After the performances, the children would leave the theater singing . . .

Source: Miriam Morton, The Arts and the Soviet Child, *1972, p. 85.*

Thus fairytale, as well as terror, was part of the childhood experience in Stalin's time; indeed, this strange combination of magic and terror was one of the distinctive features of the age.

The rehabilitation of the traditional family in 1936 meant a tacit recognition of the existence of a private sphere. At the same time, the arm of state propaganda could still reach into people's private worlds. The following extracts from a literary calendar of 1937, which would have hung on the wall of a person's flat or office, is an example of this. The calendar illustrates the way in which the Stalin regime attempted to reconstruct the country's historical memory. The calendar is partly structured around the six-day working week; in 1929, the government replaced the seven-day week with a six-day one, including one day off, and the days of 25 and 26 December were proclaimed Days of Industrialisation, with compulsory attendance at work. Each day contains the days of birth or death of certain figures in European literature and culture. The calendar also contains references to the Bolshevik tradition, and to successful writers of Stalin's time like Ilya Ehrenburg. The general thrust of the calendar is to suggest that Bolshevism is the natural culmination of European and Russian cultural history. The reference to a large number of Russian writers implicitly draws attention to the contribution of Russia to European culture. By including such figures as the French Catholic intellectuals Archbishop Fénelon and Charles Péguy, and the English poet, Rudyard Kipling, the compilers of the calendar were implying that Soviet culture was the inheritor of the full breadth of the European tradition. On the other hand, such propaganda in certain circumstances could have had a reverse effect: such a calendar would have introduced a young audience to a non-Bolshevik past. Of those referred to in the final entry of the following extracts, Gasem Lakhuti was a Tajik revolutionary poet who was a member of the Presidium of the Union of Soviet Writers, Nairi Zarian was an Armenian revolutionary poet well known for his positive descriptions of collectivisation, and Samed Vurgun was an Azerbaijani socialist poet who was strongly opposed to 'formalism' in art.

Document 10.14 The Construction of Memory

1937
LITERARY CALENDAR

January

Friday,   1st   1823: b. Alexander Petefi, Hungarian poet (d. 1849).
1st day of   1829: b. Tomazo Salvini, Italian tragedian (d. 1915).
six-day-   1887: b. A.S. Neverov, Russian writer (d. 1923).
week   1934: d. Jacob Vasserman, German writer (b. 1873).
. . .

Monday,   4th   1785: b. Jacob Grimm, German philologist and writer
4th day of   (d. 1863).
six-day-   1858: d. Elisa Rashel, French actress (b.1820).
week   1905: First edition of *Forward* – the first Bolshevik
                         newspaper.
                     1920: d. Benito Peres Galdos, Spanish writer (d. 1843).

. . .

Wednesday, 6th   1872: b. A.N.Scriabin, Russian composer (d.1915).
6th day of
six-day-
week

Thursday,   7th   1715: d. Fénelon, French writer (b. 1651).
1st day of   1847: d. N.M. Yazykov, Russian poet (b. 1803).
six-day-   1873: b. Charles Péguy, French poet (d. 1914).
week   1884: d. I.M. Fedorov (Omulevsky), Russian writer
                         (b. 1836).

Friday,   8th   1812: b. V.P. Botkin, Russian critic (d. 1869).
2nd day of   1878: d. N.A. Nekrasov, Russian poet (b. 1821).
six-day-   1889: b. Yalmari Virtanen, people's poet of Karelia.
week   1896: d. Paul Verlaine, French poet (b. 1844).
. . .

Wednesday, 13th 1703: First edition of first Russ. newspaper, *The Gazette*,
1st day of   Moscow.
six-day-   1813: b. V.V. Samoilov, Russian actor (d. 1887).
week   1830: First edition of the first Russian *Literary
                         Newspaper*.
                     1847: First edition of *The Contemporary* by Panaev and
                         Nekrasov.

. . .

Sunday,	17th	1600: b. Pedro Calderón, Spanish dramatist (d. 1681).
5th day of		1749: b. Vittorio Alferi, Italian dramatist (d. 1803).
six-day-		1863: b. K.S.Stanislavsky, people's artist of the USSR.
week		1869: d. A.S. Dargomyzhsky, Russian composer (b. 1813).
		1936: d. Rudyard Kipling, English writer (b. 1865).

. . .

Wednesday,	27th	1756: b. W.A. Mozart, German composer (d. 1791).
3rd day of		1826: b. M.E. Saltykov (Shchedrin), Russian writer
six-day-		(d. 1889).
week		1891: b. Ilya Ehrenburg, modern Russian writer.
		1936: Resolution of the TsK SSSR on the award of the order of Lenin to the poets Gasem Lakhuti, Nairi Zarian and Samed Vurgun.

Source: 1937: Literaturnyi kalendar', *Leningrad*.

The laws on marriage and the family of 1936 were an important moment in Soviet history. There was a limit to what propaganda could achieve. Private loyalties were given a chance to develop. In time, the Pavlik Morozov image would fade. The terror did not destroy the family (Thurston 1991: 567). Indeed, the family was frequently a subversive institution in Soviet life. It was through family relationships that memories of pre-revolutionary Russia or non-Soviet views of the world were encountered. For example, the family became the institution through which many young people encountered religion. Famously, grandmothers played an important role in preserving and passing on religious convictions, frequently baptising their grandchildren. In general, close parental ties could always threaten to undermine the state's hold on the individual. The following document relates to an occasion in 1927 when a young mother, in spite of the prevailing hostility towards religion, is determined to have her son baptised. The author of the extract, Evdokia Petrov, was an NKVD official, who defected to Australia in the early 1950s.

Document 10.15   Baptism

Mother went through awful conflicts on the question of having my brother Valentin christened. By this time I was a member of the Pioneers, the officially-sponsored movement for children not yet old enough to be Komsomols, or Young Communists. This meant that, young as I was, I had taken the first step towards a career under a government which had made plain its practical hostility to religion. In Moscow Mother did not go to church even at Christmas. But when Valentin was three or four months old, and had not been christened, she began to have dreams and nightmares and could not sleep at night. At last she decided to have him christened. The church opposite our home had been demolished, but there was another church a few streets away and she set out with my aunt, carrying Valentin and a kettle of hot water, as it was winter, for the total immersion which the Russian Orthodox service requires. But when they reached the church there was no priest in attendance and they came home disappointed. They went again, and again there was no priest. Then one day when they were going to market, my Mother carrying Valentin, they passed another church and went in. There was a priest there but they had no warm water. Mother decided to wait no longer and to have Valentin christened in cold water, though it hurt her to do it. But they still had no godfather for the child. However, they were not put off by this difficulty. They went out into the street and asked the old *dvornik*, or yardman, to be godfather. He agreed; Valentin was christened, and after that Mother slept soundly.

Source: Vladimir and Evdokia Petrov, Empire of Fear, *1956, pp. 109–10.*

Religion: The Russian Orthodox Church

The Bolsheviks were always hostile to religion. In some ways, their ideology was a child of the Enlightenment in that they rejected any kind of religious authority, and argued that their view of the world was the fruit of a scientific account of things. Theirs was a 'scientific socialism'. They were Utopians in the sense that they did not believe in the 'fall' of man – the idea that good and evil reside within the human being. In their view, in order to improve the human being, it was first essential to change structures. Moral improvement would start in the exterior arrangements of society and from there transform the individual. Thus, politics would be the chief agent for changing the world.

The Marxist tradition was overtly materialist, taking the view that the human being is essentially motivated by material interests rather than ethical or spiritual considerations. The pre-war edition of the *Great Soviet Encyclopedia* described religion very much in these terms.

Document 11.1   Definition of Religion

'Every religion is nothing more than a fantastic reflection in the minds of people of the external forces that rule over them in their everyday life, a reflection in which earthly forces take the form of unearthly ones' (Engels, *Anti-Düring* . . .). R[eligion] is the worship of god or gods, belief in supernatural forces, in the immortality of the soul, in life after death. R[eligion] in its very essence is anti-scientific, is the enemy of science, an obstacle to knowledge, it does not contain a grain of truth, is purely a reflection of the ignorance and oppressed nature of man . . . R[eligion] is the 'opium of the people' – Lenin called this dictum of Marx the foundation stone of Marxist teaching on religion and its struggle against it.

Religion is one of the superstructures above the material life of society. Religious ideas change in accordance with changes in the material life of society, which give them birth. To the extent that religious ideas are a distorted and inaccurate reflection of the being of people, they cannot in any way accurately reflect society's need of development, they always substitute illusions for reality . . .

Marxist-Leninism has revealed the reactionary essence of R[eligion], its class and exploitative character. Religion is a weapon of the exploiters, it serves as a means for the spiritual enslavement of the workers. Religious ideology distracts the workers from their earthly struggle by introducing a hope of heavenly deliverance.

Source: 'Religiia', Bol'shaia sovetskaia entsiklopediia, *vol. 48, 1941, p. 567.*

Officially, then, Soviet ideology understood religious belief to be the product of economic and social forces, having no existence in itself.

In 1721, Peter the Great abolished the post of Patriarch – the title given to the leader of the Russian Orthodox Church. From that time on, the Church was administered by a layman, the Chief Procurator of the Holy Synod. However, in late October 1917, the Church reintroduced the Patriarchate. Tikhon, the new Patriarch, was at once confronted with the problem of how to deal with the state. The 1918 Constitution established the formal separation of Church and State, stating that freedom of both religious and anti-religious propaganda was permitted. However, the State was not in practice neutral towards the Church and Lenin himself had a profound hatred of religion. During the Red Terror, for example, many clergy were arrested and shot. Tikhon called for spiritual opposition to the regime, but refused to take sides during the Civil War. Those who wanted a stronger stance against Bolshevism provoked a schism in 1921 when they called a Church Sobor in Karlovtsy, Yugoslavia, which gave rise to the Russian Orthodox Church Abroad. Back home, the reform-minded Renovationists, who were supported by the Bolsheviks, set up the administration of a Living Church in July 1922 and at a Sobor in April 1923 pushed through a number of church reforms. Tikhon, who was imprisoned from May 1922 to the summer of 1923, was released from house arrest after he announced that he would not be an enemy of the Soviet authorities, and after re-establishing a measure of control, died in 1925. Metropolitan Petr of Krutitsky became the *locum tenens,* pending the election of a new Patriarch. However, he was arrested in December 1925 and sent into exile. A number of possible successors were arrested before Sergei Stragorodsky, Metropolitan of Nizhny Novgorod, assumed the leadership. In 1927, he abandoned Tikhon's non-political stance towards the authorities, and declared the Church's support for the regime. It was a very controversial move, and in subsequent years there was much argument over whether his loyalty to the regime was truly in keeping with Metropolitan Petr's wishes.

Document 11.2   Metropolitan Sergei's Proclamation, July 1927

We must show, not in words, but in deeds, that not only people indifferent to Orthodoxy, or those who reject it, can be faithful citizens of the Soviet Union, loyal to the Soviet government, but also the most fervent adherents of Orthodoxy, to whom it is as dear with all its canonical and liturgical treasures as truth and life. We wish to be Orthodox and at the same time to claim the Soviet Union as our civil motherland, the joys and successes of which are our joys and successes, the misfortunes of which are our misfortunes. Every blow directed against the Union, be it war, boycott, or simply murder from behind a corner, like that in Warsaw, we acknowledge as a blow directed against us. Remaining Orthodox we remember our duty to be citizens of the Union 'not from fear, but from conscience', as the Apostle has taught us (Rom 13:5). And we hope that with God's help, by your general cooperation and support, we shall resolve this matter . . .

The founding of the Soviet government has appeared to many to be some sort of a misunderstanding, fortuitous and therefore not long-lasting. People have forgotten that for a Christian there are no fortuitous events, and what has occurred in our land, as everywhere and always, has been the work of God's Providence, unswervingly leading every nation towards its predestined goal. To such people, who refuse to accept the 'signs of the times', it may seem impossible to break with the former regime or even with the monarchy without breaking with Orthodoxy. Such an attitude of certain well-known ecclesiastical groups, expressed, of course, both in words and deeds, aroused the Soviet government's suspicion and hindered the efforts of the Holy Patriarch to establish peaceful relations between the Church and the Soviet government . . . Only impractical dreamers can think that such an immense community as our Orthodox Church, with all its organizations, may peacefully exist in the country by hiding itself from the government.

W.C. Fletcher, A Study in Survival, *1965, pp. 29–30.*

This declaration was motivated by a belief that the Church was in such a chaotic state that some measure of government protection was needed to ensure its survival. Furthermore, if the text is read carefully, it should be noted that it is the 'civil motherland' rather than the Soviet Union which is declared to be the source of the Church's 'joys and successes' (Fletcher 1971: 51–5). Nevertheless, the statement provoked widespread protest. Many saw it as a compromise of the Church's integrity, and it provoked further schisms in the Church. The impression that the Church was selling out to the authorities was strongly reinforced when on 15 February 1930 Metropolitan Sergei gave a press conference for Soviet journalists, in which he denied that the Church was being persecuted or undermined by the state.

Document 11.3   Press Conference of Metropolitan Sergei

1. Question: Does there really exist in the USSR persecution of religion and in what forms does it manifest itself? Answer: There has not been any persecution of religion in the USSR. Due to the Decree on the separation of Church and State the profession of any faith is fully free, and is not persecuted by any state organ. Moreover, the last resolution of the TsIK and SNK RSFSR about religious organisations of 8 April 1929 completely excludes even the slightest semblance of any persecution of religion.

2. Question: Is it true that the godless are closing churches and how do believers relate to that? Answer: Yes, it is true, some churches are closing. But the closure takes place not on the initiative of the [state] power, but on the wish of the population, and in certain cases even at the decision of the believers themselves.

3. Question: Is it true that priests and believers are subject to repressions for their religious convictions, are arrested and sent into exile etc.? Answer: Repressions enacted by the Soviet government, in regard to serving believers and priests, happen not because of their religious convictions, but more generally, as in relation to other citizens, for various anti-government activities.

4. Question: is freedom of religious propaganda permitted in the USSR? Answer: Priests are not forbidden to perform religious services or to give sermons (only unfortunately, we ourselves are not especially wholehearted in doing them).

5. Question: Is the news published in the foreign press true regarding cruelties perpetrated by agents of Soviet power in relation to particular priests? Answer: This news does not correspond to reality in any way. It is all pure speculation and slander, completely unworthy of serious people. Certain priests have been called to account not for their religious activity, but charged for various anti-government activities.

6. Question: How is the church governed and is there not pressure on the leadership? Answer: We have, as in the pre-revolutionary period, central and local church administrations. On the administration of these organs we have had no pressure up until now.

7. Question: Does any religious movement receive privileges from the Soviet government over other religious movements? And does the Soviet government exercise support for any one of these movements? Answer: By Soviet law, all religious organisations have the same rights.

Source: Russkaia pravoslavnaia tserkov' i kommunisticheskoe gosudarstvo 1917–1941: dokumenty i fotomaterialy, *1996, pp. 261–3.*

Metropolitan Sergei gave similar answers in a press conference to foreign journalists on 18 February 1929. His answers to questions were presented to the journalists in written form. It seems that the text of what he had to say was prepared in advance by the party and, after he had made some editorial changes, was photographed and printed abroad (Fletcher 1965: 52).

In his remarks, Metropolitan Sergei refers to the law of April 1929. This law was designed to severely impede the activities of religious organisations. The plan was to put a stop to the charitable and educational activities of churches, restrict the mobility of clergy, and confine religious ceremonies to within the church building itself. By these means, the Stalin regime hoped to drastically reduce the visibility of all that pertained to the Church and its culture.

Document 11.4   Law on Religious Associations

17. Religious organisations are forbidden: a) to set up accounts for mutual help, cooperatives, manufacturing organisations, and in general to use property at their disposal for any purposes apart from the satisfactions of religious needs; b) to exercise material support for its members; c) to organise special children's, youth, women's, prayer and other meetings, as also bible, literary, handicraft, labour, and other meetings, groups, circles, sections for the teaching of religion, and also to arrange excursions, children's playgrounds, to open libraries and readings rooms, and organise sanatoriums or medical aid. In prayer buildings and places only those books can be kept which are necessary for the maintenance of the given cult.

18. Teaching of any kind of religious belief in state, public, private educational or preschool institutions is prohibited. Such teaching may be given exclusively in religious courses created by the citizens of the USSR with the special permission of the People's Commissariat of Internal Affairs of the RFSFR, and on the territory of autonomous republics with the permission of the central executive committee of the corresponding autonomous republic.

19. The clergy and other ministers of religion may operate only in the area of residence of members of the religious association by which they are employed and in the area of the temple where they serve . . .

59. A special permission for each occasion is required for the performance of religious processions as well as the performance of religious rites in the open air . . . Applications for such permission must be submitted at least two weeks prior to the ceremony. Such permission is not required for religious services connected with funerals.

60. No special permission is required for religious processions around the religious building, where they are an integral part of the worship . . . , as long as they do not interfere with the normal street traffic.

61. All other religious processions and all performances of religious rites outside the building of the religious organisation require special permission in each particular case . . . Such permission can be obtained after the prior agreement of the executive committee in the raion where the procession, rite or ceremony is to take place.

Source: Russkaia pravoslavnaia tserkov' i kommunisticheskoe gosudarstvo 1917–1941: dokumenty i fotomaterialy, *1996, pp. 252–3, 259–60.*

Following this law in May 1929, a change to the Constitution removed the constitutional right to conduct religious propaganda. Only atheist propaganda was to be permitted.

Also on 8 April 1929, the authorities introduced a Central Standing Commission on Religion Questions (Cult Commission) to supervise and implement the new religious legislation (see Luukkanen 1997: 53). Through this institution, the party monitored local churches and kept records of those who were attending. This meant that in effect the Patriarchate was only superficially in control of its own affairs. This is illustrated by the following memorandum, by Metropolitan Sergii of Lithuania, Exarch of Latvia and Estonia, which was written for the German authorities after the Nazi invasion about the Church in the USSR, explaining its loyalty to the Soviet state and his own continuing loyalty to the Moscow Patriarchate.

Document 11.5   The Cult Commission

Riga, 20 August 1941

The Bolsheviks realized their fundamental control over ecclesiastical life through the so-called 'Commission concerning the cults'. The Central Commission was created under the Presidium of the Supreme Soviet, and it further descended into a network of corresponding local commissions. The composition of the Central Commission and of the local ones remained secret, but they were undoubtedly ruled by the GPU-NKVD. The Commission chose the so-called 'instructor concerning the cults', i.e a well-known lecturer who entered into the life of every community. Apart from the central ecclesiastical organ – the Patriarchate – he demanded from every unit the necessary information. Directly, they handed over to him lists of believers, forms with the names of those who had signed agreements for the use of a church and property, or concerning the composition of the clergy, and so forth . . .

From the above, the Patriarchate itself, as the central ecclesiastical establishment, existed, as far as the Bolsheviks were concerned, only as a prop for the sake of credulous foreigners.

The Patriarchal locum-tenens, we – the episcopy and his closest helpers – reconciled ourselves with this humiliation and disgrace for the sake of the relative preservation of the Church for the Russian people and in the hope of future deliverance from the atheistic yoke. I repeat, the position itself of the Moscow Patriarchate did not protect her members from Bolshevik persecutions at all. Many of her members suffered, many had yet to suffer, but their hour had not yet arrived, by the will of God. Metropolitan Sergii personally compared our position with chickens in the kitchen garden of a cook. The day would come when even from the small garden the next victim would be snatched. All were doomed, but the cruel cook did not lead to the chopping block immediately.

Source: Dimitry Pospielovsky, A History of Marxist-Leninist Atheism and Soviet Anti-Religious Policies, *vol. 2, 1988, pp. 196–7.*

The way in which the Soviet regime attempted to infiltrate religious organisations is illustrated by the following document. It was written after the Soviet takeover of Lithuania following the Nazi–Soviet pact by the Lithuanian head of the NKVD to one of his district superintendents. It indicates the extent to which policy towards the churches in the non-Russian republics was coordinated from Moscow. In Lithuania, as in all the other non-Russian republics, the Soviet regime was anxious to combat religious movements which might encourage political opposition or the growth of nationalism.

Document 11.6 Infiltrating the Church

Absolutely Confidential
To Comrade *Palevicius*, District Superintendent of Alytus

Section II of the [NKVD] of the USSR is at present engaged in working out a plan for agencies dealing with the clergy in the new Soviet Republics.

Wherefore, I issue the following instructions: . . .

(3) Draw up a list of Catholic and Orthodox churches and other places of worship in your district.
(4) Draw up a list of Catholic and Orthodox priests and ministers of any other sects in your district, and indicate the influence of each clergyman among the masses and in the social and political life of the country.
(5) Point out the internal dissension existing within the religious organisations or among the clergy, indicating in detail the reasons for the dissension and giving the names of the priests between whom strained relations exist.
(6) Offer your suggestions as to the best way to make use of these dissensions, so as to enlist certain people as secret agents and thus undermine the Church organisations in your district.
(7) Send on precise information on the results already obtained by your agents in their activity against Catholic and Orthodox priests and against ministers of other sects, enclosing the official forms duly completed and specify the plans followed in the operation . . .

Signed: Guzevicius
Commissar for the Interior
21 January 1941

Source: Albert Galter, The Red Book of the Persecuted Church, *1957, pp. 76–7.*

Legislative and institutional mechanisms for the control of religious behaviour were accompanied by a fierce campaign to persuade the population of the treacherous or reactionary nature of religious belief. At the forefront of this campaign was the League of the Militant Godless (LMG), which grew out of a newspaper *The Godless*, founded in December 1922 by Emelian Yaroslavsky. Yaroslavsky stressed the link between building socialism and the attack on religion. At the Second Congress of the LMG in June 1929, when it launched what it hoped would be the final destruction of religion in the USSR, one of the slogans was: 'Struggle against religion is a struggle for the Five Year Plan!' It was after this Congress that the word 'militant' was added to the title of the organisation, and it is important to see this militant tendency as part of the wider radicalism of the first Five Year Plan (see Peris 1991; also Document 4.8).

The peak of the LMG's membership came in 1932 when it reached 5,670,000 members. It declined to just a few hundred thousand in the middle of the 1930s, although membership was back up at 2 million in 1938 and 3.5 million in 1941, when the League also published ten atheist newspapers and twenty-three journals (Pospielovsky 1987: 52–61). It is probable that membership figures and successes were exaggerated. Yaroslovsky himself observed that sometimes counties were declared 'godless' when no anti-religious activity had actually taken place there (Powell 1975: 38).

A probable reason for the revival of the LMG after the decline in the mid-1930s was the discovery, in the census of 1937, that about 56 per cent of the population considered themselves believers (Peris 1998: 198). Clearly, much of the anti-religious propaganda had been ineffective. Renewed attempts were made to galvanise the LMG, and the festivals of Christian Easter and the Jewish Passover came in for particular attack. The following letter, written on 15 April 1937 against the background of the Spanish Civil War, illustrates the attempt made by the party and the LMG to associate religion with politically unreliable, reactionary or unscientific modes of belief.

Document 11.7   Activity of the League of the Militant Godless

To the Secretary of the Party Committee of the ACP(b), the Party Organization and the Secretary of the cell of the LMG

In the past year the christian feast of easter has almost coincided in time with the international proletarian feast of 1 May. This circumstance especially strengthens the responsibility for an effective and wide enough anti-easter campaign.

In the heroic struggle of the Spanish people against international fascism for their existence in freedom, in conditions of exceptional tension in the international situation when the reactionary forces of fascism are trying to stir up an unprecedented anti-soviet war, the easter feast of 'love' and 'forgiven sins' reveals especially clearly its reactionary sense and its false religious teaching. Your task is to explain to the wide masses the reactionary class character of easter and religious feasts in general and of religion as a whole. Not confining ourselves to this, we must also show the falsity and anti-scientific nature of religious faith, in particular the easter gospel legends and tales about Christ, both about having suffered allegedly for mankind and risen as god. We must oppose the priestly easter slogans of non-resistance and hypocritical love with slogans in defence of the socialist fatherland, to the aid of the heroic Spanish people, international brotherhood and the shattering blow to the fascist war-mongers infringing on the integrity and independence of the socialist homeland of the workers of the whole world.

The District Committee of the ACP(b) and the RC of the LMG draw your attention again to the fact that in a range of party organisations repeated instructions of the DC of the ACP(b) on improving the situation of anti-religious work are not being fulfilled, in particular the decree of the buro of the DC of the ACP(b) of 5 February 1937.

For this reason it is necessary to strengthen anti-religious work and party, komsomol and trade union organisations and institutions of people's education must fulfil the directives of the party on anti-religious work. Rejuvenate already existing cells of the LMG and create new ones where they have up till now not been created and in general set in motion planned, systematic and anti-religious work.

The DC of the ACP(b) and the RC of the LMG recommend the following forms of the conducting of the anti-religious campaign: lectures, reports and talks on anti-religious and actual scientific themes, plays, evenings of literary readings, amateurs' nights, concerts, etc. To illustrate lectures, reports and talks one should use visual aids, slides in several photo series – they have them in many schools.

The following basic themes are recommended for lectures and talks:

1. Two worlds – two feasts.
2. The tale of Christ and other dying and allegedly risen gods.
3. Religion and the church in the service of international fascism.
4. The Stalin Constitution and religion.
5. Is resurrection from the dead possible?
6. Science and religion and other current anti-religious themes.

Schools must help in anti-religious work with enterprises and collective farms, especially with those which sponsor them.

The following literature is recommended:

1. 'The agitator's companion', No. 5 and 8 for 1937, during which it is necessary to work through the article in No. 5 of 'the agitator's companion' – the Stalin Constitution and questions of religion at meetings of members of the trade unions and participants in collective farms.

2. In the next few days the brochure by [I.A] Kryvelev 'Against easter' will be sent out to rural party organisations and seven year secondary schools, while urban organisations and schools can get it in the RC of the LMG.

3. Literature sent to party organisations and schools in 1936.

Send a report on the course of the campaign to the DC of the ACP(b) and the RC of the LMG by 13 May 1937.
Head of cultural propaganda dept of the DC ACP(b)
Mukhin

Chmn of the RC of the LMG
Afonsky

Source: Felix Corley, Religion in the Soviet Union: An Archival Reader, *1996, pp. 117–19.*

Religion was frequently caricatured in posters and cartoons. The following cartoon of November 1937, published in the newspaper *The Godless*, conjures up the image of an anti-Soviet Vatican plot, and offers the protection of Yezhov's NKVD. The *chastushka* (ditty) beneath the cartoon, which is translated here, reinforces the message.

Document 11.8 Antireligious Cartoon and Ditty

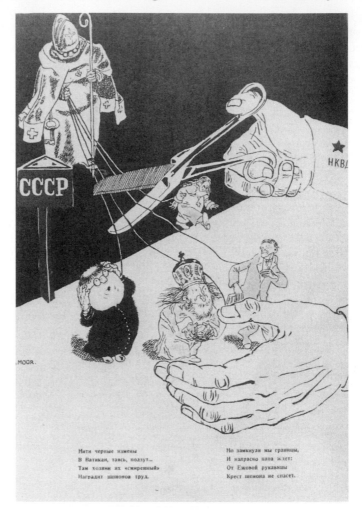

Black threads of betrayal
are crawling away to the Vatican . . .
There their 'humble' leader
rewards the labour of the spies.

But we have closed our borders,
And the Pope waits in vain:
The cross does not save the spy
From the iron rule of Yezhov.

Source: A. Luukkanen, The Religious Policy of the Stalinist State,
1929–1938, *1997, p. 148.*

Attacks on the Church under Stalin were most frequent during the first Five Year Plan and in 1936–39. By 1939, all monasteries, nunneries and seminaries had been closed down. Some 80,000 clerics, monks and nuns had lost their lives since the revolution. Roughly 35,000 priests were exiled or executed during the 1930s. Of the 163 bishops supervised by Metropolitan Sergei in 1930, only four survived the decade in office. Metropolitan Sergei presided over 30,000 parishes in 1930, and there were a further 10,000 priests in the Renovationist Church. By 1939, it is estimated that there were only 200–300 churches left open in the whole of the USSR. The administration of the Russian Orthodox Church was almost completely dismantled. Following the occupations of Moldavia, eastern Poland, the Baltic republics and Western Karelia, after the Nazi–Soviet pact, the numbers rose again, reaching an official total estimate of 4,222 churches in 1941 (Davis 1995: 11–13; Pospielovsky 1988, vol. 2: 66–8).

The attacks on the churches did not happen without fierce opposition. Throughout the countryside, in particular, there was fierce opposition, often from women. For example, attempts to close the village church in Olshanitsa in western Russia met furious resistance.

Document 11.9   Opposition to Closure of Churches

To the Western Regional Committee of the ACP(b)

The closure of the Olshanitsa church and the handing over of it for cultural needs did not take place, for the reason that almost no mass work was conducted around this question of the closure of the church . . .

This decision led to active discussion of this question by the whole population and the women especially created an aggravated attitude towards the party cell. The cell did not take this into account and conducted no work to liquidate the tensions created . . . The area executive committee . . . was satisifed, after which the representative of the Militia was sent to Olshanitsa to close the church.

The population took this as an administrative act and local anti-Soviet elements in the village used this to their purposes. The alarm was sounded at which up to 200 women (who had also stood for leaving the church at the last meeting) ran up in a group, from which sticks and stones flew at the members of the vill. soviet present, as a result of which the commission to close the church had to flee.

The RC [Regional Committee], having addressed this question . . . , suggested that the RC Agitprop travel to conduct an anti-religious month of anti-religious propaganda in the village of Olshanitsa, and to Dyatkovsky DC to develop mass work among the poor and middle part of the population of the village of Olshanitsa.

Deputy Secretary of the Regional Committee of the ACP(b)
Cherkasov
Deputy Head of the Inform.P/Dept of the RC
Pavlyukov

Source: Felix Corley, Religion in the Soviet Union, *1996, pp. 83–4.*

With the outbreak of war, the situation changed. The annexation of new territories following the Nazi–Soviet pact and then during the war as Soviet forces moved westwards, brought large numbers of Christians into the orbit of Soviet rule. As well as wishing to mobilise believers to support the war effort, the regime sought to bring religious communities under its control. In 1940, the government abandoned the six-day working week introduced in 1929 and reverted to the traditional seven-day week with Sunday as the day of rest. By the end of 1941 all anti-religious periodicals had been shut down. In 1942, there were releases of Orthodox priests from the camps, and in September 1943 the Patriarchate itself was restored after an agreement with Stalin.

Document 11.10   Restoration of the Patriarchate

The Council of Bishops of the Orthodox Church

On 8 September in Moscow there was held the Council of Bishops of the Orthodox Church, convened to elect a Patriarch of Moscow and All Russia and to form a Holy Synod under the Patriarch.

The Council of Bishops unanimously elected Metropolitan Sergei as Patriarch of Moscow and All Russia.

The Council furthermore adopted unanimously the statement addressed by Metropolitan Sergei to the Government of the USSR expressing thanks for its attention to the needs of the Russian Orthodox Church. Archbishop Grigory of Saratov read a statement to the Christians of the whole world. This document, containing an appeal for the unification of all forces in the struggle against Hitlerism, was also adopted unanimously by the Council . . .

Statement of the Council of the Most Reverend Hierarchy of the Russian Orthodox Church to the Soviet Government (September 8, 1943)

Deeply moved by the sympathetic attitude of our national leader and Head of the Soviet Government, J.V. STALIN, towards the needs of the Russian

Orthodox Church and towards our modest works, we, his humble servants, express to the Government our council's sincere gratitude and joyful conviction that, encouraged by this sympathy, we will redouble our share of work in the nationwide struggle for the salvation of the motherland.

Let the Heavenly Head of the Church bless the works of the Government with the Creator's blessing and let him crown our struggle in a just cause with the victory we long for and the liberation of suffering humanity from the dark bondage of fascism.

(Signed by Sergei, Metropolitan of Moscow and Kolomna, and eighteen other metropolitans, archbishops and bishops.)

Condemnation of Traitors to the Faith and the Fatherland (September 8, 1943)

Alongside the gratifying manifestations of patriotic activity by the Orthodox clergy and laity it is all the sadder to see manifestations of a contrary character. Among the clergy and laity there are those who, forgetting their fear of God, dare to take advantage of the common misfortune: they meet the Germans like invited guests, make themselves available for service, and sometimes commit outright treason, for example betraying to the enemy their fellows among the partisans and others who are sacrificing themselves for the motherland. An obliging conscience, of course, is always ready to suggest justification even for such conduct. But the treachery of Judas will never cease to be the treachery of Judas. Just as Judas destroyed his own soul and bodily bore an exceptional punishment even here on earth, so these traitors, preparing themselves to perish for eternity, do not avoid the fate of Cain on earth. The Fascists will suffer just retribution for their plunder, murder and other evil deeds. Nor can mercy be expected by these stooges of the Fascists who do well for themselves at the expense of their brothers and behind their backs.

The Holy Orthodox Church, Russian and Eastern, has already pronounced its condemnation of traitors to the Christian cause and betrayers of the Church. And today, gathered in the name of the Father, the Son and the Holy Spirit, we affirm this condemnation and declare that anyone guilty of betraying the cause of the Church and going over to the side of fascism is an enemy of Christ the Lord and is excommunicated, and if a bishop or cleric is removed from office. Amen.

(Signed by Metropolitan Sergei of Moscow and eighteen other metropolitans, archbishops and bishops)

Source: Robert Daniels, A Documentary History of Communism, *vol. I, 1985, pp. 289–90.*

The Russian Orthodox Church came under the supervision of the newly-created Council for the Affairs of the Russian Orthodox Church, headed by G.G. Karpov. The administration of the Orthodox Church thus came under the direct control of the state. This had its uses. For example, the Orthodox Church was used to control nationalism in the non-Russian republics. In Ukraine, the Greek Catholic 'Uniate' Church, which was seen by the regime as a source of Ukrainian nationalism, was abolished in 1946 and joined to the Orthodox Church. In 1944, a Council for the Affairs of Religious Cults, covering all non-Orthodox groups, was created in Moscow. It was designed to supervise such organisations as the All-Union Council of Evangelical Christian-Baptists, which was set up in October 1944.

The following document is from a report of 30 August 1945 by Karpov to G.F. Alexandrov in the Central Committee, and presents data and information about the state of the Russian Orthodox Church on 1 July 1945. Particularly interesting is the uneven distribution of the churches, and the influence of the church in areas that had been under German occupation.

Document 11.11 The Russian Orthodox Church in 1945

On the territory of the USSR, there are 10,243 acting churches and prayer houses. These include: in the Ukrainian SSR – 6,072; in the RSFSR – 2,297; in the Belorussian SSR – 633; in the Moldavian SSR – 615; in the Baltic republics – 343, and in the rest of the union republics – 83.

Churches and prayer houses are distributed very unevenly in the Union. The greatest quantity are in regions, subject to German occupation, where in the period 1941–1943 there was a mass opening of churches . . .

There are oblasts and krais where there are just 1–5 churches (the Primorsky and Khabarovsky krais, the Mariisky and Mordovsky ASSR, Kemerovsky, Kurgansky, Novosibirsky, Omsky, Saratovsky, Tomsky and Chitinsky oblasts . . .)

In 14 regions of the Moscow oblast there are no churches, although in the Ramenskii region [of the Moscow oblast] there are fourteen churches . . .

Representatives of believers daily visit the Council not only from the Moscow oblast, but from a number of other more distant oblasts. In personal conversations with members of the Council they cite the Constitution, the long distance to acting churches, the opening of churches in other regions, the presence of a large number of believers at a given place, and the demand for prayer for the war dead by relatives and friends . . .

In the regions where there are no active churches or very few, religious services and rites are held quite widely outside the church by unregistered priests, and sometimes by people who do not belong to the priesthood. In some places these services have a mass character.

Source: M.I. Odintsov (ed.), 'Godudarstvo i tserkov' v gody voiny', Istoricheskii arkhiv, 1995, No. 3, pp. 118–20.

Although Stalin rehabilitated the Church as an institution, it is difficult to argue that he wanted to revive religion itself. More likely, he aimed to break the Church's resistance by demoralising and corrupting it (Walicki 1995: 444). The Church revived, but in such a way as to have its spiritual authority compromised. Its leadership was to be henceforth carefully vetted by the state. The regime wanted loyalty, rather than belief.

It was one thing to seek to eradicate or control the institution of the Church; it was another to change people's minds. State rituals were not always attractive, and with official churches closing, much of the religious impulse was diverted underground. House churches, secret churches and secret communities sprang up in various places (see Fletcher 1971; Shkarovskii 1995). Popular religion flourished. For example, collectivisation and the purges led to the surfacing of apocalyptic rumours in rural areas. The *Peasant Newspaper* reported the following on 22 July 1937, implicitly suggesting that such behaviour was deeply irrational.

Document 11.12   Apocalyptic Rumours

The rumor went from izba to izba. Two nimble old women quickly ducked into the house, furtively looked round, sat down on a bench as if unwillingly. Then they heaved heavy sighs and, in response to questions, said: 'Misfortune hangs over us, women! The Day of Judgment draws near. War and famine have begun . . . Pray!'

This example is not unique in Mginsky raion. Church people have started going more and more frequently to the houses of kolkhozniks to spread their anti-Soviet talk and threaten those who do not go to church with 'The Last Judgment.'

Source: Sheila Fitzpatrick, Stalin's Peasants, *1994, p. 214.*

The spirituality of the Stalin era was shaped by the experience of persecution. It was typical of Christians to perceive their ordeals as part of a divine call for a renewed spiritual commitment. The following letter is an illustration of this. It was written by German Riashentsev, at the time the Bishop of Volokolamsk, who lived from 1923 to 1925 in exile in the Tobolsk region. Writing in a letter to a friend (Vera), he observed that it was important that they understand their trials from a divine perspective. Bishop German was repeatedly arrested, and exiled or sent to labour camps, before being shot in September 1937.

Document 11.13   Responding to Persecution

Letter to Vera

22 June 1925

Naturally each Christian must persuade himself of the logic of the position which his faith has placed him in: there are fewer churches, so be one yourself.

Also become a temple of God. Entry to many shrines has become difficult, so become a shrine and a living icon yourself. Much of the external apparatus, a lot which the faith of men, women and children depended on at a simple level has disappeared, so give them something of incomparably better standing and which is as obvious to wise men as it is to a child: the simplicity and intensity of devout humility.

It is only our spiritual stagnation which is preventing us from seeing what is happening today as a call for the strengthening of the self, and for self-knowledge and self-denial. As it says in one of our fasting prayers, now 'the time for spiritual activity has dawned.'

Source: Tatiana Goricheva (ed.), The Cry of the Spirit, *1989, p. 105.*

Many priests and believers found themselves in labour camps, where they very occasionally managed to organise prayer meetings and church services. The labour camps and prisons occasionally had the effect of encouraging a turn to religious belief or a deepening of it (Boobbyer 1999; Todorov 1999: 41). Memoirs of the camps often contain descriptions of mystical experiences (see Mihajlov 1978); and some memoirs have become widely admired (Ciszek 1975). Understanding imprisonment or suffering as a spiritual opportunity is typical of the outlook of the novelist and writer, Alexander Solzhenitysn, who was sent to the labour camps during the war for writing a critical letter about Stalin. In *The Gulag Archipelago*, Solzhenitsyn describes how the experience of imprisonment turned him towards a religious worldview, at odds with the Marxism which he had grown up with and believed in.

Document 11.14   The 'Ascent'

As soon as you have renounced that aim of 'surviving at any price', . . . then imprisonment begins to transform your formal character in an astonishing way . . .

And it would seem that in this situation feelings of malice, the disturbance of being oppressed, aimless hate, irritability, and nervousness ought to multiply. But you yourself do not notice how, with the impalpable flow of time, slavery nurtures in you the shoots of contradictory feelings . . .

You are ascending . . .

Formerly you never forgave anyone. You judged people without mercy. And you praised people with equal lack of moderation. And now an understanding mildness has become the basis for your uncategorical judgments. You have come to realize your own weakness – and you can therefore understand the weakness of others. And be astonished at another's strength. And wish to possess it yourself . . .

Your soul, which formerly was dry, now ripens from suffering. And even if you haven't come to love your neighbors in the Christian sense, you are at least learning to love those close to you . . .

It was granted me to carry away from my prison years . . . this essential experience: *how* a human becomes evil and *how* good . . . Gradually it was disclosed to me that the line separating good and evil passes not through states, nor between classes, nor between political parties either – but right through every human heart . . .

Since then I have come to understand the truth of all the religions of the world: They struggle with the *evil inside a human being* . . .

And since that time I have come to understand the falsehood of all the revolutions of history: They destroy only *those carriers* of evil contemporary with them . . . And they then take to themselves as their heritage the actual evil itself, magnified still more.

Lev Tolstoi was right when he *dreamed* of being put in prison. At a certain moment that giant began to dry up. He needed prison as a drought needs a shower of rain.

All the writers who wrote about prison but who did not themselves serve time there considered it their duty to express sympathy for prisoners and to curse prison. I . . . have served enough time there. I nourished my soul there, and I say without hesitation:

'*Bless you prison for having been in my life!*'

(And from beyond the grave come replies: It is very well for you to say that – when you came out of it alive.)

Source: Alexander Solzhenitsyn, The Gulag Archipelago, *iii–iv, 1975, pp. 610–11, 615–17.*

The decline of religion had a considerable impact on Soviet life. At one level, it simply led to the disappearance of older traditions. Some writers, however, also see a link between religious decline and the rise of the Stalinist contempt for human life. For example, the Russian religious philosopher, Nikolai Berdyaev, writing in *The Russian Revolution* (1931), criticised the very spirit of communism: he saw in it a negation of the spiritual principle in man, and thought that this was bound to have disastrous consequences (see Berdyaev 1931: 80–1). There is also evidence to link the decline of religious values with a general deterioration in the standard of public ethics and private morality, although this is difficult to measure. Dmitri Panin, who was the model for the character of Sologdin in Solzhenitsyn's novel, *The First Circle* (1968), suggested that the decline of religion after 1917 led to a loss of honesty and integrity.

Document 11.15   Religion and Moral Standards in Russia

Until 1917, in Russia, the concept of honesty was drilled into the children of families professing to be Christian and was reinforced by church, school and good literature. After the disaster of 1917 and the opening of the new Bolshevist era, this traditional process went into sharp decline. For no other reason than ingrained habit, the words *honesty, truth* and *honor* still remained in use, but the new regime encouraged people to behave in despicable and devious ways and threatened with destruction all those who did not conform. As the campaign to wipe out religion got under way, large numbers of people in all walks of life began losing their integrity. The very word *honesty* became unfashionable and was used only in a tone of cynicism or mockery. However, among the generations who had come to maturity before the national cataclysm, one still encountered decent behavior within the family or between friends.

Source: Dmitri Panin, The Notebooks of Sologdin, *1976, p. 174.*

If what Panin says is true, it is possible to read the return to traditional morality in the 1930s as expressed in Makarenko's work, for example, as an attempt by the state to fill the gap which religion had left behind.

While the Bolsheviks destroyed so much of the religious life within the USSR, a rich religious culture was preserved in the emigration (see Raeff 1990: 118–55). In the Russian Orthodox tradition, theology during the Stalin era was represented abroad by men like Sergei Bulgakov, Georgy Florovsky and Vladimir Lossky. The monastic tradition of the 'staretz' was continued by men like Staretz Siluan in Mount Athos and his disciple Archimandrite Sophrony, who founded a community in Essex, England. Outside the USSR, churches and seminaries loyal both to the Moscow Patriarchate and to the Russian Orthodox Church Abroad preserved much of the spiritual heritage of the Russian Orthodox Church.

The artist and the state | 12

The attempt to bring all aspects of Soviet life under state control was no more powerfully felt than in the arts. The Stalin regime sought to use artists and writers to mobilise the population to fulfil its directives, and had little patience with those who believed in the unique creative vision of each individual. Yet, the state's struggle to bring the arts into line brought it into conflict with some of the most brilliant and memorable personalities of the Stalin era. This conflict led to some remarkable creative achievements.

Until the late 1920s, the party continued to tolerate a certain amount of competition and freedom among writers. However, the idea that Soviet power should bring with it a new culture and a new kind of working-class literature remained popular among many writers, in particular those who belonged to the radical Russian Association of Proletarian Writers (RAPP). During the first Five Year Plan, RAPP and its journal *On the Literary Front*, spearheaded a campaign to improve the cultural level of the masses. During the trials of the bourgeois specialists, they attacked the elitism of traditional literature, sought to make the arts more accessible to the masses and encouraged workers and peasants to try their hand at writing. Many writers thus came to see their role as participants in the process of reconstructing society; the writer was now perceived not as an independent observer, but as a 'writer-fighter' (Clark 1978: 156–7).

A well-known example of this kind of literature was Valentine Kataev's novel *Time, Forward!* ([1932] 1995). During the first Five Year Plan, the party sought to use literature to mobilise the population's revolutionary energy. Kataev's novel, which reflected the agenda of Stalin's speech to managers of 1931 (see Document 4.2), described the building of the metallurgical plant at Magnitogorsk. The central idea of the novel was the speeding up of time, and thus the possibility of achieving extraordinary targets. In the novel, the philosophy of Triger, the young secretary of the local travelling edition of the newspaper *Komsomolskaia pravda* who has devoted himself to an analysis of the mixing of concrete, reflects the official party doctrine.

Document 12.1 'Time, Forward!'

To the knowledge derived from books, [Triger] had added his own theory of tempos.

It consisted of this: increase of the productivity of one machine automatically entails the increase of the productivity of others indirectly connected with it. And since all machines in the Soviet Union are connected with each other to a greater or lesser degree, and together represent a complex interlocking system, the raising of tempos at any given point in this system inevitably carries with it the unavoidable – however minute – raising of tempos of the entire system as a whole, thus, to a certain extent, bringing the time of socialism closer.

[Triger] had selected that point. He had specialised in concrete. He was convinced that accelerating the work of even one concrete-mixer would lead to accelerating the tempos of work of all the machines indirectly connected with the production of concrete.

And indirectly connected were: the water system, which supplied the water; the railroad, which brought up the cement, the sand and the gravel; and the electric station, which produced the power. So the daily requirements of sand, cement, and gravel would be increased . . .

Since, in order to strengthen the work of the water system, the electric station, the stone-crushers, and so forth, it was indispensable to accelerate not only the work of all the machines connected with it, but also the work of all the machines connected with these machines, then it became absolutely clear that with the small, and at first glance, minor matter of raising the productivity of one concrete-mixer was connected all the tremendous, complex, important, interacting system of the Five-Year Plan.

Source: Valentine Kataev, Time, Forward!, *1995, pp. 166–7.*

Just as the educational experimentation of the 'cultural revolution' of 1928–31 was quickly reined in, so too the revolutionary trend in literature and the visual arts was also terminated. Ultimately, the regime wanted subservient rather than revolutionary literature. In April 1932, the Central Committee declared that artistic organisations had become too narrowly focused, and that RAPP was to be disbanded and replaced by a new Union of Soviet Writers. The literary doctrine of the new organisation was to be 'socialist realism'. This was a doctrine which was designed to be broad enough to embrace both party and non-party members. While stressing party-mindedness, *partiinost'*, it also theoretically allowed for considerable creative initiative (Kemp-Welch 1991: 171). In practice, however, the Union of Writers was a mechanism for ensuring close state supervision of literature.

Socialist realism involved seeing reality in terms of the march of socialism. The veteran Bolshevik writer and politician, Anatoly Lunacharsky articulated it as follows in February 1933, in a report on the role of the theatre.

Document 12.2 Lunacharsky on Socialist Realism

The Socialist Realist is in complete harmony with his surroundings and with the tendencies in their development as a warrior for the morrow that is in process of realisation. But he does not accept reality as it really is. He accepts it as it will be. From this derives the need, dictated by his position as a warrior, to stylise reality in its artistic representation with the aim of re-creating it in practice.

Source: R. Taylor and I. Christie (eds), The Film Factory, *1988, p. 327.*

The main speaker at the first congress of the Union of Soviet Writers in 1934 was the widely respected writer Maxim Gorky, a long-time supporter of the Bolshevik party, who became at this time an intermediary between Stalin and the literary intelligentsia (Kemp-Welch 1991: 127). In his speech Gorky attacked what he called 'critical realism': a term he used to describe the kind of realism which was typical of nineteenth-century literature. Its weakness, he said, was its tendency to accentuate the negative. Writers, he famously declared, should regard themselves as 'engineers of the soul'; their task was not so much to describe reality, but to participate in the task of transforming it for the better.

Document 12.3 'Engineers of the Soul'

It should be realized that critical realism originated as the individual creation of 'superfluous people', who, being incapable of the struggle for existence, not finding a place in life, and more or less clearly realizing the aimlessness of personal being, understood this aimlessness merely as the senselessness of all phenomena in social life and in the whole historical process.

Without in any way denying the broad, immense work of critical realism, and while highly appreciating its formal achievements in the art of word painting, we should understand that this realism is necessary to us only for throwing light on the survivals of the past, for fighting them, and extirpating them . . .

The proletarian state must educate thousands of first-class 'craftsmen of culture', 'engineers of the soul'. This is necessary in order to restore to the whole mass of the working people the right to develop their intelligence, talents and faculties – a right of which they have been deprived everywhere else in the world. This aim, which is a fully practicable one, imposes on us writers the need of strict responsibility for our work and our social behaviour. This places us not only in the position, traditional to realist literature, of 'judges of the world and men', 'critics of life', but gives us the right to participate directly in the construction of a new life, in the process of 'changing the world'. The possession of this right should impress every writer with a sense of duty and responsibility for all literature, for all the aspects in it which should not be there.

Source: Robert Daniels, A Documentary History of Communism, *vol. 1, 1985, pp. 246–7.*

In many of the best-known socialist realist novels, there is an 'archetypal plot': a hero emerges from among the people; his 'spontaneity' is tempered by the 'consciousness' of the party; and, guided in the right direction, he leads his comrades to greater successes in the construction of socialism (Hosking 1990: 222–3). Furthermore, socialist realism required that the artist appeal to the masses, and avoid any work that could be considered elitist. To the extent that generalisation is possible, and socialist realism was a very flexible literary-political doctrine, socialist realism was a conservative artistic trend which presented a conventional view of reality in narrative form, and which at the same time reflected the viewpoint of the state. Experimentalism was frowned upon and condemned as 'formalistic'. Socialist realist principles came to apply to all spheres of cultural life. There were Unions of Artists, Film Workers, Architects, etc.

The turn to conservative principles is well illustrated in the field of architecture. In February 1931, the Soviet government launched a competition for the design of a so-called Palace of Soviets, a vast building designed to host mass assemblies and congresses. Stalin eventually chose a design by Boris Iofan, which combined classicism with elements of Art Deco, thus launching the 'retrospectivist' movement in Soviet architecture, and the final version of which was approved in February 1934. The palace was to have a 1,250-foot tower, and a 300-foot tall figure of Lenin on the top. It was a design which met with outrage amongst certain Western modernist architects, who saw in it a return to establishment architecture (Cooke 1993: 96). The grandiose palace was to be constructed near the Kremlin in the place of the Cathedral of Christ the Saviour, which was demolished in 1931. The foundations were laid, but the Second World War intervened, and it was never built.

Document 12.4   Final Project for the Palace of Soviets

[See page 191]

Source: David King, The Commissar Vanishes, *1997, p. 155.*

The clampdown on ideologically unreliable intellectuals was coordinated at the highest level. The case of theatre director Vsevolod Meyerhold, whose work exemplifed the 'naturalism' of the Stanislavsky stage tradition, is an example. The following document shows the way in which preparations were made for the closure of Meyerhold's theatre and his arrest. P. Kerzhentsev, chairman of the All-Union Committee on the Arts, sent the following letter and enclosures to Stalin and Molotov. The draft essay for *Pravda* was published on 17 December 1937.

Document 12.5   The Meyerhold Case

11 December 1937
SECRET

The All-Union Committee on the Arts of the SNK SSSR directs Your attention to the draft resolution to close down the Meyerhold Theatre.

The theatre's latest production of Gabrilovich's play 'One Life' (based on N.Ostrovsky's novel, *How the Steel was Tempered*) revealed completely that the

[Document 12.4]

theatre, as a result of its depraved line, has come to a political and creative deadend, is not in a condition to produce Soviet realistic shows and is a renegade in the family of Soviet theatres.

I attach

a) A draft resolution.
b) A draft order of the Committee.
c) A draft essay for *Pravda*. . . .

[Attachment b]

The Meyerhold Theatre in the course of all its existence was unable to free itself from the formalistic positions which are foreign to Soviet art and did not have a clear political line.

The ideological content of plays was here and there distorted to appease leftist trickery and formalistic vagaries. Many of the plays gave a distorted, slanderous presentation of Soviet reality . . .

Seeing that the Meyerhold Theatre, which has shown that it is unwilling and incapable of creating a Soviet repertoire and decisively freeing itself from formalistic errors, is alien and unnecessary for the Soviet land, it is imperative to close it down and to distribute the theatre's troupe to other theatres of Moscow and the periphery . . .

[Attachment c]

In its first essays on formalism *Pravda* especially spoke of the formalistic errors of V. Meyerhold, but he reacted to this criticism, as is usual, with a lack of seriousness and sense of responsibility . . . He did not correct his formalistic distortions in the plays of the current repertoire, and the production celebrating twenty years of the October revolution was permeated with mistakes of a formalistic and crudely naturalistic character . . .

P.Kerzhentsev

Source: T.M. Goriaeva (ed.), Istoriia sovetskoi politicheskoi tsenzury, *1997, pp. 75–81.*

Meyerhold was arrested in 1939 following a public refusal to accept the doctrine of socialist realism, and shot in February 1940.

Another figure who was accused of formalism was the composer Dmitri Shostakovich. In January 1936, Stalin attended a performance of Shostakovich's opera *Lady Macbeth of Mtsensk.* Two days later, an editorial in *Pravda* appeared, reputedly written by Politburo member Andrei Zhdanov, in which the work was criticised for its dissonance and vulgarity (see Fitzpatrick 1992: 187–8). Shostakovich, under pressure to denounce his 'formalistic' tendencies, recanted. He expressed his penitence by writing his Fifth Symphony, which premièred in Moscow in November 1937, and was subtitled 'a Soviet artist's reply to just criticism'. At the time, the work was very well received. Its final movement concluded with an heroic flourish, which could easily be interpreted as a celebration of Soviet achievements. However, in his *Testimony* of 1979, edited by Solomon Volkov, Shostakovich is quoted as saying that in reality the conclusion expressed just the opposite meaning: it was a forced celebration. He refers to the Seventh Symphony, first performed during the siege of Leningrad, in the same way, suggesting that its finale should not be understood as triumphant.

Document 12.6   Shostakovich on his Fifth and Seventh Symphonies

I think that it is clear to everyone what happens in the Fifth. The rejoicing is forced, created under some threat, as in *Boris Godunov*. It's as if someone were beating you with a stick and saying, 'Your business is rejoicing, your business is rejoicing' and you rise shakily, and go marching off muttering, 'Our business is rejoicing, our business is rejoicing.'

What kind of apotheosis is that? You have to be a complete oaf not to hear that. Fadeyev heard it, and wrote in his diary, for his personal use, that the finale of the Fifth is irreparable tragedy. He must have felt it with his Russian alcoholic soul.

People who came to the première of the Fifth in the best of moods wept. And it's ridiculous to speak of a triumphal finale in the Seventh. There's even less basis for that, but nevertheless, the interpretation does appear.

Source: Dmitri Shostakovich, Testimony, *1979, p. 140.*

There has been some doubt about the reliability of Volkov's version of Shostakovich's memoirs. Too easily, they give the impression that Shostakovich always harboured dissident attitudes. The reality was more ambiguous (Taruskin 1995: 46). Nevertheless, there is independent memoir evidence that Shostakovich did see the Fifth and Seventh symphonies as in some way an attack on Soviet totalitarianism (Wilson 1995: 159).

Shostakovich's argument that his work really involved a criticism of Soviet power illustrates the way in which artists were sometimes trying to play a 'game' with the state. A piece of work could be read at more than one level. Such ambiguity became a feature of post-Stalinist Soviet literature (see Shlapentokh 1990: 65).

Eisenstein's work also illustrates something of this 'game'. *October* (see Document 2.3) was unashamedly pro-Soviet. Likewise, *Alexander Nevsky* (1938), a celebration of the great tsar's victory over Mongol and German invaders, was a contribution to the cult of great leaders. During the Second World War, Stalin asked Eisenstein to shoot a film of *Ivan the Terrible*. The first part of the film was released in 1942, and portrayed Ivan as a sort of heroic early version of Stalin: a great tsar forced to consolidate the Russian state against internal and external enemies. Part II (1944), however, was much more complex: Ivan was presented as a dark figure, surrounded by his sinister political police, the *oprichniki*. Apparently, after years of subservience, Eisenstein decided to make a moral criticism of the regime. Certainly, he later commented that this had been his intention. In the following document, which is the account of a conversation he had with a colleague, Iosif Ilyich Yuzovsky, he claims to have been influenced by *Boris Godunov*, a play by Alexander Pushkin which portrayed a king struggling with his conscience. Stalin, when he watched the film with Beria, expressed his dislike of the film, and it was not released.

Document 12.7   Eisenstein on Ivan the Terrible, Part II

'I've even heard that, as an intellectual, I couldn't manage without the Hamlet tradition – I've dragged myself in, not Ivan.'

'There is a tradition, but it's not Hamlet.'

Eisenstein's face became extremely serious. His eyes seemed to be piercing into me. 'So you think there's some kind of tradition here?'

'I even think I know which one . . . '

'Well, tell me . . . but briefly . . . no, it's impossible!'

'Boris Godunov.'

Eisenstein burst out laughing and then crossed himself. 'Lord, can you really see it? I'm so happy, I'm so happy! Of course it's Boris Godunov: "Five years I have governed in peace, but my soul is troubled . . . " I couldn't make a film like that without Russian tradition, without that great Russian tradition, the tradition of conscience. Violence can be explained, legalised, validated, but it cannot be justified. If you are a human being, it must be atoned. The destruction of one man by another: I say yes, but, whoever I am, I find it painful, because man is the highest value. Violence is not an end, and the joy lies not in achieving that end – as it did for other classes, epochs, states . . . even peoples. The Russian will know no mercy in his just anger, but the blood he sheds will bring bitterness to his heart. To say otherwise would be to debase the nation, the human race and the great idea of socialism. This, in my view, is the most stirring tradition of the people, the nation, and the literature . . . '

Source: Leonid Kozlov, 'The Artist and the Shadow of Ivan', in R. Taylor and D. Spring (eds), Stalinism and Soviet Cinema, *1993, p. 130.*

Much has been made of the parallels between Stalin's rule and the autocratic leadership of certain Russian tsars. Eisenstein's reference to *Boris Godunov* is an indication of the influence during the Stalin era of another Russian tradition which had been very influential in nineteenth-century Russian literature: the emphasis on 'conscience'.

Artists like Eisenstein and Shostakovich faced a terrible dilemma: they could compromise with the regime and continue to work, or express their opinions openly and lose the possibility of producing anything. How hard this was to deal with is illustrated by the recently released documentation of the case against the prominent short-story writer, Isaac Babel, author of *Red Cavalry* (1920). Babel was arrested in 16 May 1939. During a series of interrogations, he confessed to being a spy and being involved in anti-Soviet Trotskyite activities. Furthermore he implicated a number of other writers in his confessions. However, during his last interrogation, Babel started to take back his testimony, declaring that he had lied and falsely implicated a number of people. He subsequently wrote three letters to the USSR Procurator General's Office, taking back aspects of his testimony, and expressing remorse for falsely accusing other writers of anti-Soviet behaviour. The following document is the third of those letters, and was written from Moscow's Butyrka prison on 2 January 1940.

Document 12.8 Babel Takes Back his Testimony

At the NKVD Inner Prison I wrote two appeals to the USSR Procurator General's Office, on 5 and 21 November 1939, stating that I had incriminated innocent people in my testimony. I do not know what has happened to these appeals. The idea that my testimony may not only not aid in ascertaining the truth but mislead the investigators causes me great torment. Apart from what I said in the deposition of 10 October, I also attributed anti-Soviet actions and tendencies to the writer I. Ehrenburg, to G. Konovalov, M. Feierovich,

L. Tumerman and O. Brodskaya and to a group of journalists . . . This is all lies, with no basis in fact. I know these people to be honest and loyal Soviet citizens. This slander was prompted by my own faint-hearted behaviour during the cross-examination.

Source: Vitaly Shentalinsky, The KGB's Literary Archive, *1995, pp. 66–7.*

Another writer who had a tense relationship with the authorities was Mikhail Bulgakov. In a personal call to Bulgakov in 1930, Stalin indicated enthusiasm for his work, and attended his play about the Russian Civil War, *The Day of the Turbins*, fifteen times during the 1930s. In spite of this apparent protection from Stalin, and evidence that he had a certain respect for Stalin, Bulgakov expressed open contempt for the regime in his great satirical novel, *The Master and Margerita*, which remained unpublished until long after his death in 1940. The hero of *The Master and Margerita* is a writer called the 'Master', who is working on a novel about Pontius Pilate.

Sections of the Master's account of Pilate's story are written into the text, and it is significant that, in Bulgakov's account, Pilate's moral dilemmas during the trial of Christ are not dissimilar to those faced by Soviet government and party members in the Stalin regime (Jones 1995: 123, 116). Most of the novel's action, however, takes place in contemporary Moscow, and revolves around the sinister visit to Moscow of a devil-figure, named Woland. At one point, after the Master has refused Woland's request to look at his novel on the grounds that he has destroyed it, Woland declares that 'manuscripts don't burn'. This phrase became famous decades later, in part because of the many manuscripts written during Stalin's time which were not published until years afterwards, some of them owing their existence to the careful filing system of the NKVD and KGB. Such texts included Bulgakov's own diary from the 1920s, which he had himself destroyed, and which emerged from the Lubianka archives at the end of the Soviet era (Shentalinsky 1995: 74–81). The phrase is an example of how a text can acquire a life and meaning of its own, detached from its original context.

Document 12.9   'Manuscripts Don't Burn'

'Let me have a look.' Woland stretched out his hand, palm uppermost.

'Unfortunately I cannot show it to you,' replied the master, 'because I burned it in my stove.'

'I'm sorry but I don't believe you,' said Woland. 'You can't have done. Manuscripts don't burn.'

Source: Mikhail Bulgakov, The Master and Margerita, *1984, p. 303.*

Some of the writings of Andrei Platonov, another great satirist, have only emerged for the first time with the opening of the KGB archives. Platonov lived safely through the Stalin years, but had difficulties with censors and publishers throughout his life. His famous novel of collectivisation, *The Foundation Pit*, was published for the first time in 1973, in the West. The novel was written in a strange, disjointed style, and its aim, according to one critic, was to illustrate the malevolent power of a 'language that has been severed from reality' (Chandler 1996: xv). Words functioned no longer to communicate thought, but as ritual formulae. The following paragraphs about the process of collectivisation, although the English translation can hardly do justice to the original Russian in this respect, highlight the absurd nature of some of the political rhetoric.

Document 12.10 Satirising the Process of Collectivisation

On the edge of the collective farm lay the Organizational Yard, and it was there that the activist and the other leading poor peasants instructed the masses; it was also where unproven kulaks were detained, along with a number of felonious members of the collective. Some of these had been confined to the Yard because they had succumbed to the petty mood of doubt, others because they had wept at a time of rejoicing and kissed their fenceposts as they were taken away into common ownership, yet others were there for some other reason, and finally there was one old boy – the watchman from the Dutch-tile factory – who had come breezing into the Orgyard on his way somewhere else and then been intercepted because of the alien look on his face . . .

The activist was also still in the Orgyard, the previous night had been wasted – no directives had descended on the collective farm and so he had initiated a stream of thought in his own head, but this had only made him feel terrified he might have overlooked something. He was afraid of letting things get out of hand, afraid that prosperity might build up in the homes of the private farmers and that he might be none the wiser. At the same time he was also worried about being overzealous – and this was why he had so far collectivized only the village horses, though he agonized over the various solitary cows, sheep and fowl, since in the hands of a rampant kulak even a goat could be a lever of Capitalism.

Source: Andrey Platonov, The Foundation Pit, *1996, pp. 94, 97.*

Platonov's work raises the question of how the Soviet experience affected the Russian language. After all, the most important continuity between the pre-revolutionary and Soviet eras was the common use of the same Russian language. After 1917, the regime itself frequently came to use words in a deliberately vague way, especially when terror was involved. It has been noted how, under Hitler, Nazi leaders played a kind of 'language game': phrases like 'shipped to the East' were euphemisms for 'execution' (Arendt 1994: 85). In the same way, phrases like 'anti-Soviet', 'kulak', 'enemies of the people' carried little hard content, and could be manipulated at will to mean whatever the regime wanted them to mean.

Platonov was never arrested. The poet Osip Mandelstam was not so fortunate. He was arrested in May 1934 for writing in 1933 an unflattering poem about Stalin which fell into the hands of the secret police. It was the main item of evidence used to convict Mandelstam, who spent the next four years in internal exile. The reference in the poem to the 'Ossete' relates to persistent rumours that Stalin was from North Ossetia, an autonomous republic in the north Caucasus.

Document 12.11   Osip Mandelstam on Stalin

We live, deaf to the land beneath us,
Ten steps away no one hears our speeches,

All we hear is the Kremlin mountaineer,
The murderer and peasant-slayer.

His fingers are fat as grubs
And the words, final as lead weights, fall from his lips,

His cockroach whiskers leer
And his boot tops gleam.

Around him a rabble of thin-necked leaders –
Fawning half-men for him to play with.

They whinny, purr or whine
As he prates and points a finger,

One by one forging his laws, to be flung
Like horseshoes at the head, the eye or the groin.

And every killing is a treat
For the broad-chested Ossete.

Source: Nadezhda Mandelstam, Hope Against Hope, *1975, p. 13.*

In May 1938, Mandelstam was arrested again, and subsequently sent to the labour camps in the Kolyma region, where he died in December 1938. On this occasion, the Union of Writers played an important role in informing on and even conspiring against him. The general secretary of the Union of Writers, V. Stavsky, wrote the following letter to Yezhov.

Document 12.12   Stavsky to Yezhov

HIGHLY CONFIDENTIAL
USSR Union of Soviet Writers, Board

People's Commissar of Internal Affairs

Comrade N.I. Yezhov
16 March 1938

Dear Nikolay Ivanovich,
Part of the literary world is very nervously discussing the problem of Osip Mandelstam.

As everyone knows, Osip Mandelstam was exiled to Voronezh 3–4 years ago for obscene libellous verse and anti-Soviet agitation. Now his term of exile had ended. At present he and his wife are living outside Moscow . . .

In practice he often visits his friends in Moscow, for the most part writers. They support him, collect money to help him, and make of him a figure of suffering, a brilliant and totally unrecognized poet. Valentin Kataev, I. Prut and other writers have openly defended him, and in outspoken terms.

In order to defuse the situation O.Mandelstam has been provided with support through the Litfond. But this does not resolve all the problems linked to O.Mandelstam.

It is not simply, or even primarily, a problem of the author himself, a writer of obscene, libellous verse about the leadership of the Party and of all the Soviet people. It is a question of the attitude of a group of notable Soviet writers to Mandelstam. I am writing to you, Nikolay Ivanovich, to seek your help.

Recently O. Mandelstam has written a number of poems. However, they are of no special value according to the collective opinion of comrades who I have requested to look at them . . .

With Communist greetings
V. Stavsky

Source: Vitaly Shentalinsky, The KGB's Literary Archive, *1993, p. 186.*

The Union of Writers was in effect an organ of censorship, and was thus part of a vast network of ideological control. The main direct organ of censorship was the Main Administration for Matters of Literature and Publishing (Glavlit), set up in 1922. Throughout the 1930s, Glavlit sought to increase its hold on all Soviet media outlets. The following document is from a report by Glavlit on its activities in 1939, and it illustrates the range of its influence.

Document 12.13   Description of the Work of Glavlit in 1939

3 March 1940
SECRET

In 1939, the organs of censorship dealt with the following: 7,194 newspapers, producing 898,418 editions, with a total print-run of 35,517,000 copies . . . ; 1,762 journals, totalling 83,035 typographical sheets, with a print-run of 268,590 copies during the year; 41,000 books, totalling 247,066 typographical sheets, with a print-run of about 600 million; all the materials of TASS; 92 broadcasting radio stations, 1,400 broadcasting radio centres with their own broadcasts; 2,357,803 postal packages of foreign literature; 70,000 libraries, from which the organs of Glavlit have removed politically harmful literature; 4,681 printing houses, whose production and output have been controlled in the light of what is produced by the presses. All this has been managed by the censorship apparatus, which totals 6,027 people, of whom 203 are in the leadership, 4,279 are censors (of them 2,199 also hold regional positions), and 545 are service personnel.

Source: T.M. Goriaeva (ed.), Istoriia sovetskoi politicheskoi tsenzury, *1997, p. 318.*

In spite of their public enthusiasm for the regime, it is likely that some members of the literary establishment were troubled about the way art became subservient to politics in the Soviet Union. An example of a man who was privately prone to disillusionment was Alexander Fadeev, head of RAPP and later the Union of Writers. Fadeev's novel *The Rout* (1927), featuring Red guerrilla detachments during the Civil War, was widely admired. Following the 20th Party Congress in February 1956, Fadeev committed suicide. In a final letter to the Central Committee, he expressed frustration at the way he had been turned into a functionary of the system, at the way artistic ideals were compromised during the Stalin era, and at the new literary establishment under Khrushchev.

Document 12.14   Fadeev's Suicide Note

13 May 1956

I do not see the possibility of going on living, since art, to which I have dedicated my life, has been ruined by the self-confidently ignorant leadership of the party, and can no longer now be repaired. The best cadres of literature . . . have been physically destroyed, or have perished thanks to the criminal connivance of those in power; the best people of literature died before their time . . .

Following Lenin's death, we were reduced to being little boys; we were crushed and ideologically frightened – and this was called the party spirit (*partiinost'*). And now, when all this could have been put right, we get the primitiveness and ignorance of those . . . who ought have been able to put it right. Literature has been put in the hands of untalented, small-minded and rancorous people . . .

I was turned into a carthorse. All my life I have trudged under the load of innumerable, dull, unwarranted bureaucratic tasks which could have been done by anyone. And even now, looking back on my life, it is unendurable to recall all the shouts, reproofs, lectures, and sermons about ideological vices which have fallen on me, – a person of whom our wonderful people should have rightly been proud in view of the inner authenticity and humility of his communist talent . . .

The complacency of those who are abandoning the great Leninist teaching, even when they bow down before it, has brought me to a complete lack of confidence in them, for we can expect worse of them than of the satrap of Stalin . . .

My life as a writer has lost its sense, and it is with the greatest joy, as a release from this rotten existence, where baseness, lies and slander fall on one, that I leave this life.

Source: A.F. Kiseleva, et al., (eds), Khrestomatiia po otechestvennoi istorii, *1946–1995, 1996, p. 471–2.*

A well-known known literary description of the terror is Anna Akhmatova's poem of 1940, in which she describes the time when she stood in line over many weeks, in order to send a food parcel to her son. The poem was subsequently included in her poem *Requiem* (1957). Like her friend Lydia Chukovskaya's book, *The Deserted House* (see Document 5.14), it captures the bleakness and unhumanity of the purges in a moving way.

Document 12.15   Akhmatova on the Purges

In the terrible years of the Yezhovshchina, I spent seventeen months in the prison queues in Leningrad. Somehow, one day, someone 'identified' me. Then a woman standing behind me, whose lips were blue with cold, and who, naturally enough, had never even heard of my name, emerged from that state of torpor common to us all and, putting her lips close to my ear (there, everyone spoke in whispers), asked me:

– And could you describe *this?*
And I answered her:
– I can.

Then something vaguely like a smile flashed across what once had been her face.

1 April 1957
Leningrad . . .

Epilogue

The hour of remembrance draws near.
Once more I hear, I feel, I see you here:

You, whom to the window they barely led,
you, who this earth no longer tread,

And you who, shaking your beautiful head,
Came here as though home, you said.

I would like to name each one in turn,
But they've taken the list; there's nowhere to learn.

From the poor words you used, which I overheard,
I have woven for you a burial shroud.

I shall remember them everywhere, always,
I shall not forget them come fresh evil days,

And if they shut my tortured mouth,
Through which a hundred million shout,

Then may you too remember me
On the eve of my remembrance day.

If they think someday in this country
To raise a monument to me,

To this solemn gesture I consent
But with the condition that it be put

Not by the sea where I was born
(My last bond with the sea is torn),

Nor in the park by the hallowed tree
Where an inconsolable shade seeks me,

But here where three hundred hours and more
I stood and no one unlocked the door.

Because even in blessed death I'm afraid
I'll forget the noise black Marias made

And the ugly way the door slammed shut
And the old woman's howl like a beast that was hurt.

And from my motionless bronze lids
May the thawing snow stream down like tears

And the prison dove coo from afar
And the boats go quietly down the Neva.

1940
March

Source: Anna Akhmatova, Selected Poems, *1971, pp. 152–3; epilogue in* Lydia Chukovskaya, The Akhmatova Journals. Vol. 1, 1938–41, *1994, pp. 225–6.*

The state's hostility to artistic freedom continued after the war, and disappointed those who had hoped that the relative freedom of the war years would pave the way for a new post-war settlement. In 1946, two Leningrad literary journals, *Zvezda* and *Leningrad* were attacked by the authorities for liberal tendencies; the latter of them was closed down altogether. In particular, Akhmatova and the short story writer, Mikhail Zoshchenko were the targets of the regime's displeasure. Once again, it was emphasised that literary works should be judged according to political criteria. In a resolution of 14 August 1946, the Central Committee stated its views.

Document 12.16 The Clampdown on *Zvezda* and *Leningrad*

Zvezda committed a crude error in granting a literary rostrum to the writer Zoshchenko, whose works are alien to Soviet literature . . . The most recent of Zoshchenko's published tales, 'The Adventures of a Monkey,' . . . is a vulgar lampoon of Soviet life and Soviet people . . .

Zvezda has also been popularizing in every possible way the productions of the writer Akhmatova . . . Akhmatova is a typical representative of the sort of empty poetry, lacking in moral content, which is alien to our people . . .

The leading workers on these journals, and primarily their editors . . . have forgotten that our journals, whether scientific or artistic, cannot be apolitical . . .

[A]ny doctrine which is devoid of moral content and apolitical, any 'art for art's sake', is alien to Soviet literature, is damaging to the interests of the Soviet people and state, and should have no place in our journals.

The insufficient moral awareness of the leading workers of *Zvezda* and *Leningrad* also led these persons to base their relations with literary figures not on the interests of the correct education of Soviet people or of the political guidance of the activities of these literary figures, but on personal interests – interests of friendship . . .

[P]ublication of the journal, *Leningrad*, is to cease, and the literary forces of Leningrad are to be concentrated around *Zvezda* . . .

Comrade A.M. Egolin is appointed editor-in-chief of *Zvezda* and will retain his position as deputy-chief of the VKP(b) Central Committee Propaganda Administration.

Source: Robert McNeal (ed.), Resolutions and Decisions of the Communist Party of the Soviet Union. Vol. 3 The Stalin Years: 1929–1953, *1974, pp. 240–2.*

The totalitarian aspirations of the Soviet regime involved a battle to ensure that only one will was at work in the country. In some ways, the most politically subversive contribution to literature during Stalin's time was the apparently apolitical literary criticism of Mikhail Bakhtin. In the 1920s, Bakhtin was associated with attempts to develop a Marxist theory of consciousness. However, his relationship with Marxism has been a matter of controversy. Although he believed that consciousness is formed in a social context, he never accepted a rigid Marxist framework. Furthermore, he embraced plurality. In his *Problems of Dostoevsky's Art* of 1929, he argued that the distinctive feature of Dostoevsky's work was the absence of a dominant authorial voice, and instead the presence of a polyphony of equally-weighted voices, of whom the author's was just one. In his essay 'Discourse in the Novel' (1935), Bakhtin wrote that there is a multiplicity of discourses ('heteroglossia') present within any unitary language. Bakhtin's work was to become one of the dominant influences of twentieth-century literary criticism.

Document 12.17 Bakhtin's 'Discourse in the Novel'

Unitary language constitutes the theoretical expression of the historical processes of linguistic unification and centralization, an expression of the centripetal forces of language. A unitary language is not something given [*dan*] but is always in essence posited [*zadan*] – and at every moment of its linguistic life it is opposed to the reality of heteroglossia . . .

A common unitary language is a system of linguistic norms . . . [These are] the generative forces of linguistic life, forces that struggle to overcome the heteroglossia of language, forces that unite and centralize verbal-ideological thought, creating within a heteroglot national language the firm, stable linguistic nucleus of an officially recognized literary language . . .

But the centripetal forces of the life of language, embodied in a 'unitary language', operate in the midst of heteroglossia. At any given moment of its evolution, language is stratified not only into linguistic dialects in the strict sense of the word . . . , but also . . . into languages that are social-ideological: languages of social groups, 'professional and 'generic' languages, languages of generations and so forth . . . And this stratification and heteroglossia, once realized, is not only a static invariant of linguistic life, but also what ensures its dynamics . . .

The living utterance, having taken meaning and shape at a particular historical moment in a socially specific environment, cannot fail to brush up against thousands of living dialogic threads, woven by socio-ideological consciousness around the given object of an utterance, it cannot fail to become an active participant in social dialogue. After all, the utterance arises out of this dialogue as a continuation of it and as a rejoinder to it . . .

The word is born in dialogue as a living rejoinder within it; the word is shaped in dialogic interaction with an alien word that is already in the object . . .

One's own discourse and one's own voice, although born of another or dynamically stimulated by another, will sooner or later begin to liberate themselves from the authority of the other's discourse.

Source: Mikhail Bakhtin, The Bakhtin Reader, *1994, pp. 89, 93–4.*

Implicit in Bakhtin's theory is the idea that a successful novel treats language as 'contested, contestable, and contesting'. It is an approach in which the didactic novel has no place (Morson and Emerson 1990: 314). Measured against such a theory, the very idea of a 'socialist realist novel' is a contradiction in terms.

The problem of ends and means

The sufferings inflicted on people by Stalinism and Nazism are not easy to explain. The contempt for human life revealed by those in power was extraordinary. The First World War, followed by Stalinism and Nazism, made the Enlightenment belief that people are essentially rational and reasonable difficult to maintain. The labour camps and the Holocaust force historians to grapple with the question of how individuals, and sometimes communities and nations, can allow themselves to support, or turn a blind eye to denunciation, deportation and genocide.

One way of exploring such questions is to ask how a society loses its sense of conscience or humanity. Throughout his biography of Stalin, Volkogonov refers to the repeated failure of those who carried out Stalin's orders to exercise their consciences; 'in such people conscience had "gone cold"' (Volkogonov 1991: 581). How, then, does the conscience of a person, party or people deteriorate? An alternative question involves asking what are the roots of European humanism, and why did the humanistic tradition prove so fragile. In discussing this theme, Nadezhda Mandelstam, wife of the poet (see Document 12.11) suggested in her memoirs that the best of the European cultural inheritance was replaced in the nineteenth century by a shallow humanism, and that this had given rise to the horrors of the twentieth century. Nadezhda Mandelstam emphasises the way in which a language, containing words built up over many generations, is the conveyor of humanistic values, and how poets, like builders, construct new visions out of the linguistic inheritance they receive. The phrase 'basic word stock' in the following extract is directly taken from Stalin's essay 'Marxism and Questions of Linguistics' (1950). Nadezhda Mandelstam clearly believed that Russia's fate in the twentieth century was tied to the overall development of contemporary European culture.

Document 13.1   Origins of European Culture

The memory of any 'builder' is a storehouse of materials used by his predecessors: their discoveries, their signs and symbols. This is how poets carry on 'the conversation begun before us' – to use Pasternak's phrase for their response to each other that knows no bounds of time and space. As transformed in the mind of the new 'builder', such borrowed elements help to bring out his purely personal feelings, thoughts, and experiences.

For [Osip Mandelstam] . . . , the original unity of the Judaeo-Christian world was far more real than its subsequent division. He saw the Mediterranean, to which he was so drawn, as a blend of Christian-Judaic with Hellenic culture . . .

The ideas at the basis of European culture and the Christian world are a priceless inheritance, like the vocabulary of the language we speak. There are always attempts to limit us to a 'basic word stock' and tawdry rationalist notions strained through the sieve of ideology. These notions were formed out of the detritus of humanism in the second half of the nineteenth century. As a result of secularization, humanism was debased and turned inside out during the twentieth century.

Source: Nadezhda Mandelstam, Hope Abandoned, *1976, p. 620–2.*

There is much debate among historians about whether it is legitimate to make moral judgments about history. Many believe that historians should seek to understand the past in all its complexity, rather than make moral judgments about it. The task of the historian is not to be a moralist (Ward 1999: 264–5). At the same time, factual judgments and value judgments are not always easy to distinguish, and there is some debate as to whether to understand events and to pass judgment on them are really different cognitive processes (Andrle 1992: 39). The challenge to remain detached, without seeming to justify terror and violence, is one which tests the historian of any turbulent epoch. In this area, the study of Nazi Germany has been permeated by discussions very similar to those concerning the Stalin regime (see Kershaw 1993: 180–96).

Some of Solzhenitsyn's analysis assumes a moral argument: the escalation of terror after 1917 can be explained by the fact that the Bolsheviks, in using violence to establish their rule, crossed certain moral boundaries. In his Nobel Prize speech of 1970, he argued that there is a dynamic relationship between violence and lies.

Document 13.2   Violence and Lies

Anyone who has once proclaimed that violence is his method is inevitably forced to choose the lie as his guiding principle. At its birth violence acts openly, is even proud of itself. But it has scarcely established itself when it feels the air around it becoming more rarified, and it cannot continue to exist without masking itself with the lie and wrapping itself up in its honied rhetoric. Violence does not always necessarily take you physically by the throat and strangle you: more often it merely demands of its subjects that they declare allegiance to the lie, become accomplices in the lie.

Source: Alexander Solzhenitysn, One Word of Truth, *1972, pp. 26–7.*

There can be little doubt that the widespread use of terror under Lenin and Stalin was partly due to a radical interpretation of the doctrine that 'the end justifies the means'. Lenin firmly believed that means should be subordinated to ends (see Lovell 1984: 18); he rejected absolute moral values in favour of the subordination of ethics to the interests of the proletariat. On 2 October 1920, speaking at the third All-Russian Congress of the Russian Komsomol, Lenin outlined his own understanding of morality.

Document 13.3   Lenin on Morality

Is there such a thing as Communist morality? Of course, there is. It is often made to appear that we have no ethics of our own; and very often the bourgeoisie accuse us Communists of repudiating all ethics. This is a method of shuffling concepts, of throwing dust in the eyes of the workers and peasants.

In what sense do we repudiate ethics and morality?

In the sense that it is preached by the bourgeoisie, who derived ethics from God's commandments. We, of course, say that we do not believe in God, and that we know perfectly well that the clergy, landlords and the bourgeoisie spoke in their own interests as exploiters. Or instead of deriving ethics from the commandments of morality, from the commandments of God, they derived them from idealist or semi-idealist phrases, which always amounted to something very similar to God's commandments.

We repudiate all morality derived from non-human and non-class concepts. We say that it is a deception, a fraud, a befogging of the minds of the workers and peasants in the interests of the landlords and capitalists.

We say that our morality is entirely subordinated to the interests of the class struggle of the proletariat. Our morality is derived from the interests of the class struggle of the proletariat . . .

When people talk to us about morality, we say: for the Communist, morality lies entirely in this compact, united discipline and conscious mass struggle against the exploiters. We do not believe in an eternal morality, and we expose all the fables about morality.

Morality serves the purpose of helping human society to rise to a higher level and to get rid of the exploitation of labour.

Source: V. Lenin, Selected Works, *vol. 2, 1947, pp. 667, 670.*

It is easy to see how such a philosophy could be used to justify any policy that the party felt to be expedient. The execution of 'enemies of the people', it could be argued, if it was in the name of the proletariat, was thoroughly legitimate; indeed, if coercion was going to produce a better set of social and political structures, it was essential to use it. Certainly, it became fashionable after 1917 to argue that violence was both politically necessary and an inevitable product of class divisions.

A literary attempt to describe the radical utilitarianism of Stalinism occurs in Arthur Koestler's novel *Darkness at Noon* ([1940] 1985). The hero of the novel was N.S. Rubashov, whom Koestler conceived of as a synthesis of certain show trial victims, and who has been likened to Bukharin. Koestler's hero is an archetypal figure: the representative of a state which does not respect individual rights, but who has now become one of its victims. The reference to Machiavelli in the following extract touches on the persistent rumour that Stalin, like Lenin, was an admirer of the Italian writer (Conquest 1992: 64–5).

Document 13.4   Darkness at Noon

It is said that No. 1 has Machiavelli's *Prince* lying permanently by his bedside. So he should: since then, nothing really has been said about the rules of political ethics. We were the first to replace the nineteenth century's liberal ethics of 'fair play' by the revolutionary ethics of the twentieth century. In that also we were right, a revolution conducted according to the rules of cricket is an absurdity. Politics can be relatively fair in the breathing spaces of history; at its critical turning points there is no other rule possible than the old one, that the end justifies the means. We introduced neo-Machiavellianism into this century . . . We were neo-Machiavellians in the name of universal reason, that was our greatness . . .

For us the question of subjective good faith is of no interest. He who is in the wrong must pay; he who is in the right will be absolved. That is the law of historical credit; it was our law . . .

I have thought and acted as I had to; I destroyed people whom I was fond of, and gave power to others I did not like. History put me where I stood; I have exhausted the credit which she accorded me; if I was right I have nothing to repent of, if wrong, I will pay . . .

No. 1 has faith in himself, tough, slow, sullen, and unshakeable. He has the most unshakeable anchor-chain of all. Mine has worn thin in the last few years . . .

The fact is: I no longer believe in my infallibility. That is why I am lost.

Source: Arthur Koestler, Darkness at Noon, [1940] *1985, p. 81.*

Through these kind of arguments, it became fashionable to state that violence was both right and inevitable. Political objectives came to override individual rights. Stalin certainly regarded individuals as means to political ends. At a Kremlin reception of 25 June 1945, he famously proposed a toast to *'vintiki'*, which literally means 'screws' or 'nuts and bolts', and is often translated as 'cogs'. Although the speech was intended to pay tribute to ordinary people, it suggests that Stalin ultimately did see individuals as cogs in a giant machine. Certainly, many Soviet citizens did not forgive him for the phrase (R.W. Davies 1989b: 81):

Document 13.5   'Vintiki'

Do not think I will say anything unusual. I have the simplest and most ordinary of toasts. I would like to drink to the health of people who have few offices and whose status is unenviable. To people who are considered *'vintiki'* in the great state machine, but without whom we – marshals and commanders of fronts and armies –, speaking crudely, are not worth a tinker's cuss. If any 'vintik' ceases to work – it's the end. I propose a toast to simple, ordinary, modest people, to *'vintiki'*, who keep our great state machine in motion in all branches of science, economy and military affairs. There are very many of them, their name is legion, because there are tens of millions of them. They are modest people. No one writes about them, they have no high status and few offices, but they are the people who maintain us as the base maintains the summit. I drink the health of these people, our respected comrades.

Source: R.W. Davies, Soviet History in the Gorbachev Revolution, *1989b, p. 80.*

The idea that the 'end justifies the means' was widely propagated in Stalin's time and doubtless played some role in the population's readiness to use violence. People were bombarded with slogans that promised a radiant future and stated that present cruelties were the necessary price to pay for future happiness. The way in which such thinking was disseminated is illustrated by the following shot and sequence of dialogue from the film *Lenin in 1918* (1939), directed by Mikhail Romm. In a conversation with Lenin, Stalin, who is sitting with a young girl in his lap, observes that cruelty towards enemies is necessary for the sake of the girl's future.

Document 13.6 Screen Shot from *Lenin in 1918*

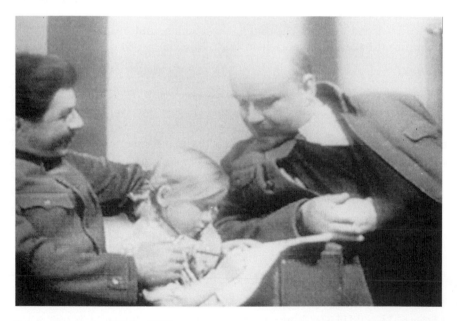

Source: Lenin in 1918, *1939.*

Document 13.7   Dialogue from *Lenin in 1918*

LENIN: Yes, it is a clear, very clear, very obvious truth: without severe repression of opposing classes, without an iron, no a steel (*stal'noi*) dictatorship, our revolution, and indeed any social revolution will inevitably perish.

STALIN: Look, Vladimir Il'ich [*pointing to the girl – editor*], for whose sake we must be merciless to our enemies. She will not live like us, but better than us.

LENIN: Better, better, better than us . . . We will not be envious of her . . . Our generation has succeeded in completing a work astonishing in its historical significance.

Source: Lenin in 1918, *1939*

The Russian population had for generations suffered at the hands of despotic leaders, and this to some degree gave rise to a passive attitude to arbitrary government. However, Soviet ideology itself reinforced such passivity. According to Nadezhda Mandelstam, the Soviet population succumbed to a belief in the idea of historical inevitability and the impotence of the individual in the face of social forces. She suggests that in the 1920s people began to exalt their own helplessness and inability to change things. They lost the inner freedom which makes it possible to affect the course of events.

Document 13.8   The Loss of a Sense of Responsibility

Everyone of us, to some degree or another, had a share in what happened, and there is no point in trying to disclaim responsibility. We may have felt utterly powerless, but at the same time, uncertain of what we had to defend, we were always only too quick to surrender. The fateful years were the twenties: it was then that people not only became convinced of their helplessness but even exalted it, learning to ridicule as old-fashioned, as a mark of backwardness, the very idea of intellectual, moral, or spiritual resistance. One could not, it was argued, hold out against the inevitable: the historical process was predetermined, as was the state of society . . .

A man possessed of inner freedom, memory, and a sense of fear is the blade of grass or wood chip that can alter the course of the swiftly flowing stream. It was cowardice that led to the horror we have lived through, and cowardice could easily plunge us back into it.

Source: Nadezhda Mandelstam, Hope Abandoned, *1976, pp. 191, 206.*

Another dimension of the question of 'ends and means' is the issue of 'lying'. There is some evidence to suggest that lying for political objectives became an acceptable part of Bolshevik political culture. Not all Bolsheviks approved of it, certainly. There were party members who were widely admired for their integrity (see Medvedev

1989: 429–30), even if they became fewer in number as Stalin consolidated his hold on power. However, even in the mid-1920s, it was generally accepted that to lie was sometimes necessary. The disillusioned Italian Communist, Ignazio Silone, writing in *The God that Failed* (1950), recalled a meeting of the Comintern Executive, in which those attending reacted with amusement to a British delegate who complained about the duplicity of a proposed course of action.

Document 13.9 'That Would be a Lie'

How can one separate the fatuous from the essential in the interminable discussions at [Comintern] congresses and meetings? What speeches should be left to the mice in the archives to criticize, and which should be recommended to intelligent people anxious to understand? I do not know. What my memory prefers to recall may to some people seem only bizarre. They were discussing one day, in a special commission of the Executive, the ultimatum issued by the central committee of the British trade unions, ordering its local branches not to support the Communist-led minority movement, on pain of expulsion. After the representative of the British Communist Party had explained the serious disadvantages of both solutions, because one meant the liquidation of the minority movement and the other the exit of the minority from the trade unions, the Russian delegate Piatnisky put forward a suggestion which seemed as obvious to him as Columbus' egg: 'The branches,' he suggested, 'should declare that they submit to the discipline demanded, and then, in practice, should do exactly the contrary.' The English Communist interrupted: 'But that would be a lie.' Loud laughter greeted this ingenuous objection, frank, cordial, interminable laughter, the like of which the gloomy offices of the Communist International had perhaps never heard before. The joke quickly spread all over Moscow, for the Englishman's entertaining and incredible reply was telephoned at once to Stalin and to the most important offices of State, provoking new waves of mirth everywhere.

Source: Ignazio Silone, The God that Failed, *1950, p. 109.*

How far this moral culture spread in the party is difficult to assess. One of the more controversial sources on the 1930s, 'The Letter of an Old Bolshevik', suggests that it became deeply entrenched. 'The Letter of an Old Bolshevik' was the purported account of a conversation between the Menshevik *émigré* historian, Boris Nicolaevsky, and Bukharin on Bukharin's visit to Paris in 1936. This document, long regarded as offering key insights into the Stalinist political system in the mid-1930s, came under fire during *perestroika* when Bukharin's widow suggested in her memoirs that the document had been a fabrication designed to destroy her husband (see Liebich 1992; Tucker 1992b). Nevertheless, for all its weaknesses, the document does offer a convincing insight into the atmosphere of the times. If Nicolaevsky is quoting Bukharin correctly, the opposition to Stalin had lost the kind of moral integrity that had characterised the pre-revolutionary opposition.

Document 13.10   The Letter of an Old Bolshevik

In former times, we 'politicals' used to observe a definite moral code in our relations with the rulers. It was regarded as a crime to petition for clemency. Anyone who did this was finished politically. When we were in jail or in exile, we refrained from giving the authorities any promise not to attempt to escape . . . But when it became necessary, under exceptional circumstances, to give such pledges, they were rigidly observed . . .

There is quite a different psychology nowadays. To plead for pardon has become a common phenomenon, on the assumption that since the party in power was 'my party', the rules which applied in Czarist days are no longer valid. One hears this argument everywhere. At the same time, it is considered quite proper to consistently deceive 'my party', since it does not fight its intellectual opponents by trying to convince them but by the use of force. This has given rise to a special type of morality, which allows one to accept any conditions, to sign any undertakings, with the premeditated intention not to observe them. This morality is particularly widespread among the representatives of the older generation of Party comrades . . .

This new morality has had a very demoralizing effect inside the ranks of the Oppositionists. The borderline between what is and what is not admissible has been completely obliterated, and many have fallen to downright treachery and disloyalty. At the same time, the new morality has furnished a convincing argument to those opposed to any *rapprochement* with the former Oppositionists, the argument being that it is impossible to believe them because they recognize in principle the permissability of telling lies.

Source: Boris Nicolaevsky, 'The Letter of an Old Bolshevik', Power and the Soviet Elite, 1965, p. 55.

These documents relate essentially to the party elite. However, it seems that, more widely, 'lying' became an essential component of the population's survival tactics. At least, that is how Nadezhda Mandelstam describes it in her memoirs.

Document 13.11   Everyday Lies

Should one lie? May one lie? Is it all right to lie in order to save someone? It is good to live in conditions where one doesn't have to lie. Do such conditions exist anywhere? We were brought up from childhood to believe that lies and hypocrisy are universal. I would certainly not have survived in our terrible times without lying. I have lied all my life: to my students, colleagues and even the good friends I didn't quite trust (this was true of most of them). In the same way, nobody trusted me. This was the normal lying of the times, something in the nature of a polite convention.

Source: Nadezhda Mandelstam, Hope Against Hope, 1975, p. 23.

The question of truth-telling and lying relates to the theme of 'subjectivity': how people's mentalities were constructed under Stalin. The assumption made by these writers is that people recognised that they were telling lies, and that they compartmentalised their lives into public and private spheres. It is doubtless true that many people understood their behaviour as a form of deceit. At the same time, the truth is more complex. Some prominent party leaders, it seems, interpreted their decision to conform, not as conscious deceit, but as a wilful choice to embrace the party line. This is illustrated by the case of G.L. Piatakov, the sixth person on Lenin's list of party leaders in his Testament, and associated with the Trotskyite wing of the party. In 1928, with the Trotskyites defeated, he repented of his mistakes, and was challenged by an associate, N. Valentinov, as to why he had changed his mind so quickly. Piatakov responded by stating that a Bolshevik should seek to submerge his personality in the party. His comments reveal the strength of the collectivist mindset in the Bolshevik party.

Document 13.12   Violence against Oneself

Bolshevism is a party which embraces the idea of bringing to life what is considered impossible, unrealisable and unattainable. It can do what to other natures, nonBolshevik natures, seems impossible. You say with surprise and reproach that I, having been excluded from the party, in order to get back into it, am ready for anything, ready to sacrifice my pride, self-respect and dignity . . . Evidently only out of a certain delicacy you did not say, but perhaps think, that the wish to return to the party as quickly as possible is inspired in me and others by a base wish to regain certain material benefits, comforts and privileges which were lost at our exclusion from the party. I agree that nonBolsheviks and in general categories of ordinary people cannot make a momentary change, revolution or amputation of their opinions. But real Bolshevik-communists are people of a special cast, a special type unlike anyone in history. *We are unlike anyone else.* We are a party consisting of people who make the impossible possible; imbued with the idea of violence, we direct *it against ourselves* and if the party demands it, if it is necessary or important, we can in an act of the will in 24 hours exclude certain ideas from our brains which we have held for years. This is absolutely incomprehensible to you, you are not in a condition to go out of your narrow 'I' and subject yourself to the severe discipline of the collective. But a real Bolshevik can do this. His personality is not confined to the limits of his 'I', but flows out in the collective which is called the party . . . Is this easy – this violent exclusion from the mind of what yesterday I considered true, but today, to be fully included in the party, I consider false? Of course not. Nevertheless, *through violence against oneself*, the necessary result is achieved . . . Such violence against oneself is keenly and painfully felt, but it is the act of resorting to this violence in order to break oneself and be in full agreement with the party that the *essence of a real ideological Bolshevik-communist*, who will to the end be linked to the party, comes out . . . [If the party requires it] *I will consider black what I considered and what seemed to be white, since for me there is no life outside the party, outside agreement with it.*

Source: N. Valentinov, 'Sut' bol'shevizma v izobrazhenii Iu.Piatakova', Novyi zhurnal, 1958, no. 52, pp. 151–3.

Learning to 'speak Bolshevik' (see Document 4.13) was not by definition a cynical exercise. Certainly, people rarely interpreted their adaptation to the new 'rules of the game' in terms of truth-telling and lying. The diary of Stepan Podlubnyi illustrates this fact. Podlubnyi came from a dekulakised Ukrainian peasant family, a fact which he concealed from the authorities until it was discovered in 1936. He had a deep sense of unease about his background. The first of the following two extracts suggests that he aspired to become a true believer. Unhappy with 'careerist' motivations for embracing the Stalinist system, he tried to refashion himself so that his private identity conformed to official Stalinist norms (Hellbeck 1996: 371). He wrote the second extract following the exposure of a work colleague as the son of a kulak. Nothing happened to the colleague, and Podlubnyi took this as an indication that he need no longer consider his own kulak background as a cause for shame, and that he could feel truly at home in the Soviet family.

Document 13.13   Believing in the System

1.6.1933 . . . Lately I've come to view my social work not as careerism, but as a system, as an intrinsic part of my body and existence, as the bread that is indispensable in order to exist, meaning not a struggle for existence, but a system that I willingly embrace. And with every day this continuity, this system, which is necessary for my organism, becomes stronger. I have noticeably reeducated myself from careerism to a system that is as necessary as food, to which I devote my time without any effort. That is good. I am happy about it.

2.3.1935 . . . This is a historical moment. Perhaps, from here on my new worldview will begin to emerge. The thought that I've been made a citizen of the common family of the USSR like everybody else obliges me to respond with love to those who have done this. I am no longer with the enemy, whom I fear all the time, every moment, wherever I am. I no longer fear my environment. I am just like everybody else, and therefore I have to be interested in various things, just like a master is interested in his farm, and not like a hireling towards his master.

Source: Jochen Hellbeck, 'The Diary of Stepan Podlubnyi, 1931–1939',
Jahrbücher für Geschichte Osteuropas, *1996, vol. 44, no. 4, pp. 359, 354.*

Podlubnyi's motivations are clearly complex, and, after his mother was arrested and accused of being a Trotskyite in 1937, his attitude to the system cooled considerably (Garros *et al.* 1995: 330). Yet, for or against the regime, he conceptualised his own identity in the terms set for him by the state. That the state could so strongly shape his self-understanding is an indication of its power.

Podlubnyi's desire to embrace public norms was in part motivated by a desire to belong. He wanted to be part of the predominant 'we' of his society. He saw the world in terms of 'insiders' and 'outsiders'. Social identity in Stalinist Russia was frequently understood in such terms. For example, it has been noted that the concepts of 'us' and 'them' were essential to how people saw themselves in the 1930s. Often, this was in terms of 'ordinary people' on the one hand ('workers', 'peasants', 'masses', etc.) and 'elites' on the other ('responsible workers', 'party members', 'new capitalists', etc.) (S. Davies 1997b: 80). Podlubnyi's worldview was his personal version of such an outlook (also on subjective identity under Stalin, see Vyleta 2000).

Podlubnyi's desire to overcome careerist attitudes suggests that for some people the Stalinist regime had partly come to represent selflessness and service: the higher moral values. This raises the possibility that people carried out party policy in the 1930s, because they had genuinely internalised Stalinist values. It was conscience rather than fear that was the motivation (see also Smith 1996: 48; Hosking 1990: 312–13). If this is true, then the Stalin regime's attempt to fashion a new Soviet man with a conscience that could be manipulated at will, must be accounted a success. Indeed, it must be counted one of the 'achievements' of totalitarian regimes that horrific acts were sometimes carried out in the name of conscience. If it is the case, it becomes difficult to divide the population neatly into victims and agents (see Hellbeck 1996: 346; also Document 7.21).

An alternative perspective on 'conscience' was provided by Vasily Grossman in his novel, *Forever Flowing*. Grossman was a Soviet journalist and novelist, who following the Second World War became increasingly disillusioned with the Soviet system (see Ellis 1994). His novel *Life and Fate* (1980) is an excellent introduction to life in the USSR during the Second World War. In *Forever Flowing*, which was very popular in samizdat in the late Soviet era, Grossman presents an example of a person's moral fragmentation (see also Todorov 1999: 141–57). He describes the return to Central Russia of Ivan Grigoryevich, after thirty years in the labour camps, following Stalin's death. During his visit to Moscow, Ivan Grigoryevich visits an old friend, Nikolai Andreyevich, who has gone on to build a distinguished scientific career. Ivan Grigoryevich's visit brings to the surface painful memories in Nikolai Andreyevich. Nikolai Andreyevich is prey to rapidly changing emotions: he first wishes to apologise to Ivan Grigoryevich for his cowardice, but he suddenly finds himself hating the man instead. He cannot remember things properly: he recalls the trial of Rykov and Bukharin to have taken place in 1937, rather than 1938. Ultimately, he is a person who has lost his integrity and cannot make an honest moral appraisal of his own past.

Document 13.14   The Disordered Conscience

For three decades Ivan had been shuttled about in prisons and camps. Nikolai Andreyevich, who always took pride in the fact that he had never made a declaration condemning and renouncing Ivan, had never once written to him. When Ivan had once written to Nikolai Andreyevich, Nikolai had asked his aged aunt to reply.

That used to seem natural; now suddenly it was a source of alarm and pangs of conscience.

He remembered a meeting that dealt with the 1937 trials, at which he had voted for the death sentence for Rykov and Bukharin . . .

After all, they had been publicly questioned by an educated, university man: Andrei Yanuaryevich Vyshinsky. After all, there had been no doubt about their guilt, not one shadow of doubt.

But now Nikolai Andreyevich remembered that there had been doubts. He had only pretended that there were none . . .

While waiting for Ivan, Nikolai Andreyevich, deeply moved, had thought how totally honest he would be with him, as he had been with no one else in his whole life. He would confess to Ivan all his pangs of conscience, set forth abjectly all his vile and bitter weakness . . .

But now, with Ivan there in front of him, he experienced a sudden turnabout of feeling. This man in a padded jacket, in soldier's shoes, his face eaten away by the cold of Siberia and the foul air of overcrowded camp barracks, struck him as alien, spiteful, hostile . . .

He burned with a desire to force Ivan to understand, to make quite clear to him that everything was different now, on a new footing, that all the old values had been wiped out, that Ivan himself was a failure, that his unhappy fate was not accidental, not just bad luck.

*Source: **Vasily Grossman**, Forever Flowing, 1997, pp. 33–4, 44–5.*

How representative of the wider party and intellectual elite is Nikolai Andreyevich's troubled conscience is difficult to assess. Nevertheless, it has been suggested that the Bolsheviks, after their initial enthusiasm for terror during the Civil War, eventually became ashamed and embarrassed by it. For example, after the Kronstadt rising in 1921, and during collectivisation, the regime constantly referred to its use of violence with 'evasion, euphemism, and denial' (Fitzpatrick 1999: 23; see also Document 12.10).

The question of 'conscience' goes beyond the realm of ordinary historical analysis: it is a metaphysical as well as an historical question as to whether a person's conscience is plastic and dependent on historical circumstances, or whether there is an essential moral core to the human being.

The capacity of people to lose their sense of identity and conscience was the main theme of Polish poet Czeslaw Milosz's book *The Captive Mind* ([1950] 1981). Milosz focused on the different ways in which Polish intellectuals came to rationalise their support for the pro-Soviet communist government which was set up in Poland after the Second World War. According to Milosz, dishonest compromise with the state led to a kind of intellectual captivity. For example, he observed that in the people's democracies of Eastern Europe, where people started to act out a role in order to preserve their social standing, they began to assume their new identities, and lost touch with their true selves (see also Walicki 1995: 489–91).

Document 13.15 'Acting in Daily Life'

Acting in daily life differs from acting in the theater in that everyone plays to everyone else, and everyone is fully aware that this is so. The fact that a man acts is . . . no proof of unorthodoxy. But he must act well, for his ability to enter into his role skillfully proves that he has built his characterization upon an adequate foundation. If he makes a passionate speech against the West, he demonstrates that he has at least 10 percent of the hatred he so loudly proclaims. If he condemns Western culture lukewarmly, then he must be attached to it in reality. Of course, all human behavior contains a significant amount of acting. A man reacts to his environment and is molded by it even in his gestures. Nevertheless what we find in the people's democracies is a conscious mass play rather than automatic imitation. Conscious acting, if one practices it long enough, develops those traits which one uses most in one's role, just as a man who became a runner because he had good legs develops his legs even more in training. After long acquaintance with his role, a man grows into it so closely that he can no longer differentiate his true self from the self he simulates, so that even the most intimate of individuals speak to each other in Party slogans. To identify one's self with the role one is obliged to play brings relief and permits a relaxation of one's vigilance. Proper reflexes at the proper moment become truly automatic.

Source: Czeslaw Milosz, The Captive Mind, *1981, pp. 55, 80–1.*

It seems that by encouraging people to participate in this ritual of 'acting', totalitarian regimes gained an inner psychological hold on people. As a scholar observed, the Stalin regime managed 'to coerce people *from within*' (Walicki 1995: 398–9).

The complexity of human motivations in Stalin's time is well illustrated by the sculpture of Khrushchev, which his family commissioned for his grave in the Novodevichy cemetery in Moscow. The sculpture was made by the dissident, Ernst Neizvestnyi, with whom Khrushchev had a famous argument about the merits of contemporary art. By constructing Khrushchev's image out of both black and white marble, Neizvestnyi presented Khrushchev as a deeply contradictory personality. Indeed, Khrushchev was complex. Although he was himself a product of the Stalinist system, he was the first to begin dismantling it. In his Secret Speech to the 20th Party Congress in 1956, he exposed many of Stalin's crimes, mainly blaming the 'cult of personality'; at the same time, he accepted the basic rightness of such policies as collectivisation, and made no mention of the negative aspects of Lenin's rule.

Document 13.16 Khrushchev's Contradictions

[See page 217]

Source: Nikita Khrushchev, Vospominaiia, *1997, between pages 416 and 417.*

[Document 13.16]

Violence, it can be argued, often has unintended consequences. It has been noted, for example, that whenever political institutions are destroyed by revolution, the new authorities have to rely on violence in order to maintain their power (Kissinger 1994: 655). The political impact of violence is a theme raised by Roy Medvedev in his exposure of Stalinism, *Let History Judge*. Medvedev, himself a Marxist who grew up in Stalin's time, had an ambivalent attitude to revolutionary violence: he sympathised with the October revolution and sought to distinguish Lenin's terror, which he regarded as necessary, from the Stalinist terror, which he condemned. His condemnation of Stalinist terror was not moral but political. By using violence on the population, the regime subsequently lost its capacity to act with popular support. This sums up one of the great dilemmas of the Stalinist state. Having been created with violence, it was extremely difficult to maintain it without fear and terror.

Document 13.17 'Vile Methods' and Popular Initiative

In the Soviet revolution there have been situations when extremely cruel methods had to be used, such as the shooting of the Tsar's family in Yekaterinburg, the sinking of the Black Sea Fleet, and the Red Terror in 1918. Still not all such methods are permissible. The revolutionary party must carefully study each concrete situation and decide which means will reach the goal at least cost and by the best route (not necessarily the quickest). Which methods should not be used in a given situation, and which should not be used in any situation, should also be determined . . .

A revolutionary party that uses vile methods inevitably loses the support of the people, and this in turn limits its possibilities of choosing methods that depend on mass action and popular initiative. Thus, vile methods are evidence of a party's weakness, not its strength. In any country a movement advocating communism must train honest, upright, and humane leaders, not sadists and cynics.

Stalin gave no thought to the problem of ends and means. To him, in the pursuit of his personal aims, all means were suitable, including the most inhumane. As a result the cause of socialism was dealt a horrendous blow.

Source: Roy Medvedev, Let History Judge, *1989, p. 672–3.*

Another perspective on this problem is provided by the Russian philosopher, Semyon Frank, who lived in emigration after 1922. Frank believed that the Russian revolutionary mentality contained a strange mixture of nihilism, moralism and utopianism (see Boobbyer 1995: 67). Writing from a religious perspective, Frank argued in his critique of utopian politics *The Light Shineth in Darkness*, first published in 1949, that the Bolsheviks tried to play God in human affairs. The function of law in a normal society should be protective, he declared; but utopian politicians frequently resorted to law in order to try to improve and transform the population, with desperate consequences.

Document 13.18 The Problem of Utopianism

The error of utopianism is based on the confusion of utterly heterogenous tasks or ideas: the hope for the conclusive transfiguration or salvation of the world, which in its essence surpasses all human powers and even lies outside the limits of the world's being . . . ; and the task of the establishment of the absolute fullness of the truth by the external organization of life, by the efforts of man . . .

History provides irrefutable empirical evidence of the fatal consequences of utopianism, of the fact that the striving to establish the kingdom of God on earth by external, human organizational measures not only turns out to be unattainable in practice, but inevitably leads to the diametrically opposed result, to the unchaining and triumph of the powers of evil, to the kingdom of hell on earth . . .

All utopians transfer the function of salvation to the law, to measures of state compulsion or, at best, moral compulsion – a function that, in essence, only the free powers of God's grace are capable of performing. Thus, the fatal consequences of the error of utopianism can be explained . . . by the fact that upon the law (the principle that in its essence has the task of the protection of the world from evil) is imposed the impossible task of the essential salvation of the world, a task that contradicts the true essence and function of the law. Since the law in its essence is incapable of performing this task, it is necessary, in a vain attempt to perform this task, to immeasurably intensify the force of the law, to have recourse to tyrannically harsh and despotic forms of the law, normalizing all aspects of human life.

Source: S.L. Frank, The Light Shineth in Darkness, *1989, pp. 166–8.*

The use of violence to build socialism surely had a real impact on Soviet history. It is difficult to avoid the conclusion that 'crime begets crime, and violence violence' (Malia 1994: 3), and thus that there was a certain moral logic to the development of events under Stalin. Such a universalist explanation must, of course, be put firmly in the context of the autocratic traditions of the Russian and Soviet state, long-term class antagonisms in Russia, and the radical utopianism of the Russian revolutionary tradition.

14 | Overview

Stalinism can partly be explained by the Soviet regime's search to catch up with and overtake the West. During the late Middle Ages, Russia had been isolated from Europe by Mongol occupation. When Russia freed itself from the Mongol yoke, and started to become a European power, it found that it lacked the technology and culture of the West. Furthermore, it was an undeveloped peasant society, embracing an enormous geographical expanse. The challenge was to change and modernise the country. Ivan the Terrible, Peter the Great, Catherine the Great, Alexander II, Witte, Stolypin – these leaders were all exercised with the problem of transforming this backward society. Defeats in the Crimean War and the First World War, as well as humiliation in the Russo-Japanese war, were a reminder of the price of failure. In 1917, the Bolsheviks inherited these traditional Russian preoccupations. Stalin thus belonged to a long line of Russian rulers who had to deal with the problem of Russia's development, and he was not alone in using the state to try and force society to embrace 'progress' more quickly. It is thus possible to understand Stalin's model of modernisation as having roots in traditional foreign policy considerations (Gerschenkron 1962: 148).

However, Russia's desire to catch up with the West was mixed with suspicion of the West. While Russian and Soviet rulers from Peter the Great onwards were fiercely impressed by Western technology and power, they were also concerned to define Russia against the West. Tsars like Nicholas I, Alexander III and Nicholas II defended their conservatism on the grounds that it was a defence against decadent Western liberalism. Suspicion of the West also pervaded the thinking of the emerging Russian intelligentsia in the nineteenth century. Slavophiles asserted that, rather than follow a Western pattern of development, Russia should pursue her own unique national calling. These suspicions continued under Soviet rule: for example, some of Stalin's rhetoric in the discussion of 'socialism in one country' in the 1920s contained strong anti-Westernism. The Soviet Union, Stalin declared, did not need the West, but could succeed on its own. Furthermore, while the Bolsheviks embraced the Marxist vision of a universal pattern of development, they also inherited Marx's ambivalent attitude to capitalism and his desire to see its destruction. Suspicion of the West thus came to be deeply embedded in the Bolshevik mentality; the West was the enemy against which Bolshevism defined its identity. It was thus an essentially 'reactive' identity: Soviet socialism, constructed as a protest against Western capitalism, was 'an anti-world to capitalism' (Kotkin 1995: 360).

To some degree, Bolshevik ideology grew out of the questions which exercised the Russian intelligentsia. More generally, however, it was one of the fruits of the age of ideologies which permeated Europe as a whole. It was an age in which visions of revolutionary transformation were widely popular. During the scientific revolution and the Enlightenment, European thinkers came to believe that a comprehensive understanding of the world could be achieved. Furthermore, they believed that if political and social structures were rationalised and mankind was re-educated, then a radical improvement of the world could be expected. Bolshevism was one of the fruits of that optimism, and although the Bolshevik ideology must now be seen as ill-conceived, the hopes that it engendered across the world should not be forgotten. Its flaw was that, like Marxism itself, it was ultimately a dualistic system of thought, combining a 'scientific' conception of history with a passion for justice and equality; terror and idealism could easily go together.

It was the combination of Russia's need for modernisation and the thinking of the Russian revolutionary intelligentsia which gave birth to the ideas of Bolshevism and eventually to Stalinism. It was to be an explosive mixture. The Russian philosopher, Sergei Bulgakov, writing in 1909, argued that the Russian revolutionary intelligentsia was imbued with a dangerous and false heroism; it was so preoccupied with changing the world that it lacked a sense of historical reality: 'The intelligentsia lives in an atmos- phere of expectation of a social miracle, of a universal cataclysm, in an eschatological frame of mind' (see Bulgakov 1977: 39). The validity of this kind of criticism of the Russian intelligentsia has been strongly debated; some historians have suggested that the Russian intelligentsia was too diverse to merit such sweeping criticism, and that its thinking reflected wider processes at work in Russian society (see Acton 1990: 97–106). These factors notwithstanding, Bulgakov's comments were prophetic of the Bolshevik caste of mind. Russian revolutionaries, both before 1917 and in power, were impatient with reality. Lenin's readiness to use terror as soon as he got into power was a reflection of that impatience, although his decision to introduce NEP and attempts to reform the party also suggest pragmatism and flexibility. There is little indication, however, that Stalin had a similar flexibility. He saw the world not as something to be accepted and worked *with*, but as material to work *upon* and to be changed. Stalin's 'revolution from above' had something of the character of the Russian intelligentsia's 'heroic' mindset.

The fact that Stalin was attempting to fulfil certain 'hero-roles' in his life (see Tucker 1974: 462–77) was not due exclusively to Bolshevik or Russian autocratic culture; it was also a feature of his own personality. Doubtless, he was a man with definite Marxist–Leninist convictions, and he justified his dictatorship on the grounds that it was necessary. Yet that was not the only thing that drove him. His personality itself seems to have been characterised by a constant and radical mistrust of the world. His policies carried the imprint of this, and as in a Shakespearean tragedy, his own flaws and frustrations were projected onto society at large. This is not to say that Soviet society of the 1930s was an exclusively Stalinist creation; it was much more complex than that. Yet, Stalin's personality was a crucial factor. His letters to Molotov reveal a man with an obsessive desire to check up on everybody around him. He was afraid of losing control, and he projected this fear onto the country he ruled. It is perhaps this fearfulness that gave some of his actions their impulsive and arbitrary quality (see Thurston 1996: 1–2). The case of Stalin suggests that the totalitarian and the impulsive dictator can exist easily in the same person: these two processes – the careful, systematic consolidation of political power and its arbitrary use – are fully compatible.

It is here that the weakness of the modernisation model of the Stalin regime lies. It does not take into account the biographical and political origins of Stalinism. It assumes that political considerations were ultimately subordinate to economic ones, that the mechanisms of supreme power evolved to support a particular model of economic change (Malia 1999: 390). However, it can also be argued that the essence of Stalinism is to be found not in the strategy of modernisation, but in the consolidation and nature of Stalin's dictatorship. All the evidence suggests that, while Stalin had a vision for transforming society and building socialism, he was also interested in the accumulation of power for its own sake. In this he was no different from Hitler and Mussolini. By 1933, a highly personalised system of decision-making had evolved in the Soviet Union, which allowed Stalin to bypass the formal political institutions (see Rees 1995a: 106–8). Power in the Soviet Union was centralised to an extraordinary degree. Although such a system of personalised rule was not new in history, new techniques of propaganda meant that the regime could aim to control the social psychology of the population in a way that was unprecedented. It was in the face of this mixture of highly centralised rule and psychological control that 'totalitarian' explanations of Stalinism acquired and have retained their enduring attraction.

The weakness of totalitarian explanations is that, while they offer a generally accurate description of the totality of Stalin's control over the mechanisms of central government, they do not do justice to the contradictions and inefficiencies of Stalin's rule. Except perhaps in his last declining years, Stalin had a firm grip on the levers of power and was central to all policy-making. Yet, that is not to say that all his decision-making was coherent. Indeed, the Stalin revolution was full of contradictions. The desire to imitate the Western industrial advance by telescoping an equivalent process of development into just a few years had certain consequences. Everything had to be done in a hurry, the Stalinists argued, otherwise it might be sabotaged by 'enemies'. This led to an outcome where, although policies were sometimes successful in the short term, they were frequently counterproductive in the long term. Stalinism was an attempt at an historical short-cut. It was the outcome of a desire to reap the fruits of civilisation without putting down roots first, and it led to certain systemic tensions which Stalin's successors had to try to unravel. There is a danger in rereading the history of the Stalin era in the light of the collapse of the Soviet Union in 1991. Nevertheless, it is also clear that many of the tensions which brought about the regime's collapse owed their existence to Stalin's policies.

The Stalin regime's 'successes' were in a quantitative sense very impressive – if one ignores the human costs that they entailed. The country was transformed. An urban, industrialised, educated society emerged out of a rural and backward one. At the time of Stalin's death, the USSR was a superpower capable of producing the atomic bomb and soon of sending men into space. Stalin, of course, was not solely responsible for this. Indeed, it could be argued that some of the intellectual and institutional foundations for these achievements were put in place before he came to power, indeed before the Soviet Union existed. Nevertheless, the Stalinist achievement was, in 'great power' terms, phenomenal: the Soviet Union became a global power with an ideology capable of attracting world-wide support. Beneath the surface, however, the achievements were fragile ones.

For all its quantitative successes, Stalinism as a system of government lacked the ability to embrace complexity. Policies were ill-conceived and impulsively introduced, and as a result usually had unintended consequences. Collectivisation, while it gave the state control over the peasantry, led to a stagnant agricultural sector, which was a profound burden on the Soviet leadership in subsequent decades. The Five Year Plans, while they provided the industrial base for victory in the Second World War, also involved the formation of a huge, unaccountable bureaucracy which proved a barrier to future change. Public ownership of wealth led to a population which was cynical with state property and had no compunction about stealing from the state. The suppression of the non-Russian nationalities and aspects of Russian culture led to deep-seated national grievances, which exploded into life when they were given a chance in the 1980s. Terror and propagandistic methods, while they helped to mobilise popular support for the regime in the short term, also deprived people of the intellectual freedom needed to question and reform the system. The deification of Soviet leaders and the party would ultimately lead to high levels of cynicism. Time and again, Stalinist policies led to consequences which were ultimately detrimental to the system itself. The more the Stalin regime forged ahead and achieved certain short-term successes, the more in the long term it laid the foundations for future stagnation, and the instability which would arise when reform was attempted.

Another major weakness of the Stalinist model of modernisation was that it was not accompanied by the development of sound political institutions. Just as Nicholas II's regime modernised, but refused to create institutions which could absorb the political interests created by the process, so also Stalin and his successors failed to integrate the Soviet population into the political process. They tried instead to buy the population's political subservience with stability and prosperity, and the party elite's support with privileges. When the Soviet economy, which remained a command economy until the end, got into trouble in the 1980s, the deal broke down, and the whole political system was plunged into crisis. It was a system that proved unable to reform itself. The Soviet political system lacked accountability: as a one-party state, the regime was accountable only to itself. Supervisory mechanisms, like the Workers' and Peasants' Inspectorate, were themselves subject to the party. Legal as well as political institutions were lacking. Here there was an underlying tension, which was never resolved. The regime never overcame 'the irreconcilable conflict between an arbitrary personal despotism and the regulatory order needed by the bureaucratic administration of modern states' (Kershaw and Lewin: 1997b: 356; see also Rittersporn 1991: 19).

Not only did the Stalin regime fail to 'modernise' its political institutions. As totalitarian theorists observed, there was a lack of a functioning civil society. Certainly, there was a *society*, as social historians have shown. Nevertheless, in spite of this, there was never what political theorists call an independent *civil society* in Stalin's Russia, if 'civil society' is taken to mean an independent cultural sphere capable of giving rise to new forms of social and political initiative. Trials, arrests and the widespread practice of denunciation had a terrible effect on human relationships. People got into the habit of sharing their thoughts only with a very small circle of friends. The underlying reason why the regime did not permit the emergence of an independent civic sphere was probably because it lacked self-confidence. Here, the issue of revolutionary violence was important. The party, having established its control through the use of force, was fearful of political freedom and popular scrutiny. Thus there was never established the kind of legitimacy which a regime must have if it is to be long-lasting and adaptable.

Instead of a civil society, where people might take initiative, there emerged a culture where the primary aim was to survive. Everybody was affected by the transformation of the Soviet Union under Stalin, and had to find new ways of coping. In both the countryside and the towns, there emerged a set of practices typical of the era. As well as learning the technical skills needed to prosper in an industrialised country, people learned the 'tactics of the habitat': the strategies of life which they needed to employ in order to survive in cramped conditions and times of scarcity (Kotkin 1995: 154). Certain personality traits became typical: '*Homo Sovieticus* was a string-puller, an operator, a time-server, a freeloader, a mouther of slogans. But above all, he was a survivor' (Fitzpatrick 1999: 227). There was in these 'rules of the game' an element of resistance as well as conformity; while people used the right phrases, they still played the system to their own advantage. At the same time, the population, while learning the new 'rules of the game' in order to survive, was also in some way corrupted by them. For obvious reasons, people learned to be silent in the face of arrests and terror, and not to ask questions that might indicate a lack of ideological vigilance.

It would be wrong to strictly demarcate Russian and Soviet culture. As so often happens in history following a period of revolutionary change, principles of continuity reassert themselves (see Carr 1958: 8). The restoration of certain conservative values in the 1930s contributed to that process, although conversely the family, Russian literature and the Church were themselves reinvented in a Stalinist image. Some of these principles of continuity were dangerous to the system: certain ethical and religious values, the respect for 'conscience' and hatred of 'lies' which were so central to Russian literature and Orthodoxy, were never extinguished and were always a threat to arbitrary despotism. Furthermore, the past was present in the minds of people. Although the regime made a serious attempt to reconstruct the national public memory, it could not always reach into the individual mind. Older generations could remember the pre-revolutionary era well. Indeed, with the rehabilitation of the traditional family in the 1930s, a sphere of life where private loyalties and memories could be passed on, came to be tacitly accepted. Another way in which culture is transmitted is through language. The Soviet attempt to build a new society could only take place through the medium of an inherited language: Russian. Russian culture, and the Russian language itself, survived Stalinism, even if it was itself remoulded by the experience of it. Finally, the regime itself embraced certain aspects of the Russian autocratic tradition for itself; Stalin saw himself as preserving and building on Russia's imperial legacy. Continuities are, of course, inevitable. Political revolution does not lead immediately to cultural revolution. Mentalities change slowly, and are not passed on by the state alone, but through the whole range of people's life experiences.

The Russian liberal historian, Boris Chicherin, observed in 1858 that history punishes those who do not accept the gradualness of historical evolution: 'History administers cruel lessons to rash innovators . . . History, like nature, does not make leaps' (Hamburg 1992: 57). The Stalin regime is a good example of this. The Stalin revolution led to some remarkable, indeed 'heroic' successes: the Soviet Union became a superpower; some people benefitted materially, and many were given opportunities which they would not otherwise have had. Yet millions died or were repressed; 'doublethink' became a constant habit of mind; and life for ordinary people was hard and often full of fear. Furthermore, the system which was created was itself full of tensions, and its dynamism was short-lived. What began as a radical and violent attempt to move the country forward foundered in its own contradictions. The price of Stalinist dynamism was Brezhnev-era stagnation. The attempt to reform the system in the 1980s would lead it to collapse and bring the Soviet peoples yet further trouble.

Bibliography

Acton, E. (1990) *Rethinking the Russian Revolution* (London: Edward Arnold)

Ades, D., Benton T., Elliot D. and Whyte, I.B. (1995) *Art and Power: Europe under the Dictators, 1930–1945* (London: Hayward Gallery)

Akhmatova, A. (1971) *Selected Poems*, ed. W. Arndt, translation of 'Requiem' by R. Kemball (Ann Arbor, MI: Ardis)

Alliluyeva, S. (1967) *20 Letters to a Friend*, trans. P. Johnson (London: Hutchinson)

Alliluyeva, S. (1969) *Only One Year*, trans. P. Chavchavadze (London: Hutchinson)

Altrichter, H. (1991) 'Insoluble Conflicts: Village Life Between Revolution and Collectivization', in S. Fitzpatrick, A. Rabinowitch and R. Stites (eds), *Russia in the Era of NEP* (Bloomington: Indiana University Press)

Andrle, V. (1992) 'Demons and Devil's Advocates: Problems in Historical Writing on the Stalin Era', in N. Lampert and G. Rittersporn (eds), *Stalinism: Its Nature and Aftermath* (Basingstoke: Macmillan)

Antonova, I. and Merkert, I. (1996) *Moskva-Berlin/Berlin-Moscau, 1900–1950* (Munich: Galart)

Arendt, H. (1979) *The Origins of Totalitarianism* (San Diego: Harcourt Brace Jovanovich)

Arendt, H. (1994) *Eichmann in Jerusalem: A Report on the Banality of Evil* (Harmondsworth: Penguin)

Art into Life: Russian Constructivism, 1914–1932 (1990) (Seattle: The Henry Art Gallery, University of Washington, Seattle)

Baburina, N. (ed.) (1984) *The Soviet Political Poster 1917–1980* (Harmondsworth: Penguin Books)

Bailes, K.E. (1978) *Technology and Society under Lenin and Stalin* (Princeton, NJ: Princeton University Press)

Bakhtin, M. (1994) *The Bakhtin Reader* ed. P. Morris (London: Edward Arnold)

Bakhurst, D. (1991) *Consciousness and Revolution in Soviet Philosophy* (Cambridge: Cambridge University Press)

Barber, J. (1981) *Soviet Historians in Crisis* (Basingstoke: Macmillan)

Barber, J. and Harrison, M. (1991) *The Soviet Home Front, 1941–1945* (London: Longman)

Barbusse, H. (1935) *Stalin: A New World Seen Through One Man*, trans. V. Holland (New York: International Publishers)

Beevor, A. (1998) *Stalingrad* (London: Viking)

Berdyaev, N. (1931) *The Russian Revolution* (London: Sheed & Ward)

Bergman, J. (1998) 'Valerii Chkalov: Soviet Pilot as New Soviet Man', *Journal of Contemporary History*, vol. 33, no. 1, pp. 135–52

Beria, L. (1994) 'Pis'ma iz tioremnogo bunkera', *Istochnik*, no. 4, pp. 3–14

Bialer, S. (1969) *Stalin and his Generals* (New York: Pegasus)

Bialer, S. (1980) *Stalin's Successors* (Cambridge: Cambridge University Press)

Bol'shaia sovetskaia entiklopediia (1929–1947) General editor O.Iu. Shmidt (vols 50–55 K.E.Voposhilov) (Moscow: Gos. Inst. 'Sovetskaia Entiklopediia')

Bol'shaia sovetskaia entiklopediia (1949–1958) General editor S.I. Vavilov (Moscow: Gos. Nauch. Izd.)

Bonnell, V.E. (1997) *Iconography of Power* (Berkeley, CA: University of California Press)

Bonwetsch, B. (1997) 'Stalin, the Red Army and the Great Patriotic War', in I. Kershaw and M. Lewin (eds), *Stalinism and Nazism* (Cambridge: Cambridge University Press)

Boobbyer, P.C. (1995) *S.L. Frank* (Athens Ohio: Ohio University Press)

Boobbyer, B. (1999) 'Religious Experiences of the Soviet Dissidents', *Religion, State and Society*, Vol. 27, no. 3–4 , pp. 373–90

Boym, S. (1994) *Common Places: Mythologies of Everyday Life in Russia* (Cambridge, MA: Harvard University Press)

Bown, M. (1998) *Socialist Realist Painting* (New Haven, CT: Yale University Press)

Bown, M. and Taylor, B. (eds) (1993) *Art of the Soviets* (Manchester: Manchester University Press)

Broszat, M. (1969) *Der Staat Hitlers* (Munich: Deutscher Taschenbuch Verlag)

Buckley, M. (1996) 'Why be a Shock Worker or a Stakhanovite?', in R. Marsh (ed.) *Women in Russia and Ukraine* (Cambridge: Cambridge University Press)

Bukharin, N.I. (1988) 'Politicheskoe zaveshchanie Lenina', *Kommunist*, no. 2, pp. 93–102

Bukovsky, V. (1978) *To Build a Castle*, trans. M. Scammell (London: André Deutsch)

Bulgakov, M. (1984) *The Master and Margerita*, trans. M. Glenny (London: Flamingo)

Bulgakov, S. (1977) 'Heroism and Asceticism: Reflections on the Religious Nature of the Russian Intelligentsia', in B. Shragin and A. Todd (eds), *Landmarks*, trans. M. Schwartz (New York: Karz Howard)

Carr, E.H. (1958) *Socialism in One Country 1924–1926*, vol. 1, (London: Macmillan)

Carr, E.H. (1978) *The Russian Revolution from Lenin to Stalin* (London: Macmillan)

Carr E.H. and Davies, R.W. (1969) *Foundations of a Planned Economy 1926–1929*, vol. 1, part 1 (London: Macmillan)

Chandler, R. (1996) 'Introduction', in A. Platonov, *The Foundation Pit* (London: Harvill)

Channon, J. (1988) 'Stalin and the Peasantry: Reassessing the Postwar Years, 1945–1953', in J. Channon (ed.), *Politics, Society and Stalinism in the USSR* (Basingstoke: Macmillan in association with School of Slavonic and East European Studies University of London)

Chuev, F. (1992) *Tak govoril Kaganovich* (Moscow: Otechestvo)

Chuev, F. (1993) *Molotov Remembers* (Chicago: Ivan R. Dee)

Chukovskaya, L. (1967) *The Deserted House*, trans B. Werth (London: Barrie and Rockliff)

Chukovskaya, L. (1994) *The Akhmatova Journals, vol. 1, 1938–1941*, trans. M. Michalski and S. Rubashova, poetry translated by P. Norman (London: Harvill)

Churchill, W. (1954) *The Second World War*, vol. IV (London: Cassell and Co. Ltd)

Ciszek, W.J. with Flaherty, D. (1975) *He Leadeth Me* (Garden City, NY: Doubleday, Image)

Clark, K. (1978) 'Little Heroes and Big Deeds: Literature Responds to the First Five-Year Plan', in S. Fitzpatrick (ed.) *Cultural Revolution in Russia* (Bloomington: Indiana University Press)

Clark, K. (1981) *The Soviet Novel* (Chicago: University of Chicago Press)

Cohen, S. (1973) *Bukharin and the Bolshevik Revolution* (New York: Alfred Knopf)

Conquest, R. (1986) *Harvest of Sorrow* (London: Hutchinson)

Conquest, R. (1989) *Stalin and the Kirov Murder* (London: Hutchinson)

Conquest, R. (1992) *The Great Terror* (London: Pimlico)

Cooke, C. (1993) 'Socialist Realist Architecture: Theory and Practice,' in M. Bown and B. Taylor (eds), *Art of the Soviets* (Manchester: Manchester University Press)

Cooper, J., Dexter, K., and Harrison, M. (1999) 'The Numbered Factories and Other Establishments of the Soviet Defence Industry, 1927–67: A Guide' (Birmingham: Soviet Industrialisation Project Series SIPS Occasional Paper, No. 2, CREES, University of Birmingham)

Cooper, J., Perrie, M. and Rees, E.A. (eds) (1995) *Soviet History 1917–1953: Essays in Honour of R.W. Davies* (New York: St Martin's Press)

Corley, F. (1996) *Religion in the Soviet Union: An Archival Reader* (Basingstoke: Macmillan)

Curtis, M. (1969) 'Retreat from Totalitarianism', in C. Friedrich *et al.* (eds), *Totalitarianism in Perspective: Three Views* (London: Pall Mall Press)

Daniels, R. (ed.) (1972) *The Stalin Revolution* (Lexington, MA: Heath and Co.)

Daniels, R. (1985) *A Documentary History of Communism*, 2 vols (London: I.B. Tauris & Co.)

Davies, R.W. (1980) *The Industrialization of Soviet Russia 1: The Socialist Offensive: The Collectivisation of Soviet Agriculture 1929–1930* (London: Macmillan)

Davies, R.W. (1989a) *The Industrialization of Soviet Russia 3: The Soviet Economy in Turmoil 1929–1930* (London: Macmillan)

Davies, R.W. (1989b) *Soviet History in the Gorbachev Revolution* (London: Macmillan)

Davies, R.W. (1997) *Soviet History in the Yeltsin Era* (Basingstoke: Macmillan)

Davies, R.W. (1998) *Soviet Economic Development from Lenin to Khrushchev* (Cambridge: Cambridge University Press)

Davies, R.W., Harrison, M. and Wheatcroft, S.G. (eds) (1994) *The Economic Transformation of Russia* (Cambridge: Cambridge University Press)

Davies, R.W. and Khlevniuk, O. (1997a) 'Gosplan', in E.A. Rees (ed.), *Decision-Making in the Stalinist Command Economy, 1932–37* (Basingstoke: Macmillan)

Davies, S. (1997a) *Popular Opinion in Stalin's Russia* (Cambridge: Cambridge University Press)

Davies, S. (1997b) '"Us against them": Social Identities in Soviet Russia, 1934–41', *Russian Review*, vol. 56, no. 1, pp. 70–89

Davis, N. (1995) *A Long Walk to Church* (Boulder: Westview Press)

Degras, J. (1952) *Soviet Documents on Foreign Policy. Vol. II, 1925–1932* (London: Oxford University Press, Geoffrey Cumberlege)

Degras, J. (1953) *Soviet Documents on Foreign Policy. Vol. III, 1933–1941* (London: Oxford University Press, Geoffrey Cumberlege)

Deutscher, I. (1959) *The Prophet Unarmed: Trotsky 1921–1929* (London: Oxford University Press)

Deutscher, I. (1967) *Stalin* (Oxford: Oxford University Press)

Djilas, M. (1962) *Conversations with Stalin*, trans. M. Petrovich (London: Rupert Hart-Davis)

'Dobit'sia Polnogo Razoblacheniia', (1994) *Istochnik*, no. 6, pp. 112–14

Druzhnikov, I. (1997) *Informer 001: The Myth of Pavlik Morozov* (New Brunswick: Transaction Publishers)

Dunham, V. (1976) *In Stalin's Time* (Cambridge: Cambridge University Press)

Dunmore, T. (1980) *The Stalinist Command Economy* (Basingstoke: Macmillan)

Dunstan, J. (1997) *Soviet Schooling in the Second World War* (Basingstoke: Macmillan)

Dyker, D. (1985) *The Future of the Soviet Economic Planning System* (Armonk, New York: M.E. Sharpe)

Ellis, F. (1994) *Vasily Grossman: the Genesis and Evolution of a Russian Heretic* (Oxford: Berg)

Erickson, J. (1975) *The Road to Stalingrad* (London: Weidenfeld and Nicolson)

Fainsod, M. (1963) *How Russia is Ruled* (Cambridge, MA: Harvard University Press)

Filtzer, D. (1986) *Soviet Workers and Stalinist Industrialization* (London: Pluto Press)

Filtzer, D. (1998) 'Stalinism and the Working Class in the 1930s', in J. Channon (ed.), *Politics, Society and Stalinism in the USSR* (Basingstoke: Macmillan)

Fitzpatrick, S. (1979a) *Education and Social Mobility in the Soviet Union, 1921–1934* (Cambridge: Cambridge University Press)

Fitzpatrick, S. (1979b) 'Stalin and the Making of a New Elite', *Slavic Review*, vol. 38, no. 3, pp. 377–402

Fitzpatrick, S. (1982) *The Russian Revolution 1917–1932* (Oxford: Oxford University Press)

Fitzpatrick, S. (1992) *The Cultural Front: Power and Culture in Revolutionary Russia* (Ithaca, NY: Cornell University Press)

Fitzpatrick, S. (1993) 'The Impact of the Great Purges on Soviet Elites: A Case Study from Moscow and Leningrad Telephone Directories', in J.A. Getty and R. T. Manning (eds), *Stalinist Terror* (Cambridge: Cambridge University Press)

Fitzpatrick, S. (1994) *Stalin's Peasants* (New York: Oxford University Press)

Fitzpatrick, S. (1996) 'Signals from Below: Soviet Letters of Denunciation of the 1930s', *Journal of Modern History*, vol. 68, no. 4, pp. 831–66

Fitzpatrick, S. (1997) 'Editor's Introduction: Petitions and Denunciations in Russian and Soviet History', *Russian History/Histoire Russe*, vol. 24, nos. 1–2, pp. 1–9

Fitzpatrick, S. (1999) *Everyday Stalinism* (New York: Oxford University Press)

Fitzpatrick, S. (ed.) (2000) *Stalinism: New Directions* (London: Routledge)

Fletcher, W.C. (1965) *A Study in Survival* (London: SPCK)

Fletcher, W.C. (1971) *The Russian Orthodox Church Underground, 1917–1970* (Oxford: Oxford University Press)

Frank, S.L. (1989) *The Light Shineth in Darkness*, trans. B. Jakim (Athens, OH: Ohio University Press)

Franklin, B. (ed.) (1973) *The Essential Stalin* (London: Croom Helm)

Friedrich, C. and Brzezinski, Z. (1956) *Totalitarian Dictatorship and Autocracy* (New York: Friedrich. A. Praeger)

Galter, A. (1957) *The Red Book of the Persecuted Church* (Dublin: M.H. Gill and Son Ltd)

Garros, V., Korenevskaya, N. and Lahusen, T. (eds), (1995) *Intimacy and Terror*, trans. C.A. Flath (New York: The Free Press)

Geldern, J. von and Stites, R. (eds) (1995) *Mass Culture in Soviet Russia* (Bloomington: Indiana University Press)

Gerschenkron, A. (1962) *Economic Backwardness in Historical Perspective* (Cambridge, MA: The Belknap Press of Harvard University)

Getty, J.A. (1985) *The Origins of the Great Purges* (Cambridge: Cambridge University Press)

Getty, J.A. (1991) 'State and Soviet under Stalin: Constitutions and Elections in the 1930s', *Slavic Review*, vol. 50, no. 1, pp. 18–35

Getty, J.A. (1993) 'The Politics of Repression Revisited', in J.A. Getty and R.T. Manning (eds), *Stalinist Terror* (Cambridge: Cambridge University Press)

Getty, J.A. and Manning, R.T. (eds) (1993) *Stalinist Terror* (Cambridge: Cambridge University Press)

Getty, J.A. and Naumov, O.V. (eds) (1999) *The Road to Terror* (New Haven, CT: Yale University Press)

Gill, G. (1990) *The Origins of the Stalinist Political System* (Cambridge: Cambridge University Press)

Ginzburg, E. (1967) *Into the Whirlwind*, trans. M. Harari, (London: Collins/Harvill)

Glavatsky, M.E. *et al.* (eds) (1995) *Khrestomatia po istorii Rossii, 1917–1940* (Moscow: Aspekt Press)

Goldman, W. (1993) *Women, the State and Revolution* (Cambridge: Cambridge University Press)

Gordon, M. (1941) *Workers Before and After Lenin* (London: E.P. Dutton)

Goriaeva, T. (ed.) (1997) *Istoriia sovetskoi politicheskoi tsenzury* (Moscow: ROSSPEN)

Goricheva, T. (ed.) (1989) *The Cry of the Spirit* (London: Collins)

Gorinov, M. *et al.* (eds) (1995) *Moskva voennaia 1941–1945* (Moscow: Moskgosarkhiv)

Gorodetsky, G. (1999) *The Grand Delusion: Stalin and the German Invasion of Russia* (New Haven, CT: Yale University Press)

Graham, L. (1967) *The Soviet Academy of Sciences and the Communist Party 1927–1932* (Princeton, NJ: Princeton University Press)

Graham, L. (1993) *Science in Russia and the Soviet Union* (Cambridge: Cambridge University Press)

Graziosi, A. (1992) 'The Great Strikes of 1953 in Soviet Labor Camps in the Accounts of their Participants: A Review', *Cahiers du monde russe et soviétique*, Vol. xxxiii, No. 1, pp. 419–46

Gregor, R. (ed.) (1974) *Resolutions and Decisions of the Communist Party of the Soviet Union, Vol. 2, The Early Soviet Period, 1917–1929* (Toronto: University of Toronto Press)

Grigorenko, P.G. (1983) *Memoirs*, trans T. Whitney (London: Harvill Press)

Grossman, V. (1997) *Forever Flowing*, trans T.P. Whitney (Evanston, IL: Northwestern University Press)

Hamburg, G. (1992) *Boris Chicherin and Early Russian Liberalism* (Stanford, CA: Stanford University Press)

Harris, J. (1992) 'The Growth of the Gulag: Forced Labour in the Urals Region, 1929–31', *Russian Review*, vol. 56, no. 2, pp. 265–80

Harrison, M. (1985) *Soviet Planning in Peace and War* (Cambridge: Cambridge University Press)

Harrison, M. (1996) *Accounting for War* (Cambridge: Cambridge University Press)

Heitlinger, A. (1979) *Women and State Socialism* (London: Macmillan)

Hellbeck, J. (1996) 'The Diary of Stepan Podlubnyi, 1931–1939', *Jahrbücher für Geschichte Osteuropas*, vol. 44, no. 4, pp. 344–73

Heller, M. and Nekrich, A. (1986) *Utopia in Power*, trans P.B. Carlos (New York: Summit Books)

Hindus, M. (1988) *Red Bread*, ed. R. Suny (Bloomington: Indiana University Press)

History of the Communist Party of the Soviet Union/ Bolsheviks/A Short Course (1939) (Moscow: Foreign Languages Publishing House)

Holloway, D. (1994) *Stalin and the Bomb* (New Haven, CT: Yale University Press)

Holmes, L. (1991) *The Kremlin and the Schoolhouse* (Bloomington: Indiana University Press)

Holmes, L. (1997) 'Part of History: The Oral Record and Moscow's Model School No. 25, 1931–1937', *Slavic Review*, vol. 56, no. 2, pp. 279–306

Holt, A. (ed.) (1977) *Selected Writings of Alexandra Kollontai* (London: Allison and Busby)

Hosking, G. (1990) *A History of the Soviet Union* (London: Collins)

Hughes, J. (1991) *Stalin, Siberia and the Crisis of the New Economic Policy* (Cambridge: Cambridge University Press)

Hughes, J. (1996) *Stalinism in a Russian Province* (Basingstoke: Macmillan)

Inber, V. (1971) *Leningrad Diary*, trans. S.M. Woff and R. Grieve (London: Hutchinson)

Jakobson, M. (1993) *Origins of the Gulag* (Lexington, KY: University Press of Kentucky)

Jones, M. (1995) 'The Gospel According to Woland and the Tradition of the Wandering Jew', in L. Milne (ed.), *Bulgakov: The Novelist-Playwright* (Reading: Harwood Academic Publishers)

Joravsky, D. (1961) *Soviet Marxism and Natural Science* (London: Routledge and Kegan Paul)

Kaplan, C.S. (1985) 'The Impact of World War II on the Party', in S.J. Linz (ed.) *The Impact of World War II on the Soviet Union* (Totowa, NJ: Rowman and Allenheld)

Karklins, R. (1989) 'The Organization of Power in the Soviet Labour Camps', *Soviet Studies*, vol. 41, no. 2, pp. 276–97

Kassof, A. (1965) *The Soviet Youth Program* (Cambridge, MA: Harvard University Press)

Kataev, V. (1995) *Time, Forward!*, trans. C. Malamuth (Evanston, IL: Northwestern University Press)

Keep, J. (1999) 'Wheatcroft and Stalin's Victims: Comments', *Europe-Asia Studies*, vol. 51, no. 6, pp. 1089–92

Kemp-Welch, A. (1991) *Stalin and the Literary Intelligentsia, 1928–39* (Basingstoke: Macmillan)

Kenez, P. (1992) *Cinema and Soviet Society 1917–1953* (Cambridge: Cambridge University Press)

Kershaw, I. (1993) *The Nazi Dictatorship* (London: Edward Arnold)

Kershaw, I. and Lewin, M. (eds) (1997a) *Stalinism and Nazism* (Cambridge: Cambridge University Press)

Kershaw, I. and Lewin, M. (1997b) 'Afterthoughts', in I. Kershaw and M. Lewin (eds) *Stalinism and Nazism* (Cambridge: Cambridge University Press)

Khlevniuk, O.V. (1995a) 'The Objectives of the Great Terror', in J. Cooper *et al.* (eds), *Soviet History, 1917–1953* (Basingstoke: Macmillan)

Khlevniuk, O.V. (1995b) *In Stalin's Shadow: The Career of 'Sergo' Ordzhonikidze*, trans. D. Nordlander (Armonk, New York: M.E. Sharpe)

Khlevniuk, O.V. *et al.* (eds) (1995) *Stalinskoe politbiuro 30-e gody* (Moscow: 'AIRO – XX')

Khrushchev, N. (1971) *Khrushchev Remembers*, ed. E. Crankshaw, trans. S. Talbott (London: Sphere Books Ltd)

Khrushchev, N. (1997) *Vospominaniia* (Moscow: Vagrius)

King, D. (1997) *The Commissar Vanishes: The Falsification of Photographs and Art in Stalin's Russia* (Edinburgh: Canongate)

Kiseleva, A.F. *et al.* (eds) (1996) *Khrestomatiia po otechestvennoi istorii, 1946–1995* (Moscow: Gumanitarnyi izdatel'skii tsentr 'VLADOS')

Kissinger, H. (1994) *Diplomacy* (New York: Simon and Schuster)

Koenker, D.P. and Bachman, R.D. (1997) *Revelations from the Russian Archives* (Washington, DC: Library of Congress)

Koestler, A. (1985) *Darkness at Noon*, trans. D. Hardy (Harmondsworth: Penguin in association with Jonathan Cape)

Kolakowski, L. (1977) 'Marxist Roots of Stalinism', in R. Tucker (ed.), *Stalinism* (New York: W.W. Norton, and Co.)

Koloskov, A.G. and Gevurkova, E.A. (eds) (1995) *Istoriia otechestva v dokumentakh 1917–1991. Vol. 3 1939–1945* (Moscow: 'ILBI')

Kopelev, L. (1981) *The Education of a True Believer*, trans. G. Kern (London: Wildhood House)

Korotkov, A.V. *et al.* (eds) (1995) 'Posetiteli kremlevskogo kabineta I.V. Stalina 1938–1939', *Istoricheskii arkhiv*, no. 5–6, 4–64

Kotkin, S. (1995) *Magnetic Mountain* (Berkeley, CA: University of California Press)

Kozlov, L. (1993) 'The Artist and the Shadow of Ivan', in R. Taylor and D. Spring (eds), *Stalinism and Soviet Cinema* (London: Routledge)

Kozlov, V.A. (1996) 'Denunciation and its Functions in Soviet Governance', *Journal of Modern History*, vol. 68, no. 4, pp. 867–98

Krasil'nikov, A. (ed.) (1997) 'Rozhdenie GULAGA: Diskussii v verkhnikh eshelonakh vlasti', *Istoricheskii arkhiv*, no. 4, pp. 142–56

Kravchenko, V. (1947) *I Chose Freedom* (New York: Garden City Publishing Co.)

Krementsov, N. (1997) *Stalinist Science* (Princeton, NJ: Princeton University Press)

Kuromiya, H. (1988) *Stalin's Industrial Revolution* (Cambridge: Cambridge University Press)

Kuromiya, H. (1993) 'Stalinist Terror in the Donbas: A Note', in J.A. Getty and R.T. Manning (eds) *Stalinist Terror* (Cambridge: Cambridge University Press)

Lane, C. (1981) *The Rites of Rulers* (Cambridge: Cambridge University Press)

Larina, L.I. (1993) *Istoriia otechestva v dokumentakh 1917–1991, vol. 3, 1921–1939* (Moscow: 'IBLI')

Leggett, G. (1981) *The Cheka* (Oxford: The Clarendon Press)

Lenin, V.I. (1947) *Selected Works*, 2 vols (London: Lawrence and Wishart)

Lewin, M. (1968) *Russian Peasants and Soviet Power* (Evanston, IL: Northwestern University Press)

Lewin, M. (1975) *Lenin's Last Struggle* (London: Pluto)

Lewin, M. (1985) *The Making of the Soviet System* (London: Methuen)

Lewin, M. (1993) 'On Soviet Industrialization', in W. Rosenburg and L. Siegelbaum (ed.), *Social Dimensions of Soviet Industrialization* (Bloomington: Indiana University Press)

Lewin, M. (1997) 'Bureaucracy and the Stalinist State', in I. Kershaw and M. Lewin (eds), *Stalinism and Nazism* (Cambridge: Cambridge University Press)

Lieberman, S. (1985) 'Crisis Management in the USSR: The Wartime System of Administration and Control', in S. Linz (ed.), *The Impact of World War II on the Soviet Union* (Totowa, NJ: Rowman and Allanheld)

Liebich, A. (1992) '"I am the Last" – Memories of Bukharin in Paris', *Slavic Review*, vol. 51, no. 4, pp. 767–81

Lih, L.T., Naumov, O.V. and Khlevniuk, O.V. (eds) (1995) *Stalin's Letters to Molotov 1925–1936* (New Haven, CT: Yale University Press)

Lih, L.T. (1995) 'Introduction' in Lih, L.T. Naumov, O.V. and Khlevniuk, O.V. (eds) *Stalin's Letters to Molotov* 1925–1936 (New Haven, CT: Yale University Press)

Linz, S. (ed.) (1985) *The Impact of World War II on the Soviet Union* (Totowa, NJ: Rowman and Allanheld)

Lomagin, N.A. (1995) 'Nastroeniia zashchitnikov i naseleniia Leningrada v period oborony goroda, 1941–1942', in V.M. Kovalchuk *et al.* (eds), *Leningradskaia Epopeia* (St Petersburg)

Lovell, D.W. (1984) *From Marx to Lenin* (Cambridge: Cambridge University Press)

Luukkanen, A. (1994) *The Party of Unbelief* (Helsinki: SHS)

Luukkanen, A. (1997) *The Religious Policy of the Stalinist State, 1929–1938* (Helsinki: SHS)

McCagg, W.O. (1978) *Stalin Embattled 1943–1948* (Detroit: Wayne State University Press)

McNeal, R. (ed.) (1974) *Resolutions and Decisions of the Communist Party of the Soviet Union, Vol. 3, The Stalin Years, 1929–1953* (Toronto: University of Toronto Press)

Makarenko, A.S. (1954) *A Book for Parents*, trans. R. Daglish (Moscow: Foreign Languages Publishing House)

Malia, M. (1994) *The Soviet Tragedy* (New York: The Free Press)

Malia, M. (1999) *Russia Under Western Eyes* (Cambridge, MA: The Belknap Press)

Mandelstam, N. (1975) *Hope Against Hope*, trans. M. Hayward (Harmondsworth: Penguin)

Mandelstam, N. (1976) *Hope Abandoned*, trans M. Hayward, (Harmondsworth: Penguin)

Mandelstam, O. (1979) 'Humanism and the Present', *Mandelstam: The Complete Critical Prose and Letters*, ed. J. Harris, trans. J. Harris and C. Link (Ann Arbor, MI: Ardis)

Manning, R.T. (1987) 'State and Society in Stalinist Russia', *The Russian Review*, vol. 46, no. 4

Manning, R.T. (1993a) 'The Great Purges in a Rural District: Belyi Raion Revisited', in J.A. Getty and R.T. Manning (eds), *Stalinist Terror* (Cambridge: Cambridge University Press)

Manning, R.T. (1993b) 'The Soviet Economic Crisis of 1936–1940 and the Great Purges', in J.A. Getty and R.T. Manning (eds), *Stalinist Terror* (Cambridge: Cambridge University Press)

Markov, V. and Sparks, M. (eds) (1966) *Modern Russian Poetry* (London: Macgibbon and Kee)

Marples, D.R. (1992) *Stalinism in Ukraine in the 1940s* (Basingstoke: Macmillan)

Medvedev, R. (1989) *Let History Judge*, ed. and trans. G. Shriver (Oxford: Oxford University Press)

Medvedev, Z. (1969) *The Rise and Fall of T.D. Lysenko*, trans. I. Lerner (New York: Columbia University Press)

Meek, D. (1957) *Soviet Youth* (London: Routledge and Kegan Paul Ltd)

Merridale, C. (1990) *Moscow Politics and the Rise of Stalin* (London: Macmillan)

Mihajlov, M. (1978) 'Mystical Experiences of the Labor Camps', in *Kontinent2* (London: Hodder and Stoughton/Coronet)

Millar, J. and Nove, A. (1976) 'Was Stalin Really Necessary? A Debate on Collectivisation', *Problems of Communism*, vol. 25, no. 4, pp. 49–62

Millar, J.R. (1976) 'What's Wrong with the Standard Story', in J.R. Millar and A. Nove, 'Was Stalin Really Necessary?', *Problems of Communism*, vol. 25, no. 4, pp. 50–5

Milosz, C. (1981) *The Captive Mind*, trans. J. Zielonko (New York: Vintage Books)

Mommsen, H. (1966) *Beamtentum in Dritten Reich* (Stuttgart: Deutsche Verlags-Anstalt)

Morson, G.S. and Emerson, C. (1990) *Mikhail Bakhtin* (Stanford, CA: Stanford University Press)

Morton, M. (1972) *The Arts and the Soviet Child* (New York: The Free Press)

Moskoff, W. (1990) *The Bread of Affliction* (Cambridge: Cambridge University Press)

Murina, Iu. (1993a) 'Nadezhde Sergeevne Alliluevoi Lichno ot STALINa,' (correspondence 1928–1931) *Istochnik*, no. 0, pp. 9–22

Murina, Iu. (1993b) 'Iosif Beskonechno Dobr,' (Diary of Maria Svanidze 1933–1937) *Istochnik*, no. 1, pp. 4–34

The New Soviet Constitution (1936) (The Anglo-Russian Parliamentary Committee)

Nicolaevsky, B. (1965) *Power and the Soviet Elite* (New York: Praeger)

1937: Literaturnyi kalendar' (Leningrad: Gosizdat, 'Khudozhestvannaia literatura')

Odintsov, M.I. (ed.) (1995) 'Godudarstvo i tserkov' v gody voiny', *Istoricheskii arkhiv*, no. 3, pp. 118–35

Orwell, G. (1984) *Nineteen Eighty-Four* (Harmondsworth: Penguin in association with Martin Secker and Warburg)

Overy, R. (1997) *Russia's War* (Harmondsworth: Penguin)

Panin, D. (1976) *The Notebooks of Sologdin*, trans. J.Moore (London: Hutchinson)

Pashukanis, E. (1951) 'The Soviet State and the Revolution in Law', in V.I. Lenin *et al.*, *Soviet Legal Philosophy*, introd. J. Hazard and trans H. Habb (Cambridge: Harvard University Press)

Peris, D. (1991) 'The 1929 Congress of the Godless', *Soviet Studies*, vol. 43, no. 4, pp. 711–32

Peris, D. (1998) *Storming the Heavens: The Soviet League of the Militant Godless* (Ithaca, NY: Cornell University Press)

Perrie, M. (1998) 'Nationalism and History: The Cult of Ivan the Terrible in Stalin's Russia', in G. Hosking and R. Service (eds), *Russian Nationalism Past and Present* (Basingstoke: Macmillan)

Petrov, V. and Petrov, E. (1956) *Empire of Fear* (London: André Deutsch)

Pipes, R. (1964) *The Formation of the Soviet Union* (Cambridge, MA: Harvard University Press)

Pipes, R. (ed.) (1996) *The Unknown Lenin* (New Haven, CT: Yale University Press)

Platonov, A. (1996) *The Foundation Pit*, trans. R. Chandler and G. Smith (London: Harvill Press)

Pomerants, G. (1998) *Zapiski gadkego utenka* (Moscow: Moskovskii rabochii)

Popov, V.P. (1992) 'Golod i gosudarstvennaia politika (1946–1947 gg)', *Otechestvennye arkhivy*, no. 6, pp. 36–60

Popov, V.P. (1993) *Rossiiskaia derevnia posle voiny (Iiun' 1945 – Mart 1953)* (Moscow: 'Prometei')

Pospielovsky, D. (1987–88) *A History of Marxist-Leninist Atheism and Soviet Anti-Religious Policies*, vol. 1 1987, vols 2 and 3 1988 (Basingstoke: Macmillan)

Powell, D.E. (1975) *Anti-Religious Propaganda in the Soviet Union* (Cambridge: The MIT Press)

Preobrazhensky, E.A. (1979) 'Economic Equilibrium in the System of the USSR', in D. Filtzer ed. *The Crisis of Soviet Industrialisation* (Armonk, New York: M.E.Sharpe)

Radzinsky, E. (1996) *Stalin*, trans H. Willetts (London: Hodder and Stoughton)

Raeff, M. (1990) *Russia Abroad* (New York: Oxford University Press)

Rakovsky, C. (1981) 'The Five-Year Plan in Crisis', *Critique*, no. 13, pp. 7–54

"Rasstrel po l'i kategorii', *Izvestiia*, 3 April 1996, p. 5

Rassweiler, A.D. (1983) 'Soviet Labor Policy in the First Five-Year-Plan: the Dneprostroi Experience', *Slavic Review*, vol. 42, no. 1, pp. 230–43

Rassweiler, A.D. (1988) *The Generation of Power: The History of Dneprostroi* (New York: Oxford University Press)

Razumov, A. Ya (ed.) (1998) *Leningradsky martirolog 1937–1938* (St Petersburg: Izd. Rossiiskoi natsional'noi biblioteki)

Rees, E.A. (1987) *State Control in Soviet Russia: The Rise and Fall of the Worker's and Peasants' Inspectorate, 1920–1934* (Basingstoke: Macmillan in association with the Centre for Russian and East European Studies University of Birmingham)

Rees, E.A. (1995a) 'Stalin, the Politburo and Rail Transport Policy', in J. Cooper, M. Perrie, E.A. Rees (eds), *Soviet History 1917–1953* (Basingstoke: Macmillan)

Rees, E.A. (1995b) *Stalinism and Soviet Rail Transport 1928–1941* (Basingstoke: Macmillan)

Rees, E.A. (ed.) (1997) *Decision-Making in the Stalinist Command System* (Basingstoke: Macmillan)

Rees, E.A. (1998a) 'Stalinism: The Primacy of Politics', in J. Channon (ed.) *Politics, Society and Stalinism in the USSR* (Basingstoke: Macmillan)

Rees, E.A. (1998b) 'Stalin and Russian Nationalism', in G. Hosking and R. Service (eds) *Russian Nationalism Past and Present* (Basingstoke: Macmillan)

Reese, R.(1993) 'The Red Army and the Great Purges', in J.A. Getty and R.T. Manning (eds), *Stalinist Terror* (Cambridge: Cambridge University Press)

Reichman, H. (1988) 'Reconsidering Stalinism', *Theory and Society*, no. 17, pp. 57–90

Reiman, M. (1987) *The Birth of Stalinism* (London: I.B.Tauris and Co. Ltd)

Report of Court Proceedings in the Case of the Anti-Soviet 'Bloc of Rights and Trotskyites' (1938) (Moscow: People's Commissariat of Justice of the U.S.S.R.)

Rhodes, A. (1993) *Propaganda, the Art of Persuasion: World War II*, ed. V. Margolin (Wigston, Leicester: Magna Books)

Riasanovsky, N.V. (1985) *The Image of Peter the Great in Russian History and Thought* (New York: Oxford University Press)

Rigby, T.H. (ed.) (1966) *Stalin* (Englewood Cliffs, NJ: Prentice-Hall Inc.)

Rittersporn, G.T. (1991) *Stalinist Simplifications and Soviet Complications* (Reading: Harwood Academic Publishers)

Rittersporn, G.T. (1993) 'The Omnipresent Conspiracy', in J.A. Getty and R.T. Manning (eds), *Stalinist Terror* (Cambridge: Cambridge University Press)

Rosenberg, W.G. and Siegelbaum, L. (eds) (1993) *Social Dimensions of Stalinist Industrialization* (Bloomington: Indiana University Press)

Rothstein, R.A. (1995) 'Homeland, Home Town and Battlefield,' in R. Stites (ed) *Culture and Entertainment in Wartime Russia* (Bloomington: Indiana University Press)

Russkaia pravoslavnaia tserkov' i kommunisticheskoe gosudarstvo 1917–1941: dokumenty i fotomaterialy, (1996) (Moscow: Izd. Bibleisko-Bogoslovskii Institut sv. apostola Andreia)

Sakharov, A. (1990) *Memoirs*, trans. R. Lourie (London: Hutchinson)

Sakwa, R. (1989) *Soviet Politics* (London: Routledge)

Sakwa, R. (1999) *The Rise and Fall of the Soviet Union* (London: Routledge)

Schapiro, L. (1972) *Totalitarianism* (Basingstoke: Macmillan)

Schapiro, L. (1977) *The Origin of the Communist Autocracy* (London: Macmillan)

Scherer, J. *et al.* 'The Collectivization of Agriculture and the Soviet Prison-Camp System', *Europe-Asia Studies*, vol. 45, no. 3, pp. 533–46

Schlesinger, R. (ed.) (1949) *The Family in the U.S.S.R.* (London: Routledge & Kegan Paul Limited)

Schultz, K. (1990) 'Building the "Soviet Detroit": the Construction of the Nizhnii Novgorod Automobile Factory, 1927–1932', *Slavic Review*, vol. 49, no. 2, pp. 200–12

Scott, J. (1989) *Behind the Urals*, ed. S.Kotkin (Bloomington: Indiana University Press)

Service, R. (1998) 'Joseph Stalin: The Making of a Stalinist', in J. Channon (ed.), *Politics, Society and Stalinism in the USSR*, (Basingstoke: Macmillian)

Shalamov, V. (1994) *Kolyma Tales*, trans. J. Glad (Harmondsworth: Penguin Books)

Shearer, D. (1996) *Industry, State and Society in Stalin's Russia 1926–1934* (Ithaca, NY: Cornell University Press)

Shentalinsky, V. (1995) *The KGB's Literary Archive* (London: The Harvill Press)

Sholokhov, M. (1977) *Virgin Soil Upturned*, trans. S. Garry (Harmondsworth: Penguin Books)

Shostakovich, D. (1979) *Testimony*, ed. S. Volkov (London: Hamish Hamilton)

Shkarovskii, M. (1995) 'The Russian Orthodox Church versus the State: The Josephite Movement, 1927–1940', *Slavic Review*, vol. 54, no. 2, pp. 365–84

Shlapentokh, V. (1990) *Soviet Intellectuals and Political Power* (London: I.B. Tauris and Co. Ltd)

Siegelbaum, L. (1988) *Stakhanovism and the Politics of Productivity 1935–1941* (Cambridge: Cambridge University Press)

Silone, I. (1950) in Arthur Koestler *et al.*, *The God that Failed* (London: Hamish Hamilton)

Slovar' tiuremno-lagerno-blatnogo zhargona (1992) (Moscow: 'Kraia Moskvy')

Smith, E.E. (1967) *The Young Stalin* (London: Cassell)

Smith, K. (1996) *Remembering Stalin's Victims* (Ithaca, NY: Cornell University Press)

Soifer, V.N. (1994) *Lysenko and the Tragedy of Soviet Science*, trans. L. and R. Gruliow (New Brunswick, NJ: Rutgers University Press)

Sokolov, A.K. (ed.) (1998) *Obshchestvo i vlast'* (Moscow: ROSSPEN)

Solomon, P.H. (1996) *Soviet Criminal Justice under Stalin* (Cambridge: Cambridge University Press)

Solzhenitsyn, A. (1972) *'One Word of Truth'*, (London: The Bodley Head)

Solzhenitsyn, A. (1974 and 1975) *The Gulag Archipelago*, i–iv, trans H. Willetts (London: Collins and Harvill Press)

Souvarine, B. (1939) *Stalin* (London: Secker and Warburg)

Spiro, H.J. (1968) 'Totalitarianism', *International Encyclopaedia of the Social Sciences*, vol. 16, ed. D. Sills (The Macmillan Company and The Free Press)

'Stalin i krizis proletarskoi diktatury,' (1990) *Izvestiia* TsK KPSS, no. 12, pp. 180–99

Stalin, Generalissimo (n.d.) *War Speeches* (London: Hutchinson)

Stalin, J.V. (1940) 'Foundations of Leninism', *Leninism* (London: Lawrence and Wishart Ltd)

Stalin, J.V. (1952–1967) *Works*, Vols 1–16 (Moscow: Foreign Language Publishing House)

Starkov, B. (1993) 'Narkom Ezhov,' in J.A. Getty and R.T. Manning (eds), *Stalinist Terror* (Cambridge: Cambridge University Press)

Stites, R. (1978) *The Women's Liberation Movement in Russia* (Princeton, NJ: Princeton University Press)

Stites, R. (1991) 'Bolshevik Ritual Building in the 1920s', in S. Fitzpatrick, A. Rabinowitch and R. Stites (eds), *Russia in the Era of NEP* (Bloomington: Indiana University Press)

Stites, R. (ed.) (1995) *Culture and Entertainment in Wartime Russia* (Bloomington: Indiana University Press)

Strumilin, S.G. (1963) 'Industrializatsiia SSSR i epigony narodnichestva', *Izbrannye proizvedeniia (2): na planovom fronte* (Moscow: Izd. Akad. Nauk. SSSR)

Suny, R. (1997) 'Stalin and his Stalinism: Power and Authority in the Soviet Union 1930–1953,' in I. Kershaw and M. Lewin (eds) *Stalinism and Nazism* (Cambridge: Cambridge University Press)

Taniuchi, Y. (1981) 'A Note on the Ural-Siberial Method', *Soviet Studies*, vol. xxxiii no. 4, pp. 518–47

Taruskin, R. (1995) 'Public Lies and Unspeakable Truth, Interpreting Shostakovich's Fifth Symphony', in D. Fanning (ed.), *Shostakovich Studies* (Cambridge: Cambridge University Press)

Tauger, M.B. (1991) 'The 1932 Harvest and the Famine of 1933', *Slavic Review*, vol. 50 no. 1, pp. 70–89

Taylor, R. (1996) 'The Illusion of Happiness and the Happiness of Illusion: Grigorii Aleksandrov's *The Circus, Slavic and East European Review*, vol. 74, no. 4, pp. 601–19

Taylor, R. (1999) 'Singing on the Steppes for Stalin: Ivan Pyr'ev and the Kolkhoz Musical in Soviet Cinema', *Slavic Review*, vol. 58, no. 1, pp. 143–59

Taylor, R. and Christie, I. (eds) (1988) *The Film Factory* (Cambridge, MA: Harvard University Press)

Taylor, R. and Spring, D. (eds) (1993) *Stalinism and Soviet Cinema* (London: Routledge)

Tchernavin, T. (1936) *We Soviet Women* (New York: E.P. Dutton and Co., Inc.)

Thurston, R. (1986) 'Fear and Belief in the USSR's "Great Terror": Response to Arrest 1935–1939', *Slavic Review*, vol. 45, no. 2, pp. 213–34

Thurston, R. (1991) 'The Soviet Family during the Great Terror, 1935–41', *Soviet Studies*, vol. 43, no. 3, pp. 353–74

Thurston, R. (1996) *Life and Terror in Stalin's Russia, 1934–1941* (New Haven, CT: Yale University Press)

Timasheff, N. ([1946] 1972) *The Great Retreat* (New York: Arno Press)

Todorov, T. (1999) *Facing the Extreme: Moral Life in the Concentration Camps* (London: Weidenfeld and Nicolson)

Trifonov, Y. (1953) *Students* (Moscow: Foreign Languages Publishing House)

Trotsky, L. (1972) *The Revolution Betrayed* (New York: Pathfinder Press)

Tucker, R. (1972) *The Soviet Political Mind* (London: George Allen & Unwin Ltd)

Tucker, R. (1974) *Stalin as Revolutionary* (New York: W.W. Norton and Co.)

Tucker, R. (1977) 'Stalinism as Revolution from Above', in R. Tucker (ed) *Stalinism* (New York: W.W. Norton, and Co.)

Tucker, R. (1992a) *Stalin in Power* (New York: W.W. Norton and Co.)

Tucker, R. (1992b) 'On the "Letter of an Old Bolshevik" as an Historical Document,' *Slavic Review*, vol. 51, no. 4, pp. 782–5

Tumarkin, N. (1983) *Lenin Lives! The Lenin Cult in Soviet Russia* (Cambridge, MA: Harvard University Press)

Ulam, A. (1974a) *Expansion and Coexistence* (New York: Holt, Rinehart and Winston, Inc.)

Ulam, A. (1974b) *Stalin: The Man and His Era* (London: Allen Lane)

Valentinov, N. (1958) 'Sut' bol'shevizma v izobrazhenii Iu.Piatakova', *Novyi zhurnal*, no. 52, pp. 140–61

Vasilevsky, A. (1975) *Delo moei zhizni* (Moscow: Izd. politicheskoi literatury)

Vinogradov, V. *et al.* (eds) (1995) *Sekrety Gitlera na Stole u Stalina* (Moscow: Izd. Ob'edineniia 'Mosgorarkhiv')

Viola, L. (1987) *The Best Sons of the Fatherland* (New York: Oxford University Press)

Viola, L. (1993) 'The Second Coming: Class Enemies in the Soviet Countryside, 1927–1935', in J.A. Getty and R.T. Manning (eds), *Stalinist Terror* (Cambridge: Cambridge University Press)

Viola, L. (1996) *Peasant Rebels under Stalin*, (New York: Oxford University Press)

Volkogonov, D. (1991) *Stalin*, trans. H. Shukman (London: Weidenfeld and Nicolson)

Volkov, V. (2000) 'The concept of *kul'turnost'*: notes on the Stalinist civilizing process', in S. Fitzpatrick (ed.) *Stalinism* (London: Routledge)

Von Hagen, M. (1997) 'From Great Fatherland War to the Second World War', in I. Kershaw and M. Lewin (eds), *Stalinism and Nazism* (Cambridge: Cambridge University Press)

Voznesensky, N. (1948) *The Economy of the USSR during World War II* (Washington, DC: Public Affairs Press)

Vucinich, A. (1984) *Empire of Knowledge* (Berkeley, CA: University of California Press)

Vygotsky, L. (1962) *Thought and Language*, ed. and trans. by E. Hanfmann and G. Vakar (Cambridge, MA: MIT Press)

Vyleta, D.M. (2000) 'City of the Devil – Bulgakovian Moscow and the Search for the Stalinist Subject', *Rethinking History*, vol. 4, no. 1, pp. 37–54

Vyshinsky, A. (1951) 'The Fundamental Tasks of the Science of Soviet Socialist Law', in V.I. Lenin *et al.*, *Soviet Legal Philosophy*, intr. J. Hazard and trans. H. Habb (Cambridge, MA: Harvard University Press)

Walicki, A. (1995) *Marxism and the Leap to the Kingdom of Freedom* (Stanford, CA: Stanford University Press)

Ward, C. (1999) *Stalin's Russia* (London: Arnold)

Watson, D. (1996) *Molotov and Soviet Government* (Basingstoke: Macmillan)

Werth, N. (1997) 'Un Etat contre son People'. in S. Courtois *et al.*, *Le libre noir du communisme* (Paris: Robert Laffont)

Wheatcroft, S. (1996) 'The Scale and Nature of German and Soviet Repression and Mass Killings, 1930–45', *Europe-Asia Studies*, vol. 48, no. 8, pp. 1319–53

Wheatcroft, S. (1999) 'Victims of Stalinism and the Soviet Secret Police: The Comparability and Reliability of the Archival Data – Not the Last Word', *Europe-Asia Studies*, vol. 51, no. 2, pp. 315–46

Wilson, E. (1995) *Shostakovich: A Life Remembered* (London: Faber and Faber)

Wipper, R.Iu. (1947) *Ivan Grozny*, trans. J. Fineberg (Moscow: Foreign Languages Publishing House)

Young, G. (1997) *Power and the Sacred in Revolutionary Russia* (University Park, Pennsylvania: The Pennsylvania State University Press)

Zaloga, S. and Grandsen, J. (1984) *Soviet Tanks of World War II* (London: Arms and Armour Press)

Zhukov, G.K. (1971) *The Memoirs of Marshal Zhukov* (London: Jonathan Cape)

'Znaio, Chto Vy ne Nuzhdaetsia v Pokhvaklakh' (1994) *Istochnik*, no. 6, pp. 82–98

Index